Some books by Roger Kahn

My Story (with Pete Rose, 1989)
Joe and Marilyn (1986)
Good Enough to Dream (1985)
The Seventh Game (1982)
But Not to Keep (1978)
A Season in the Sun (1977)
How the Weather Was (1973)
The Boys of Summer (1972)
The Battle for Morningside Heights (1970)
The Passionate People (1968)

Inside Big League Baseball
(juvenile, 1962)

The World of John Lardner
(editor, 1961)

ROGER KAHN

GAMES WE USED TO PLAY

A Lover's Quarrel with the World of **S P O R T**

Ticknor & Fields · New York · 1992

For information about permission to reproduce
selections from this book, write to Permissions,
Ticknor and Fields, 215 Park Avenue South,
New York, New York 10003.

Library of Congress Cataloging-in-Publication Data

Kahn, Roger.
Games we used to play / Roger Kahn.
p.   cm.
ISBN 0-395-59351-4
1. Sports—United States.   I. Title.
GV583.K34   1992
796'.0973—dc20   91-24982
CIP

Printed in the United States of America

DOH 10 9 8 7 6 5 4 3 2 1

In Memoriam
O.R.K., 1902–1989

And for K.C.J.,
so vibrantly alive

CONTENTS

GAMES
WE USED
TO PLAY

Introduction:
A Dancer
in the Wind

In 1965, when all the men were lean and the women in bikinis stirred, to say the least, the heart, we used to play Sunday softball beside a sunbright white-sand beach.

It was a time when we all could afford to summer in Easthampton, as Ring Lardner and Grantland Rice had before us, and the weekends were wonders of parties and song, surfing with children and, to tell the truth, drinking immoderate quantities of Bombay gin and Dewar's Scotch.

The drying-out period was a Sunday softball double-header, which began promptly at ten A.M., when a church bell bid those of another bent to prayer. We had fine ball players. Buna O'Connor, who worked in a local laundromat, threw from third base with a major league arm. Cy Rembar, the lawyer who turned gallantry into money by defending *Lady Chatterley's Lover* against obscenity charges — the case kept coming up in different states and Rembar kept collecting additional fees — played a creditable shortstop. Artie Blaustein, a professional World Federalist who squired an always-changing cast — the women had different names but a similar pale beauty — threw rising fast balls, curves, and once, when he knew a woman I loved was sitting in the stands, a delightful shoulder-high change of pace that I clubbed beyond the left fielder toward the sea.

But only once. The games were so competitive that we actually chose up sides to make certain that the teams had different personnel each Sunday. Had we played the same nine against nine every week, fist fights would have begun along about Bastille Day.

Women watched but were not permitted on the field until that Sunday when Suzanne Storrs appeared. She was one of Artie Blaustein's friends, an actress who had been selected as Miss Utah, then finished sixth in the Miss America contest at Atlantic City. She knew the Book of Mormon but not our baseball rules, and she walked out from behind the backstop, positioned herself in foul territory and, not entirely innocently, stretched. She wore a white blouse and tight white slacks. The stretching done, Suzanne lay on her belly about a yard beyond the foul line halfway between third and home.

No one, least of all Blaustein, knew what to say, so no one said anything. There Suzanne remained through both games of a double-header, moving languorously from time to time. I was playing second base, so Suzanne stirred in my field of vision. I am fortunate not to have been struck in the mouth by a bounding ball.

We repaired to the beach, where a samaritan bore a jug of cranberry juice mixed with vodka, and after a bit Lenny Listfield, the first baseman, said, "Did you happen to notice that girl who was wearing white?"

"Notice?"

Listfield's wife, Helen, herself attractive, spoke up: "Oh, do you mean the one with fat thighs?"

Lenny said, "Helen, fat thighs like that you should have," and an extended silence followed. That seemed to bother Lenny the most, and out of nowhere he said to me, "Do you find that you root for Jewish major leaguers more than for players who aren't Jewish?"

"Not really. I know lots of the players, and I root for the ones I've come to like."

Listfield considered that for a time. He had just passed his fortieth birthday. Then he said it. Bartlett should have been there. Lenny Listfield said: "I *used* to root Jewish. Now I root old."

Like Listfield, I have come to root old, and on August 11, 1986, I watched in delight as Pete Rose, who was forty-five, went five-for-five against the San Francisco Giants. The effort must have been exhausting, and Rose was subdued when he met the press afterward in his office, a green windowless hutch in the depths of a large cement coffee cup called Riverfront Stadium. He wore only a towel, and he leaned forward in fatigue. His chin was on his forearms as questions came.

"Do you happen to know who holds the National League record for most five-hit games?"

"If I'm not mistaken," Rose began. Rose uses that phrase only when he is certain of his facts. "If I'm not mistaken, it was Max Carey with nine. I hold the record now."

"What does that mean to you, Pete?"

He closed his eyes. He was terribly tired. He opened his eyes and said, "A slightly larger stone on my grave."

Once you have been a newspaperman, part of you remains a newspaperman. To this day I mentally revise leads, reposition stories — and occasionally fire a columnist in the morning when I read the *New York Times*. On the night of August 11, 1986, I imagined at once a pretty fair sports page for Cincinnati the next day. The lead headline would read: "FIVE FOR FIVE AT 45." Below that, side by side, pictures of Rose lashing his bat and Rose in weariness after the game. Print a large box detailing Rose's five hits, with the pitcher's name, the count, and a description of each one. Three were lines-drive singles. One was a bloop single. One was a rocketing double.

Everybody rooting old, from Lenny Listfield to Ronald Reagan, if either happened to be in Cincinnati, would respond. For one night, anyway, Pete Rose had defeated time. Even young people could thrill to his excellence.

The Cincinnati papers played things differently. Their headlines focused on confusion in the Reds' front office about an announcement that first baseman Tony Perez would retire. Rose's batting was only the secondary story.

I asked a young Cincinnati journalist why he had handled matters as he did, and he told me: "The editors say I'm not supposed to write the games. They say television and radio have the games. I'm supposed to write something else."

"Like controversy?"

"Exactly."

Arguments distress me, and I subsided, but the episode was troubling. Controversy is a staple of sports reporting, but insofar as you can control these things, you save it for slow times. Long ago Pee Wee Reese of the Brooklyn Dodgers made this comment on the sporting press: "Watch out for them rainy days."

During 1988 Don Mattingly, the Yankees' gifted and controlled first baseman, began suddenly to talk about feelings of unhappiness. He never mentioned George Steinbrenner by name, but he went into an extended soft-voice monologue, saying that "they" (code for Steinbrenner) offer the players only money and that there were many fine athletes on the Yankees, who in addition to money deserved respect. Steinbrenner replied with a relatively subdued statement, arguing that he wasn't making a million dollars a year to play ball and he wasn't the one playing badly, as the Yankees indeed had.

The press had a big day and properly so. Before Mattingly spoke, the Yankees had played a dull, flat ball game, without news value except to emphasize that the team was going through a dull, flat period. A bigger story would have been this: have Mattingly go five for five, like Rose, then hold forth on unhappiness and lack of love. Didn't happen.

What is news? is a question that draws almost as many answers as, what is truth? A pragmatic response is that news is what newspaper editors and television producers decide it is. Their judgments are inexact, subject to whim, pressures from advertisers, demands for ratings and circulation, passion for attention, and finally the other events of the day. News itself is inexact. There is no one formula. Often, as with Perez, minor stories are wildly overplayed. More often, I suspect, great stories go unreported because journalists don't find out about them or, more frequently than one might think, don't recognize the good story that has just bitten them on the bun. Once in a while a fine story is passed over because the journalist decides that printing it is not worth hurting all the people who would be wounded.

I break down stories into three categories: hard news, soft news, and gossip. Let's give Steinbrenner a break, put him back in business, and proceed. Here is hard news:

New York — George M. Steinbrenner III, back as managing partner of the New York Yankees, today announced that he is moving the team to Paris, France. Mr. Steinbrenner and French officials displayed contracts signed yesterday. This marks the first time a major league baseball team has moved to a foreign country. "I got tired of my fans getting mugged in parking lots," Steinbrenner said, "and the favorable exchange rate means I can buy four free-agent pitchers."

Here is soft news:

New York — George M. Steinbrenner III today threatened to move the Yankees to Paris unless President George Bush cleaned up the Bronx. "And I mean cleaned up," Steinbrenner said. "I want the borough leveled and turned into a National Forest patrolled by the 82nd Airborne. They're back from Kuwait now."

In the hard news story, Steinbrenner actually is moving. He has signed a contract. In the soft news story, he is only threatening, and what he would settle for is a new parking garage, federally funded.

Here is gossip:

Paris — Special Yankee batting coach Mickey Mantle was spotted at Moulin Rouge last night with famed exotic dancer Fifi LaRue.

A technocrat would point out that the Mantle item isn't news and is of interest primarily to Mickey, Fifi, and Mrs. Merlyn Mantle. And the technocrat would be wrong. No less a personage than Robert Frost said that his abiding interests were poetry, teaching, farming, and gossip. Gossip is commercial, and people love it without always wanting to admit they love it. Its tenor has changed somewhat — more overt sexual stuff appears now — but Grover Cleveland's sex life was news in the nineteenth century. (It was claimed, accurately, that he had fathered an illegitimate child.)

I can imagine no story that doesn't fall into one of the three categories, although some overlap. SOVIETS DISMANTLE NUCLEAR MISSILE. Hard news. BUSH CALLS DEMOCRATS UNPATRIOTIC. Soft. HART RUMORED BETWEEN SHEETS WITH CUTIE. Gossip that worked its way up to hard news when Hart had to quit the 1988 presidential race.

Defining the present is a tricky business. Although it is true that winners get to rewrite history, we can be reasonably certain about the past. Rome rose and fell. Charlemagne reigned. Thomas Jefferson wrote the Declaration of Independence. The past is both reasonably certain and secure. But the future hasn't happened yet, so we can imagine anything we please, from heaven to hell.

A few years back Ronald Reagan suggested we were approaching a shining city on a hill. Someone else foretold that the city and all the world would be blown up in a thermonuclear explosion. Each believed his vision. Neither anticipated war in Mesopotamia. Time presides.

The crowded and confusing present is the question. Presently, or at least for the recent season of 1988, local and national radio and local, national, and cable television invested $366 million in broadcasting major league baseball games. (That total has grown, but 1988 is the latest season for which I can get entries that are both comprehensive and believable.) Compared to figures on the national debt, the number may seem small. But it is not small, not small at all. Indeed, the number has revolutionized aspects of the game as diverse as the salaries ball players earn to how we perceive a double play. (At least three times these days: as the double play happens, as it is rerun, and as it is re-rerun in slow motion.)

It is a personal prejudice, but I'm not much interested in what a baseball player earns. A good reporter can find out the salary of any professional athlete, and the last few years have given us a frenzy of money stories on sports pages. Rankings of managers, pitchers, quarterbacks by income. Things like that. Stock market tables disguised as sports stories.

I *am* interested in how an athlete performs. But describing the movement, control, and confluence of a catch is more difficult than setting down a series of names and dollar figures. That factor, and the pervading editorial belief that money is hot, money sells, money is sexy, explains the invasion of the dollar sign.

Enormous salaries change the way a game is played in subtle and generally underreported ways. Some champions now retire while in their twenties. Bjorn Borg, the great tennis star, built a home in Monaco, high above the income tax line, and withdrew from competitive tournaments before he was thirty. Commentators speak of burnout, but before an athlete can indulge himself in that, he has to afford to burn out. The hungry athlete runs till all his footpads blister. He runs for glory and for his next meal.

Pete Rose was always what baseball people call "a hard sign." Even when he had to bargain for himself, Rose pushed for the last $1,000, and later he engaged as his attorney Reuven Katz, who elevated baseball contract negotiation to a diabolical art form.

"But once I signed the contract, I put all that behind me," Rose says. "Good contract, or one I didn't like, it was behind me. Then I went out and played as hard as I could. In twenty-four years as a major league player, I never got sick once during a season." Rose expanded a bit. "The money's been good, but on the field the best way for me was to have fun. You know what the most fun is? Winning."

The Rose is the Rose, and I shall have some more to say on that in a later chapter. Other ball players, generally in a younger generation, take a different approach. During the classic baseball competitions of the 1950s, the average salary of a Brooklyn Dodger was about $20,000. Raises came grudgingly and in small increments. It was *vital* for the Dodger players to reach the World Series, because by doing that they could earn an additional $6,500 — each man's typical share of Series proceeds — in a single October week.

That money meant the ball player could move to a nicer house, make a down payment on a bowling alley, or, in the case of Billy Cox, a great third baseman who didn't like to be bothered, build a fence around his property in Pennsylvania.

Recent World Series shares have reached as high as $100,000 per man. That sum means a great deal to a reserve player — indeed he may double his annual salary in a week — but not that much to stars, what with salaries at $5 million annually. A rising player who wants to get rich may concentrate on individual performance, steal thirty bases, and hit thirty home runs. He then takes his case to a baseball arbitrator. Individual ball players have won extraordinary raises on the basis of one outstanding year and a generous estimate of how they are likely to perform in years ahead. Early in 1991 one player increased his salary in a single arbitration by $2,250,000 a year. (That's more than twice what Babe Ruth earned across an entire career of some note.)

Isn't having a great year and driving toward a World Series the same thing? Not precisely. Far from a ball field, a wonderful young player has said, "I don't care all that much whether the team wins or loses. What I really want is good stats [statistics] to take into arbitration." To begin with, this athlete has an attitude problem: the object of the game is to achieve team victory. Second, how willing would he be to risk injury, make a running catch against a fence, even when a game is on the line? He can't amass stats while disabled. One can go on from there and make a fairly long list of specifics where personal goals and team goals are not the same.

As the numbers were broken down by an industry publication called *Broadcasting*, the New York Mets led the twenty-six clubs in 1988 with an income of $17 million for electronic rights. The Yankees were second at $16.5 million. No other club's revenues exceeded $10 million, which tells us at once that New York, for all its potholes, muggers, and beggars, remains the richest market in the land.

The weakest broadcasting contracts were in Cleveland and San Francisco, $3 million each, with most of the other teams bunched around $5 million, give or take the salary of a starting pitcher or two. This confirms something we have suspected. Different teams start out with different budgets. The bankroll each general manager takes to the poker table is not the same.

Frank Cashen did a brilliant job in assembling the recent Mets; he is a far-ranging character, a journalist and lawyer before he gave his career to baseball. Television helped Cashen pay Dwight Gooden, Ron Darling, Darryl Strawberry, and Keith Hernandez all at once, and Cashen was intelligent enough to invest heavily in the Mets' farm system, which was superb. That probably means another Gooden, another Strawberry is on the way.

But if a bankroll were all, the Minnesota Twins would not have reached, much less won, the 1987 World Series. The Twins started that season with only $4 million guaranteed in the broadcasting pot, fourth in the American League West and less than a quarter of what the Mets and the Yankees, who did not make that World Series, were guaranteed. Then, in 1990, Oakland and Cincinnati, gave us a surprising Series. The minor surprise was that Cincinnati won. It was astonishing that two teams from such modest markets were there at all.

What can one conclude? Today, as always, it takes intelligent management to assemble a championship team, and money helps. I think that is more accurate than the converse: it takes money to assemble a championship team, and intelligence helps. We have seen fine ball clubs arise in such lesser markets as Houston and Kansas City, and a woeful team play in Philadelphia, where 1988 broadcast rights were a fine, round $10 million. We saw the Yankees, with such wonderful and expensive athletes as Don Mattingly and Dave Winfield, taste ashes. Various Yankee managements have been unable to assemble a competent pitching staff. Late in the season, particularly, a marginal pitching staff comes apart. Given the choice of good pitching and a weak team or the reverse, sound baseball men — better baseball men than Steinbrenner — opt for pitching. The cliché is that you never have enough pitching, and when I heard that from a former Yankee president, Gabe Paul, I said, "Except for the Dodgers of Koufax and Drysdale."

"As a matter fact," Paul said, "I was running the Reds at the time, and the Dodger people were on the phone a lot trying to get one more right-hander, one more left-hander."

Broadcasting money affects the balance of baseball, but the change is only in degree. New York has always been the richest market, and at different periods the Giants, the Dodgers and, most of all, the Yankees capitalized and ruled their leagues. What *is* different, and a little frightening, is that broadcasting people now dominate not only the play of baseball but the reporting.

After suspending Pete Rose for umpire-bumping in 1988, the late A. Bartlett Giamatti, then president of the National League, called in both Cincinnati broadcasters, Marty Brennerman and Joe Nuxhall, and reprimanded them for what they said on the air. He could do this because Brennerman and Nuxhall were employed by the Reds, and thus subject to supervision by the league.

Giamatti rationalized by saying that the two had agitated the crowd at Riverfront Stadium almost to riot by criticizing the umpiring and that crowd control was the greatest problem facing baseball. Both points may have been accurate, but another issue muddied the situation. Giamatti violated the spirit if not the letter of the First Amendment, which allows for a certain amount of journalistic misbehavior.

Giamatti could have fined and suspended Brennerman and Nuxhall as surely as he fined and suspended Rose. But how can people report properly on the moderately large business of major league baseball when officers of Major League Baseball, Inc. have the power to fire them for excesses in reporting? It cannot be done. (In different cities and at different networks, announcers have individual arrangements. But in practice everyone, even as strong an individual as Vince Scully, works at the sufferance of the baseball rulers.) Thomas Boswell, a good baseball reporter, works only at the sufferance of the rulers of the *Washington Post*. If Giamatti had disliked one of Boswell's pieces, all he could have done was pout or compose a letter to the editor.

A few seasons ago a Cincinnati outfielder was so dazed by "recreational" drugs that he was unable to pull on his stirrup, the red sock that goes over the white understocking called a "sani." As you learn when first pulling on a uniform, the stirrup goes under the arch of your foot. The outfielder kept trying to jerk on the stirrup from heel to toe, which is impossible. After a while someone helped him to a training table, where he lay down. He missed the game and didn't care until the next day.

It isn't good for baseball's business or baseball's image to disclose that yet another major leaguer is a drug addict. If you report that and name the athlete in print, you have to be certain of your facts. (I'm not naming the outfielder here because he has since entered rehabilitation and has enough trouble.) The item is, to say the least, hard news. But if you were announcing a ball game, you'd *have* to skip the drug story, as indeed Nuxhall and Brennerman did. That isn't theory. That is simply the way things work in the marriage of sports and the broadcasting industry.

In practice, of course, such announcers as Vince Scully and Joe Garagiola have become popular public figures; baseball executives would shun a confrontation. But the training of announcers leads them away from truth when truth gets ugly. Under Walter O'Malley, Scully heard repeatedly that stories should be "positive." Don't think like a journalist. Think Dodger blue. Garagiola was a better ball player than he admits, but it is ludicrous to compare his early training as a St. Louis catcher with the training he might have gotten elsewhere in the state, say at the University of Missouri school of journalism.

The best announcers, indeed Scully and Garagiola, are wonderfully entertaining. But with outside censorship, self-censorship, and the nature of their trade, announcers can offer baseball, and the rest of us, only an enormous lollipop, a gigantic valentine.

Let's say, just for purposes of reasoning, that this is the position of the right. Our portion of the world is wonderful the way it is. The lollipops are luscious. Against this view there is a developing position of the left, fueled by academicians. Sport is generally *frightful* as it is. Accepting the illusions of sport, the hype of sport, is a narcotic as dangerous as a fifth martini.

In the compositions of the antisports left, one finds useful facts mixed with error and questionable conclusions. One academic writes that the more decadent a society, the more bloody its sports. (He is building toward an indictment of football.) As examples he cites imperial Rome, with its gladiators; Montezuma's Mexico, where losing athletes were disemboweled; and Hitler's Germany. I hope this is not a horrific joke, identifying the Holocaust as sport. The most popular sports during the Nazi era were bloodless: soccer and such standard Olympic events as foot racing, at which Nazis did very well in 1936.

At work here is advocacy journalism and all that goes with that. Excess. Exaggeration. Valentines. Diatribes. Love letters. The first victim is reasoned discourse.

Does major league baseball maintain racial quotas and thereby limit the number of blacks who can work in the big leagues? I believe that some teams do. One executive told me not very long ago: "We can't have an all-black team. No whites would pay to see an all-black team play."

I don't know any way legally to prove the existence of baseball quotas. One thing on which lawyers agree is that conspiracy is a hard case to nail. Except for Mr. Nixon, conspirators don't tape-record themselves.

An academic named Richard Lapchick compiles statistics showing that most major league ball players convicted on drug charges are black. That is so, but what does it mean? Does baseball police blacks more strictly than whites? In 1983 I owned the Utica Blue Sox in the New York–Penn League, a summer recounted in *Good Enough to Dream*. We had one visitor from the baseball establishment, the late Dale Long, once a hard-hitting first baseman, then working for the minor league umbrella organization. Long visited Murnane Field in Utica with questions and observations. Our physical plant was terrible, Long said. I said it was the only field in town, and Long knew that.

He asked about attendance, were we paying our bills? Did we have any problems where he could help? It was a serious and pleasant meeting. Everything Long asked he had a right to ask. Neither racism nor drugs entered our discussion.

Several weeks later a few players, as far as I know white, smoked pot on the Blue Sox team bus after a victory. That bothered me, not for what it was but as a defiance of the authority of the manager and myself. Jim Gattis, the manager, said he'd like to handle the issue at a team meeting, and if I was dissatisfied I could take over.

At the meeting Gattis said, "You want to know what our drug policy is? If we catch you doing drugs, you go home. You won't be a professional ball player anymore. End of meeting." It would have been difficult to take over after that, and I didn't have to. No player smoked pot in front of us again. I believe that racism and drugs are separate issues. So do the intelligent baseball people I know.

The sporting left, like the sporting right, is not interested primarily in balance or even in reaching fair conclusions. Each begins as an advocate, one con, one pro. That is not my favorite kind of journalism.

When Bob Cooke was sports editor of the *New York Herald Tribune*, he told me, "Always go to the ball park with an open mind. Never mentally write your lead before the game." He said that in 1952, and it still applies.

If you were covering the New York Mets against a weak team, say the old Atlanta Braves, you could be right more often than wrong in guessing during batting practice that the Mets were going to win. Before the national anthem, you could write the following lead:
"The Atlanta Braves made a terrible mistake last night. They showed up at Shea Stadium."

That is not a new joke, which wasn't Cooke's point. Observe the ball game and the ball players. Structure your story on the basis of what you see and hear. That is sportswriting. The lead above is joke writing, which may pay better, but there aren't as many jobs.

In short, you have to be willing to be surprised. Whether you are considering data or dialogue, you cannot do the job very well if you reach your conclusion in advance. Major sports have become a division of the entertainment business; ball games are now "copyright performances." But at opera and theater, the last act is preordained. I have seen five productions of *Hamlet*, and in every one the prince was killed. We know that as we buy tickets. If we know who is going to win the World Series in advance, we had better pay a call on the district attorney.

The view that sport is narrow is narrow itself. A few years ago I wrote monthly articles for *Esquire* magazine that ran under the heading SPORTS. Restless one year, I said to the editor, the late Harold T. P. Hayes, that I'd like to change to general pieces. Hayes said a change would cause problems because the magazine had sold advertising to a tobacco company and the contract provided that the ads would run on the page facing the beginning of my sports column. "But as far as I'm concerned," Hayes said, "you can write anything you want, so long as you call it sports." That sort of thinking made Hayes the successful editor he was. Race, sex, drugs, and even death interplay with sports as surely as fast balls and touchdowns.

In April 1987 a producer of "Nightline," the ABC interview program that stars Ted Koppel, asked if I would appear and comment on the fortieth anniversary of Jackie Robinson's major league debut. The season was about to open, and Commissioner Peter Ueberroth decreed that second base in every ball park be painted with a 42, Robinson's number. I thought baseball should have been that respectful of Robinson in life, which it was not, and I agreed to travel to a studio. To my agent's dismay, ABC offered no appearance fee but did provide a white-chauffeured limousine almost as long as my driveway.

"Nightline" is live, as advertised. You sit before a camera with a small receiver in one ear, and Koppel paces and guides the program. But you need not be unprepared. That afternoon a producer discussed a number of topics and wanted to know if I would respond to a question like this: "What would Jackie Robinson think about the condition of blacks in baseball today?"

I said to go ahead and ask. The producer said the other guest would be Al Campanis, the general manager of the Los Angeles Dodgers, who were opening in Houston.

An easy, incomplete response to the question could have taken these lines. In Robinson's major league era, 1947 through 1956, there were almost no black utility players. Blacks who were not stars were sent to the minors or released. That blacks can get jobs as back-ups now is an indication of some progress. But as I say, that answer is incomplete and doesn't take into account Robinson's feelings as I knew them.

In the New York studio at 11:29, Koppel spoke to me through the ear plug. "I grew up in England, so I don't know very much baseball. You'll have to carry the show." That woke me. Nobody carries "Nightline" but Ted Koppel.

After taped preliminaries we went live, and Koppel immediately asked the Robinson question. I offered a forthright answer. Robinson believed in capitalism and equal opportunity, and he would not be happy because no black owned a major league team, no black was a general manager, and no black was managing on the field.

Koppel assimilated that in his quick, restrained way and addressed the next question to Al Campanis in the Astrodome: "Is Mr. Kahn's statement true, and if it is, to what do you attribute it?"

Campanis confirmed that I was correct and maintained that blacks lacked the "necessities" to manage. He meant qualifications.

Koppel announced a commercial break and said nothing during that period. When the program went live again, Koppel asked if Campanis wanted to state his position once more. Campanis did, making his situation worse, and finally added that blacks couldn't win Olympic swimming medals, either, because "they lack buoyancy."

Koppel said, "How about the fact that blacks don't have access to pools?"

Campanis continued in an inane way and simply refused to be checked. I would not endorse what he was saying. After a few minutes I couldn't have helped him if I had wanted to. Repelled by his thinking and his words, I finally said, "I understand, Al. Blacks have the intelligence to work in the fields. The cotton fields and the ball fields. But do they have the intelligence to manage in the major leagues? Of course not."

After the program was finished, Koppel said by telephone that he wished he had had a black guest. That seemed irrelevant. Then he told me that the ABC switchboard was lighting up and I'd do well to anticipate phone calls. The next day a reporter wanted to know if Campanis was drunk. I had no idea. I talked to reporters from the *New York Times* and the *Los Angeles Times* and went on a radio program with Rachel Robinson, Jackie's widow. I left the other messages unanswered. I had called attention to a nasty situation. That was a decent journalistic accomplishment. Let the spotlight move now from the interview to the situation.

Peter O'Malley, president of the Dodgers, disassociated himself from Campanis's remarks but said Campanis would be retained. Then he changed his mind and fired Campanis. (One inside view had Dodger management unhappy with Campanis's work. He had made a few mistakes. The Dodgers of 1987 were awful. In this version, which may be cynical, the Dodger chiefs wanted Campanis gone before "Nightline." The television debacle provided an excuse.)

A few days later at Shea Stadium, Eric Davis of the Reds said, "I saw you get Campanis on TV."

"I didn't get him. He got himself."

"Maybe, but you threw in a few zingers."

Davis is young and gifted and black. I didn't know quite what to say. I went off and watched the game. Afterward I said, "Eric, can you swim?"

"I'm a good swimmer."

"Campanis says you lack buoyancy."

That drew a wide grin, and Davis said, "I was just putting you on."

Splashy as "Nightline" was, the story remains under my definition of soft news: words rather than action. At the time three blacks, Maury Wills, Larry Doby, and Frank Robinson, had managed in the major leagues. The same was true eighteen months later. Since then a fourth black manager, Cito Gaston, has appeared, but major league managing remains overwhelmingly white. Had "Nightline" proceeded differently, I might have gotten to another point. Managers run games and change pitchers. General managers pick the twenty-four men who make up the active roster. In essence the general managers are the employers. And there has never been a black major league employer, a black general manager. Not one.

Sexism in sport is more complicated than it may appear. Since no one can argue seriously, at least with me, for female major league shortstops or Chicago linebackers, a pattern of prejudice was first evident at newspapers. During the 1950s the *New York Herald Tribune* employed one woman in the sports department. She was a secretary. The *Times* employed a reporter, Maureen Orcutt, but she was limited to covering women's golf.

Sports Illustrated used an attractive woman interviewer during the 1950s, one Joan Flynn Dreyspool, with uneven results. In a break from the standard interviewing tactics of the time, Dreyspool said to Walter Alston, a taciturn man who managed the Dodgers, "Your eyes are a lovely blue. They match the blue letters on your uniform." The door to Alston's office was closed, and he talked into Dreyspool's tape recorder for a long time.

Sportswriters laughed at the piece. One more *Sports Illustrated* tactic to draw attention to itself, like sending William Faulkner to cover the Kentucky Derby. ("First came Boone," Faulkner began.) There simply were no women working in sports departments, and few men gave it any thought.

In early 1976 I was taken to lunch by Patricia Ryan, who had risen through the ranks and become articles editor of *Sports Illustrated*. In just a few years she had developed a reputation for honoring commitments, encouraging writers, and handling stories with care and skill. Pat wanted a series covering as much as I could of a single season of baseball in America.

Soon I found myself living the life of a political candidate. Jet trips to Tulsa; Portland, Oregon; San Juan; St. Louis; Sarasota. I lacked some of a candidate's perks. I had to deal with my own baggage and save a series of tattered receipts from hotels and rent-a-car agencies so that the *Time* bureaucracy would honor my expense account.

After I considered subjects from the Berkshire Brewers in Pittsfield, Massachusetts, to Little League players in Carolina, Puerto Rico, it came time to pay attention to major league baseball. I planned a trip to Chicago, there to see how Bill Veeck was surviving with a last-place White Sox team, and then on to Cincinnati, where a great Reds team was going to play a series against the Dodgers, almost as good.

To help on this leg of the voyage, *Sports Illustrated* offered a reporter, Melissa Ludtke, a twenty-five-year-old New Englander who, it developed, was organized and hard-working.

In the press box at Comiskey Park I sat beside Veeck; we had been friends for fifteen years. Bill could do many things at once — when we met he was watching television, reading a book, and addressing one of his children at the same time — but watching a ball game required all his concentration. There was none of the flashy promoter once the game began; he studied the play and chain-smoked.

Ludtke took a seat in the second row of the press box and kept score. The White Sox fell behind Kansas City and then rallied with a winning home run in the eighth inning. Now you knew you were in a Bill Veeck ball park. Fireworks burst above the scoreboard. When the explosions ceased, the loudspeakers blared the famous chorus from the *Messiah*.

"Hallelujah," I said to Veeck.

"It's supposed to be fun," he said.

Afterward I led Ludtke from the press box to the Bard's Room at Comiskey Park, where Chicago writers and baseball people had gathered for chatter and drink since the days of Ring Lardner. She ordered a Scotch and water. The bartender served her but a few minutes later approached me. "Your secretary will have to drink in the hall."

"She's not a secretary, she's a reporter, and if she has to drink in the hall, I'll drink there, too."

"Sir, I'm just telling you what they told me to say."

We drank in a windowless, airless, ocher hall, and the next day I called Veeck. "They're not my rules," he said. "The baseball writers make the rules for the Bard's Room."

"Somebody ought to talk to the writers. The woman is a working reporter."

Next day Melissa was admitted to the Bard's Room. She took all this in without much comment, a quiet young woman who liked sports and did her work well. It surprised me to read in the *New York Times* of December 30, 1977:

> Time, Inc. and a female reporter for *Sports Illustrated* who was denied access to locker rooms to interview players during the World Series at Yankee Stadium brought suit yesterday against the commissioner of baseball, the president of the American League, the New York Yankees, Mayor Beame and other city officials for depriving her of the opportunity to cover baseball to the same extent as her male colleagues and competitors.

The female reporter was identified as "26-year-old Melissa Ludtke." Next day Bowie Kuhn, the lawyer who was commissioner, told the *Times*: "We consider our approach of providing female reporters with interview facilities adjacent to the teams' dressing room completely appropriate."

My first reaction was that once again *Sports Illustrated* was sending Faulkner to the Derby, calling attention to itself. Curiously, or not so curiously, the case was assigned to a woman judge, and Constance Baker Motley ruled on September 27, 1978, that all reporters, regardless of sex, must be granted equal access to clubhouses.

Ludtke celebrated by writing in the *New York Times*: "I, and others like me, were presented as women who wanted nothing more than to wander aimlessly around a locker room, to stare endlessly at naked athletes. . . . Nothing could be further from the truth."

When women first were permitted into clubhouses for interviews, that fact itself became a story. Now we had women covering other women covering ball clubs. Then a new interplay developed. A ball player who had placed a towel over his loins disliked one woman's questions. By way of response, he dropped the towel. The verbal equivalent of that action is less offensive, but only by degree.

The ambiance of a locker room is changed by the presence of women. A good interviewer wants to help his subject relax, to speak freely and comfortably. Since Judge Motley's ruling, exhibitionist athletes have exhibited themselves and shy athletes have indicated discomfort. Neither sort of behavior lets a dressing room story develop as it once did.

The Ludtke case had headline — and therefore some symbolic — value, but the equal opportunity case strikes me as weak. Suppose Ludtke wanted to try out for Othello. Her sex would get in the way. Her equal opportunity in Shakespeare would be to read for the part of Desdemona.

Reasonable equal opportunity in sports journalism calls for opening the field to women and paying them fairly. All editing positions and the great majority of reporting assignments can be handled as well by women as by men. You don't have to enter the locker room to write a column, cover golf or boxing, report a baseball trade or league action against a professional football player whose urine sample reveals traces of cocaine. If I were to go back to my earlier years and supervise a sports department, I would hire the best people I could, regardless of sex. When I gave out assignments, I would certainly know which reporter was which, and make differentiations. Feature stories go to the most accomplished writers. Gambling rumors go to street-smart types, preferably with a background of police reporting. Men's locker rooms go to men. Women's locker rooms go to women. I wouldn't want anyone who had difficulty with that working for me.

The feminist author Barbara Seaman mentioned once that she was attending a meeting of the organization Women Against Pornography. "I'd like to go," I said.

"You can't." Nudity was not the issue, Seaman said, although "sadistic" photos would be displayed. Rather, the women wanted to talk about pornography among themselves. The presence of a man might get in the way and lead to argument, self-censorship, or exhibitionist speeches. I had no trouble with that. The ladies of WAP wanted their clubhouse closed to men. So be it.

The sporting left sees sex as sexism. The sporting right looks away and says, "Say, that split-fingered fast ball really dipped." Another body of information is neither left nor right but simply commercial and mindless. This area consists of books by athletes with ghosts, who want to tell distressing stories provided the book advance is $100,000 or more.

One editor at a successful publishing house says that he gets seventy-five such proposals a year. Some reach print, and occasionally one makes a best-seller list. "I really have trouble with someone who wants to confess that he used heroin or cocaine," the editor said, "and asks for an advance. He's trying to make a profit from crime."

Typically these books attack aspects of the sports establishment, sometimes properly, but the rest of what they have to say is so shrill, impulsive, and often inaccurate that whatever serious message lies within is canceled.

It is a mistake — understandable, but still a mistake — to expect sports to function on a more exalted level than the rest of the country. Sports hucksters would have us believe that it does. They describe a droll world of sports, featuring great good fellowship and genial sessions of beer drinking, where no one gets drunk and certainly no one approaches alcoholism. Some believe in this sportsworld of the huckster. It doesn't exist. Sports reflects light. It does not originate light. The moon versus the sun.

The one exception, the day Branch Rickey invited Jackie Robinson to play in the major leagues, was a magnificent exception. I agree with Bowie Kuhn that it was the greatest moment in the history of American sport. Robinson made almost all of us focus on bigotry. When we looked away, if we had looked carefully, we were never again the people we had been.

I've seen venality and worse, but at the end I hope I have the breath to say I've had a glorious time playing sports and watching sports and writing sports. Jackie Robinson and Carl Furillo; Melissa Ludtke and Red Smith; Johansson and Patterson, Ali and Foreman; Stengel and Mattingly; George M. Steinbrenner III and Peter Edward Rose I. What a collection!

And once, a woman of twenty-two, poised and balanced on water skis as she proceeded to cross to and fro against the wake, poised and balanced, a dancer in the wind.

Isn't that the idea, to experience the glory? The French, who understand a great deal, believe it is.

Let the games begin.

Roger Kahn
Croton-on-Hudson, New York
May 1991

Willie Who?

The eloquence of Adlai Stevenson, the obscenity of Joe McCarthy, and the underestimated judgment of President Dwight Eisenhower, who declined to send forces to Vietnam. And then there was Willie Mays. With Mays in the army during 1952 and '53, the New York Giants finished second and fifth. The anticipation of Mays's return turned the Giant camp at Phoenix into a febrile rooting section.

The first of the two stories here is an effort to restore reason. Then I saw Willie.

Phoenix, Arizona, February 27. Willie Mays is due to arrive in the Giant camp on Tuesday — not a day too soon. By Wednesday half the Giant party will have left the desert sun, flown to Cooperstown, and started remodeling the Hall of Fame to include ten busts and five portraits of Willie.

It's only human to wonder whether this is man or superman coming to join the Giants. In my case the wonder takes the form of questions, and after I have asked every authority within earshot of the swimming pool where I hang out, a good portrait of Willie Mays has emerged.

Willie is ten feet nine inches tall. He can jump fifteen feet straight up. Nobody can hit a ball over his head.

Willie's arms extend roughly from 157th Street to 159th Street. This gives him ample reach to cover right and left as well as center field.

Willie can throw sidearm from the Polo Grounds to Pittsburgh. No one has ever measured the length of his longest overhand throw.

Willie's speed is deceptive. The best evidence indicates he is a step faster than electricity.

Willie hits balls that even Willie couldn't catch.

Willie does more for a team's morale than Marilyn Monroe, Zsa Zsa Gabor, and Rita Hayworth, plus cash.

That's about all there is to Mays except that every authority added: "And if you think that's something, wait till you see him."

It won't be hard to tell he's about to arrive. Bare desert mountains rim the Phoenix horizon. A sound of golden horns from beyond the mountains will herald Willie's approach. When he alights from his plane eyes will be dazzled. Women will gasp. Children will cheer! Grown men will weep.

It is hard to realize what measure of man Willie is, particularly hard after spending a couple of years among Dodgers, all good men but none super. There is, however, one point that will penetrate into the deepest reaches of Flatbush and East New York. Before Mays went into service, the Giants won a pennant. Maybe Willie really isn't ten feet nine inches tall. Maybe that's just the way he looks to the Dodgers.

Phoenix, Arizona, March 2. This is not going to be a plausible story, but then no one ever accused Willie Mays of being a plausible baseball player. This is simply the implausible truth.

Willie, discharged from the army yesterday, arrived in the Giant camp this morning after an all-night plane ride from Washington. He came directly to the ball park and waited impatiently for a chance to play in an intrasquad game. When the chance came and Willie was allowed to pinch-hit in the fifth inning, he hit a 400-foot home run.

He went to center field and had no chances until the seventh inning. Then, with Bill Gardner on first, Harvey Gentry slammed a long drive to right center. Willie raced to the right center-field fence, speared the ball one-handed, whirled, threw a strike to first base, and doubled Gardner. And then, when Bill Taylor blasted a tremendous wallop to dead center, Willie galloped fifty feet back and caught the ball over his shoulder.

Last August Mays suffered a broken bone in his left foot. After that a brief October appearance with the barnstorming team of major leaguers was the only baseball Willie had played until today. Just wait until he gets into shape.

What Willie did on the field was just one part of the implausibility. His arrival in the Giant camp was as unobtrusive as a bolt of lightning. The brightness of his yellow sweater was partly hidden by a brown sports jacket when Willie cruised into camp and headed for the clubhouse. On the field, in a whisper at first, Giants began telling other Giants, "Willie's here."

Sal Maglie, a pitcher who needed Mays's center fielding last season, stepped out of the shower room to shake Willie's hand.

"Where ya been?" Mays asked.

"In the shower," Maglie said.

"That's what I thought," Mays said and giggled.

His voice ranges from soprano to falsetto, and his giggle is two octaves higher.

Monte Irvin, Mays's old roommate, came into the locker room.

"How's your game, Roomy?" he asked.

"What game?" Mays asked.

Irvin smiled and shook his head.

"You mean pool?" Willie said. The rest of the clubhouse broke up.

Photographers were converging on Mays. They took his picture while he was buttoning his Giant shirt, tying his baseball shoes, and shaking hands with everyone in sight. "I wanna get out and hit," Mays complained.

"You're too late," said coach Fred Fitzsimmons.

"Just one more," said the photographers.

Looking on the verge of tears, Mays submitted to several more. His ordeal was not yet over. As Willie started to trot down the runway to the field, manager Leo Durocher threw both arms around the rookie in a wild greeting and wrestled him back into the clubhouse. Finally Willie emerged to meet the press.

"Durocher says he's depending on you," a reporter said.

"I don't know nothing about that," Willie said. "If I worry, I don't play good. So I don't read the papers."

"Have you signed a contract yet?"

"No," Willie said, "but I'm easy to sign. I love to play."

"There's a story out of Fort Eustis that says you want $20,000."

"That man Stoneham would take a gun and shoot me if I asked for that," Willie said. "You know those reporters. Sometimes they write on their own."

"I guess," a reporter suggested, "you'd play for nothing."

"Now you're going on your own," Willie said.

"How'd you hit in the army, Willie?"

"About .420 the first year and .389 the second. Around twenty-nine homers in the two years. There was some good pitchers, but a lot of them wasn't so good."

"How about your hitting this season?"

"I'm going for .300 and maybe twenty homers."

A private first class on his discharge from Fort Eustis, Mays spent twenty-one months attached to the Special Service Division of the Second Army. He weighs 180, which he thinks is 5 pounds too heavy, but he's in good shape because he's been playing basketball. He'll be twenty-three on May 6, has a total of 155 major league games under his belt, and was earning about $13,000 when he entered the service. That's what he will earn this season, too.

The first time Mays went to bat, Durocher was chatting with reporters and watching Willie out of one eye. "I figure that I can take my chances with the kid," Leo kidded as the count went to two and two. Then came the homer. "That's what I mean," Durocher said.

1954

Intellectuals and Ball Players

After the 1957 season, the Giants deserted Manhattan and Willie Mays had to spend years swatting high drives into San Francisco gales. That cost him the chance — and he had a great one — to break Babe Ruth's home run records.

The Dodgers deserted Brooklyn at the same time, and people asked less frequently if baseball was a business. Baseball had been a business since at least 1869, when the Red Stockings, the first professional team, organized in Cincinnati.

A year later the Cincinnati Daily Gazette *published an editorial concerned about commercial influences and gambling in what was then called Base Ball. Did the Troy, New York, Haymakers throw a game in 1870 to the Red Stockings? Wait for the film.*

This piece, about a less discussed alliance, marked, I believe, the debut of baseball in the Phi Beta Kappa magazine.

The late Hiram Haydn, revered editor, suggested the essay, but since the rate he could pay was tiny, Haydn sought to soften me with a lunch that was begun, as so many 1950s lunches began, with pellucid martinis. We talked lit, from Abelard to Zola, until at length an odd transfiguring light appeared in Haydn's gaze.

"About baseball," he said, softly. "I was a right-handed batter myself. Then one day, in a pick-up game when I was twenty-two years old, I decided to hit left-handed for a lark. Darned if I didn't

*wallop the ball over the fence." The light in Haydn's eyes burned
like the sun. "And then I knew," said this great editor, who was
approaching the age of sixty, "that if only I had started out batting
left-handed, I could have made the major leagues."*

*How touching it was to hear this version of the dream that does
not die.*

The romance between intellectuals and the game of baseball is,
for the most part, one-sided to the point of absurdity. A large
percentage of intelligent Americans evaluate the four hundred men
who play major baseball as demigods. A large percentage of the
muscular four hundred rate intellectuals several notches below
umpires.

Neither point of view is necessarily conscious, but the uncon-
scious, as they say in the trade, will out. Intellectuals considering
baseball occasionally retreat behind cultivated cynicism, which
ranges in phrase from the stock remark about bread and circuses
to more thoughtful indictments of false values and commercialism.
Similarly, some ball players, whose closest contact with printed
matter occurs when they run their hands across the photographs in
Playboy, protest, "I know all about that reading stuff." Both false
fronts are transparent to the practiced eye.

During a term I spent covering major league baseball for a newspaper in New York, both of my eyes were given plenty of practice.
As social evenings wore on, the guest who had first pointedly
skirted a discussion of Mickey Mantle's swing to analyze late
Beethoven quartets ("so vague, so illusory, yet so magnificent")
would usually come a circle and ask at midnight, "How does
Mickey do it? I mean is it in his wrists or is it just plain brawn?"
Far more common and far more enjoyable was the unaffected egg-
head who avoided the whole complexity of a façade. Simply and
directly, he would begin, "What's Leo Durocher really like?" or
"How do you hold a slider?" or "Is there any chance of the old
bent-leg slide coming back?"

Bright ladies generally steer clear of such technical discussions, but that is not to say they give baseball much berth. One woman who applied herself brilliantly to interpreting Wallace Stevens and somewhat less successfully to illustrating his work in nonrepresentational painting, returned from her first baseball game in many years with a series of representational sketches of Stan Musial, a graceful man with sloping shoulders, who has been among the game's outstanding batters for fifteen years.

"What's this?" someone remarked in surprise when he was shown the Musial sketches. "The last time we talked you said you were going to paint the poem about the blackbird."

"I know," the lady said, "but I had to try my hand at sketching this man. He moves so beautifully."

Ball players generally are noncommittal about painting, but written words and men who write, they agree, are things to be approached carefully, like land mines. Better still, they are not approached at all.

The ball player's first postschool contact with the printed word ordinarily comes through the sports columns of a newspaper. All is well when the player is successful, but as soon as he makes an important error or strikes out at a critical time, there is a headline, an article, a box score, and possibly a feature story documenting and publicizing his failure. Even assuming a happy school experience with books, something rather rare among athletes, sports-page reading in itself can be traumatic. Baseball writers and baseball players have a relationship which resembles that of teacher and pupil, or surgeon and patient, or Ben Gurion and Nasser.

One veteran baseball writer on the *New York Times* suffered a painful back injury while covering the Yankees twenty-five years ago and still remembers what happened after he limped into the trainer's room in the clubhouse at Yankee Stadium. No less a figure than Lou Gehrig walked in as the trainer was laboring over the reporter.

"Writer?" Gehrig asked, pointing to the tortured wraith who was yelping in pain.

"Uh huh," said the trainer. "Yup."

"Good," Gehrig said, quite seriously.

It is not really a long jump for a ball player to go from a *Times* reporter to Tolstoy, Yeats, or Marcus Aurelius. They all write, don't they, or they all wrote? Well, wouldn't it be just as well if all their backs were broken so they'd stop taking all those swipes at ball players? Joe Trimble of the New York *Daily News*, who wrote of an awkward Yankee first baseman named Nick Etten when he signed an $18,500 contract, "The $500 is for his fielding," was chased through a train by Etten and escaped only by locking himself inside a ladies' rest room. Try telling Etten that Tolstoy and Trimble are different kinds of writers and you would be pushed headlong over your nuance.

One ball player, Pee Wee Reese, enjoys reading. He wisely ignores the sports pages whenever the Dodgers lose. "If I don't see what they write about us when we get beat," he says, "I'm that much ahead." Reese has few unpleasant associations with the act of reading.

Another Dodger, a pitcher named Carl Erskine, is well versed in Kipling and Robert W. Service. He even eased a descent through fog one night by reciting the entire "Cremation of Sam McGee" loudly and clearly over the rumbling and creaking of what I believed to be a doomed DC 4.

Still another pitcher, Mal Mallette, who had unsuccessful trials with both the Dodgers and the Yankees, became spellbound by the lore and legend of Thomas Wolfe during the summer he played for Asheville. The next winter Mallette began to write himself; soon afterward, when his pitching arm went bad, he switched to journalism. Mallette is now a successful sports editor, fittingly enough, in Asheville.

These instances, sadly, are exceptional. I have it on excellent authority that the first book Mickey Mantle finished reading was his own ghosted autobiography. "Not started," my source carefully explains, "just finished."

Perhaps the entire case of baseball men versus the written word comes down to an incident involving Charlie Dressen, the sincere, ineloquent former manager of the Washington Senators. Gesturing at a copy of *Crime and Punishment* a young sportswriter had carried into the dugout, Dressen asked immediately, "What's that?"

"Huh?" the reporter said. "Oh, that — that's a book."

"I know," Dressen said, "but what kind of a book?"

"A novel. A tragic kind of novel."

Dressen, then over fifty, nodded, dropped his guard, and said, "You know I never read a book in my whole life."

"You ought to," the reporter said, too eagerly. "It would help you make speeches and things like that."

"Nah," Dressen said, closing the discussion, "I've got by pretty good up to now without books. I ain't gonna start making changes."

From the grandstand or, more significantly, on a twenty-one-inch television screen, the attitude of a baseball player toward a book and the whole process of thought it implies is undetectable. Nor is it germane. How does he move? Does the curve ball bother him? Can he throw? These are the relevant questions. Any sensitive intellectual moved by the majesty of a Ted Williams home run is bound to be disturbed that the Williams he meets is not a man to match the deed but an egocentric emotionalist who seems most of all to need a spanking.

But Williams's personality has no more to do with his home runs than Wagner's personal habits had to do with Siegfried's horn call. From even the best box seat, the petulance and ignorance that Ring Lardner noted inside dugouts subside to less than sound and fury. I don't think intellectual spectators should be troubled by the private attitudes of athletes and fortunately I don't believe that they are. They are all players in a drama larger than themselves. There is classic tragedy within major league baseball tragedy that catches and manipulates the life of every athlete as surely as forces beyond the heaths manipulated Hardy's simple Wessex folk into creatures of imposing stature.

Major league baseball is an insecure society: it pays lavish salaries to athletes, and then, when the men reach thirty-five or so, it abruptly stops paying them anything. But the tragedy goes considerably deeper than that. Briefly, it is the tragedy of fulfillment.

Years ago each major leaguer, like his friends, wanted desperately to become a major leaguer. Whenever there was trouble at home or in school or with a girl, there was the sure escape of baseball — not the stumbling, ungainly escape of the ordinary ball player but a sudden metamorphosis into hero. For each major leaguer was a star in his neighborhood or in his town years ago and each lived with the unending solace that there was one thing he could always do with grace and skill and poise. Somehow, he believed once with the most profound faith he possessed, if he ever did make the major leagues, everything would then become ideal. A major league baseball team is a collection of twenty-five youngish men who have made the major leagues and discovered that in spite of it, life remains distressingly short of ideal. A bad knee still throbs before a rainstorm. Too much beer still makes for an unpleasant fullness. Girls still insist on tiresome preliminaries. And now there is a wife who gets headaches and a baby who has colic. No, despite the autograph hunters, things are a long way from ideal. In retrospect, they may have been better years ago, when the dream was simple and vague. Among the twenty-five youngish men of a ball club who individually shared a common dream now fulfilled, cynicism and disillusion are as common as grass. So Willie Mays angrily announces that he will henceforth charge $500 to be interviewed, and Duke Snider shifts his dream site from a ball park to an avocado farm near the Pacific, and Pee Wee Reese tries to fight off depression by saying: "Sure I dreamt about baseball when I was a kid, but not the night games. No sir. I did not dream about the lights."

For most men the business of shifting and reworking dreams comes late in life, when there are older children upon whose unwilling shoulders the tired dreams may be deposited. It is a harsh, jarring thing to have to shift dreams at thirty, and if there is ever a major novel written about baseball, I think it will have to come to grips with this theme.

The imaginative intellectual whose legs go bad when he is twenty-two is more fortunate than he knows. His dream, the one in which he strikes out Williams, Mantle, and the boss on nine pitches, is good for the rest of his life. If it dims at any time he has only to visit a ball park for a recharge.

By its nature, the watching of baseball appeals most strongly to imaginative people. The average major league game lasts approximately two hours and forty-five minutes. There is action for perhaps fifteen minutes of that time. The rest is either inaction or suspense, depending on imagination and point of view.

The pitcher throws, the batter looks, the umpire says, "Strike," and the game is on. The batter steps quickly out of the batter's box, knocks his bat against his shoe spikes to loosen what little dirt has become lodged there. From a good seat, or on a large screen, it is possible to see his lips move as he mutters toward the umpire. What did he say? Possibly, "One-thirty is a helluvan early time to start a game, ain't it, Charley?" The umpire shakes his head. "Hell, I wish I had your money," he says. "I wouldn't complain about nothing." Then it is time for another pitch, but if the imaginative man chooses to believe so, there is already a feud flaring between the umpire and the batter. Didn't the batter mutter? Didn't the umpire shake his head? "Come on," our imaginative man demands of the umpire, "call them right."

By the time the eighth inning arrives, the visiting team is one run ahead, but the home club starts an interesting rally. The leadoff man singles to right, the next man doubles off the center-field wall, sending the runner to third, and now the home club's toughest man marches up to bat. The catcher flashes a sign, and the pitcher shakes his head violently. The catcher tries another sign. Again the pitcher shakes his head. When it happens a third time, the imaginative spectator remembers an anecdote from his treasury of baseball stories.

"He doesn't want to pitch to him," the spectator remarks. "It's like the time in thirty-seven when Lefty Gomez was pitching to Jimmy Foxx and the catcher ran through every sign and still Gomez was shaking his head. So the catcher charged out to the mound and Gomez said, 'I just don't want to throw this guy *any-thing*.'"

The imaginative man has had time to tell this anecdote, which, with other names, dates from either the early Bill Stern [a fanciful broadcaster of the time] or the late Abner Doubleday era, because the game itself has come to a new standstill. The visiting manager has called time out so that he can walk to the pitcher's mound and discuss matters with the pitcher and catcher, plus an unwanted fourth hand, the veteran shortstop, who, to the manager's annoyance, invariably seems to have managerial theories of his own. Before leaving the dugout, the manager placed his right hand to his left ear lobe, a signal that ordered the pitcher, "Shake him off for a while so we can give the relief pitcher more time to warm up." This signal was given too subtly to be noticed by anyone but the pitcher. Consequently it did not interfere with the Gomez anecdote.

As the four worried men talk intensely, the imaginative fan again can only guess at the dialogue. Actually, the manager opens with sarcasm: "Well, that was a great nothing ball you just threw."

"You come all the way out here to tell me that?" the pitcher says.

"Is he tired?" the manager asks the catcher.

The pitcher glares at the catcher, who then shrugs.

"He's tired," says the shortstop. "Didn't you see the way he —"

"I didn't ask you," the manager says. "Is he tired?"

"He threw that last guy a nothing ball," the catcher says cautiously.

"Okay," says the manager. "Stick a fork in him. He's done." The manager waves to the bullpen, and a new pitcher begins a long walk into the game.

Ten minutes later, when the game resumes, the imaginative fan has thought of two further anecdotes and, in addition, has come to a personal conclusion. "If I'd had someone like that manager to give me pitching tips," he thinks, "I might have been out there myself."

The batter hits the relief pitcher's third pitch into the left-field grandstand, and the imaginative fan, once again identifying with the home team, jumps triumphantly to his feet, slaps a stranger on the back, and glows until dinner, when his wife asks why he did not take her to the ball game or, better yet, devote some time to doing what his family wants for a change and go rowing in the park. The imaginative man can offer no good answer. If he is wise, he does not try.

Football is violence and cold weather and college rye. Horse racing is animated roulette. Boxing is smoky halls and kidneys battered until they bleed. Tennis and golf are better played than watched. Basketball, hockey, and track meets are action heaped upon action, climax upon climax, until the onlooker's responses become deadened.

Baseball is for the leisurely afternoons of summer and for the unchanging dreams. I do not suggest that major league baseball can take the place of the late Beethoven quartets, merely that the two frequently coexist in harmony within the thoughts of the American intellectual. I think this is in no way incongruous. The one came out of a life that was like thunder; the other cost four hundred men — the ringing roster of the major leagues — their dreams.

1957

The Life and Death of Howie Morenz

Very few survive who saw him play, but awe remains. Was Morenz as good a hockey player as Wayne Gretzky? We only know that Morenz, like Ruth and Dempsey, was the best in the times in which he lived.

It was always speed with Howie Morenz, and in the end it was speed that killed him. Like the fury-driven hero of an ancient tragedy, Morenz was destined to die young. The forces that whipped him through life and through the game of hockey were strong and relentless and finally fatal. His body gave out when he was thirty-four years old.

Probably Morenz was the greatest hockey player who ever lived. Certainly he was the most exciting and the most idolized. Although soon it will be nineteen years since Morenz died, memories project a picture of him alive and swift and young.

He is wearing the *bleu-blanc-rouge* of Les Canadiens, number 7 on his back, the puck at the end of his stick as he glides swiftly across the ice of Montreal's famous Forum. First he is circling behind his own goal. A little hop signals the start of his charge. Skating from the hips with long, easy strides, Morenz gains speed. The crowd at the Forum rises in waves as he skates past, and the cheering comes in waves, too, rolling down the tiers of seats louder and louder. As if to match the crescendo's rise, Morenz drives himself still faster toward the goal. In his path, two defensemen brace their heavy frames. Suddenly Morenz is upon them, hurling his body into the air as though he would jump over the two men. The crowd is on its feet and screaming. Morenz breaks through. A final feint, a goalie's lunge, a hard, quick shot into the open corner of the cage. Morenz has scored. While the Forum rocks with sound, he skates easily back to center ice for the next face-off.

Howie Morenz came to Montreal from the Ontario railroad city of Stratford in 1923, when he was twenty. Before he turned twenty-one, he had been nicknamed "The Stratford Streak." When he explained that actually he was from an Ontario village called Mitchell, he became "The Mitchell Meteor." Soon he was "Phantom of the Ice" and "Hurtling Howie" and "The Marvel of Hockey" and "The Canadien Catapult." It was no easier to contain his speed in six nicknames than in one.

Once, in a forty-four-game season, Morenz scored forty goals. He could defend and pass as well. Although he never played at more than 165 pounds, Morenz body-checked with ferocity. He was so swift, so skillful, so fearless that the wildly nationalistic French-Canadians of Montreal were undisturbed when they discovered his secret sin. Morenz's ancestry was German.

Off the ice, the pace was almost as fast. He was a relentless golfer, whose mighty drives dropped his scores into the seventies. He was a passionate horse player, losing like everybody else. He sang and he played a ukulele. He changed suits twice, sometimes three times a day. He wore spats. He had an easy wit and an easier smile that played about his puckish mouth. He was a charming and cosmopolitan young man living swiftly in the charming, cosmopolitan city of Montreal.

Then, suddenly, he was no longer quite so young. After eleven seasons with the Canadiens, he was traded. He cried, and Montreal cried with him. Although he seemed to be faltering, finally, he was still a hero. Two years later a new syndicate purchased the Canadiens. Their first move was to reacquire Morenz.

It was then, at thirty-four, that Morenz came back. As December of 1936 began, Morenz again heard cheers of triumph. He responded in the way he knew. He responded with speed.

On the night of January 28, 1937, in the midst of the greatest comeback in hockey history, Morenz sped down ice for the last time. In the first period of the Canadiens' game with the Chicago Black Hawks, a furious charge carried him past the left side of the goal. He hurtled into the stick of a tall Chicago defenseman named Andy Blair. Then he crashed into the boards. The point of his left skate embedded itself in the wood. Morenz fell, and as he did, the second Chicago defenseman, Earl Siebert, skated into him. By the time Morenz's body struck the ice, four bones in his left leg and ankle had snapped. He did not try to rise.

At Hospital St. Luc the fractures were set. Morenz slept under sedation, and within three days the pain faded. On March 8, more than five weeks later, the bones were knitting well, and at 11:30 that night Morenz got out of his hospital bed to relieve himself. Then he fell to the cold floor. An embolism stopped his heart. He died instantly.

A game between the Canadiens and the Montreal Maroons was scheduled for the following night, a Tuesday. Morenz's wife, Mary, asked that it not be postponed. Before the face-off, a bugler played "The Last Post." Then the Canadiens stumbled to defeat.

On Thursday, March 11, Morenz's coffin was taken to the Forum and placed upon boards laid over center ice. Morenz's teammates stood about the casket, an honor guard. A Presbyterian minister conducted services. More than 10,000 men and women sat silent in the Forum. Another 15,000 stood bareheaded in the street. When the services were over, a cortege moved slowly up Mount Royal. There, in a simple grave facing the clean, white mountains of the north, Morenz was buried. He had lived less than half of three score years and ten.

There was a night in 1930 when Morenz was hurling himself at defensemen with fury. The Canadiens were playing the Bruins at Boston Garden. But on this evening Morenz's charges were less effective than spectacular. One Boston defenseman was Eddie Shore, the square-shouldered bruiser of the ice, and the other was Lionel Hitchman, a tall angular back-liner. Between Hitchman and Shore, Morenz, whose slightness was belied by his somewhat jowly appearance, was outweighed by roughly 200 pounds. Whenever Howie charged, Shore brush-checked him toward Hitchman, and Hitchman then attempted to check Morenz clear back to Montreal, 300 miles. Three times Morenz was driven yards backward. Then the powerful defensemen saw Morenz launch a fourth charge at them. Shore nudged Howie toward Hitchman, who dove into Morenz. For the fourth time Morenz went down. When he got up, he was smiling.

"Don't you sons of bitches ever get tired?" he asked.

The story has a sequel. The next time the Bruins and Canadiens met, Hitchman and Shore were prepared for another violent night. As they expected, Morenz came roaring down center ice the first time he got his stick on the puck. The defensemen were about to resume their one-two-*oof* act when Morenz swerved, skated around both of them, and scored. His smile this time was only sightly brighter than it had been when he was picking himself up off the ice.

Another game with the Bruins. A face-off deep in Canadien ice that matched Morenz with Ralph (Cooney) Weiland. When the referee dropped the puck, Morenz and Weiland moved sticks with equal speed and wedged the puck between them. Abruptly it flew into the air. Weiland tapped the puck with his hand, and it dropped behind Morenz. Weiland then poked a shot into the Canadien cage. Boston won by one goal.

Hours later Elmer Ferguson, sports columnist for the Montreal *Herald*, was asleep in his room at Boston's Hotel Manger, dreaming whatever sports columnists dream. He heard a knock.

"Who's there?"

"Howie," came the voice through the door. "It's me. Morenz."

Ferguson flipped on the bed lamp. A look at his watch showed him that it was four A.M. He let in Morenz. "Howie, this is no time to get me up," Ferguson said. "Whatever it is, couldn't it wait? Why don't you go back to bed?"

"I haven't been to bed," Morenz said.

"Where have you been, Howie?"

"Walking."

"Walking where?"

"Just up and down. Up and down the streets. I lost that game."

"Don't be silly," Ferguson said. "The whole team lost the game."

"People are going to figure that I lost it, Fergy. That face-off was the thing. He got around me."

This grim reaction to defeat was not unusual. Whenever the Canadiens were beaten at the Forum, Morenz walked to a night club run by Lou Hill. (Morenz walked a great deal and at a pace that made conversation difficult.) Hill was proud of the famous performers who visited his place — such notables as Texas Guinan — but Morenz seldom noticed the acts or the celebrities. He marched into the club with his gray eyes bright but his boyish face drawn. After checking his hat and coat, he regularly sat by himself at a small table. Usually he put his head down.

The waiters were under order not to speak to Morenz nor bother him, and to keep other patrons at a distance. For half an hour Morenz brooded. Then Hill walked over. As he approached, so did a waiter carrying a tray of salt and pepper shakers. Hill and the tray arrived at Morenz's table simultaneously.

"Well, Howie," Hill opened. "How did it go?"

Before breaking silence, Morenz smiled. His face looked quite young. "Like this, Lou," Morenz answered. "I'm here." He picked up a salt shaker and place it on the tablecloth. "Two of them are coming down there." He picked up two pepper shakers and planted them to represent rival players. Then, a hockey Napoleon playing with toy soldiers, Morenz ran through the key points of the game, manipulating salt and pepper shakers. After half an hour he stalked off into the Montreal winter night and, following another session of rapid-paced walking through stone-splitting cold, went home.

One must travel slowly and with great care to trace the beginnings of the boy who was christened Howarth Morenz. He was born on June 21, 1902, and before either the boy or the new century was a decade old, a pattern of life was set. Howie was the youngest child in a family of six. His youth was an advantage since a brother, Ezra, had already searched Mitchell, Ontario, for the finest place to skate. The river Thames, Ezra found, was ideal, and on a bank of the Thames Howie Morenz first pulled on a pair of skates. He was seven.

The form of hockey he played was primitive. A piece of coal served as the puck, the sticks were cut-down broomsticks. As goalie, Howie was entitled to wear pads — magazines tucked inside his stockings. When Morenz finally got out of the goal mouth, it was under embarrassing conditions. At thirteen he landed a job with his first organized team, the "Mitchell Juveniles," and in his first game he allowed twenty-one goals. By popular demand, Howie was made rover, a vague position that vanished when hockey teams were reduced in size from seven to six men.

In his teens Morenz was a skater of furious speed. A friendly referee grabbed Morenz one night after he had landed several punches but scored no goals. "Listen kid," Lou Marsh, the referee, said. "Don't let everyone out there make a fool of you. Don't let 'em get your goat. Don't fight 'em. Let them get the penalties. You get the goals." Morenz was seventeen when Marsh spoke to him. He never forgot the referee's words.

On August 10, 1923, Morenz, at twenty, reached another decision. He placed Leo Dandurand's check and a Montreal Canadiens contract into an envelope and mailed both to Montreal. He enclosed a letter:

Dear Sir,
    I am enclosing check and contract to play hockey with your club owing to several reasons of which family and work are the most to

consider I find it impossible to leave Stratford. I am sorry if I have caused you any expense or inconvenience and trust you will accept the return contract in a sportsmanlike way. I would like to continue to play in my hometown.

Dandurand was a sports promoter first and a sportsman second. Under the early draft rules, he owned Morenz. Subsequently, seeking free agency, Morenz made a trip to Dandurand's office at Montreal's Hotel Windsor.

"I would like to be released," Morenz said.

"I am sorry," Dandurand said. "I will not release you."

Morenz wept. He was young and strong and miserable. If he wanted to play hockey at all, he'd have to play in Montreal.

Dinner with the Dandurand family cheered Morenz somewhat. Howie, in turn, cheered Dandurand when the Canadiens' training camp opened at Grimsby, Ontario. In his first turn around the rink, Morenz skated full speed. Dandurand turned to Cecil Hart. "The Lord had his arms around me when we signed him."

Left wing to Morenz's center was Aurel Joliat, a native of Ottawa, who was of Belgian descent. Joliat and Morenz were a magnificent combination. The freshman Morenz scored thirteen goals in forty-four games; the sophomore Joliat scored fifteen. The Canadiens won the Stanley Cup in the spring of 1924. That season the Canadiens played in the Mount Royal arena, but the following season the Forum opened. Before long the Forum had become a temple.

When Morenz left Stratford, he broke cleanly, but he had been thoroughly warned about Montreal. Then, as now, Anglos whispered about the French. Didn't they make sexy motion pictures? Didn't the rich ones keep mistresses? Morenz reacted happily. He did not cloister himself and he did not go wild. He lived with one of Dandurand's friends, a man named Alex Moore. He had a penchant for spending money on good clothes and good food, but he managed to keep his head.

Over the next two seasons, the National League expanded by adding teams in New York, Boston, and Pittsburgh. Morenz loved the American trips. New cities to see. New arenas in which to skate. New crowds to cheer him. In his second season he scored twenty-seven goals.

On trips Morenz carried his ukulele and crooned during train rides. His special favorite was called "If I Had a Girl Like You." When the team was home he took to bursting in on the Dandurands and demanding breakfast. "Where is it," he asked amiably on bitter winter mornings. "Where's my breakfast?" His smile warmed Dandurand and his wife, so presently breakfast was on the table. He smiled evenings after games, too, and drank fine beer and fell in love with a girl named Mary MacKay.

In the spring of 1926, Morenz married Mary and with marriage came golden years. On ice he was like a whirling wind. "He's not number 7," complained Roy Worters, goalie for the New York Americans. "He's number 77777. Just a blur." Off the ice there were trips with Mary, and banquets and parties and, in 1927, a son.

In 1928 the Canadiens won the divisional championship. They won the next four in a row. This was one of hockey's great teams, but it had one undisputed star. There was no question. In French, Howie Morenz was *l'homme-éclair*.

He did not slow down all at once, and his salary continued to rise, but there were signs that fate was beginning to turn around. At first, of course, Morenz hardly noticed. He had lived a great deal, but he was still a youthful man.

The Canadiens won the Stanley Cup in the spring of 1930 and again in the spring of 1931. Twice in succession and three times in all, Morenz was awarded the Hart Trophy as the most valuable player in hockey. But when he tried the restaurant business as a wedge against the day when he could no longer play hockey, the business didn't work. Then, in 1932, the Toronto Maple Leafs won the Stanley Cup. The Canadiens were eliminated in the first round. Next there was a fight between Cecil Hart and Dandurand. Hart left. And there was the raise Howie wanted that Dandurand would not grant.

In 1932–33, Morenz scored only fourteen goals. The next season he scored eight; before it was over, Pit Lepine had replaced him as center alongside Joliat and Johnny Gagnon, called "The Black Cat of Chicoutimi." Morenz was thirty. At the end of the season, Leo Dandurand traded him to Chicago. The night he was traded, Morenz walked the streets of Montreal in brisk despair.

Morenz was neither happy nor successful in Chicago. The Black Hawks shipped him to New York for a journeyman, no cash. That he was traded for a routine player seared Morenz; with the Rangers he seemed to burn out.

While Morenz was in eclipse, so were the Canadiens. Crowds fell to 2,500 some nights. In 1936 the owners of the Forum bought the franchise. Dandurand went off to run a racetrack in New Orleans. The new group called on Cecil Hart to be their coach. Hart's first move was to bring his friend home to Montreal.

Logically, Morenz was through. He was thirty-four, and his body carried the scars of fast hockey. He was all played out. Yet at the Canadiens' training camp outside Montreal, Morenz managed to be everywhere, talking to youngsters, cheering old friends; a little speed seemed to have come back into the legs.

When the 1936–37 season opened, the Canadiens rolled. There were new names now like Toe Blake and Paul Haynes, and still there was Joliat and once again Morenz. At the Forum the Canadiens,who had finished last the year before, came alive. This was a final chance and Morenz knew it. He drove again, and checked, and the Canadiens were what they once had been, an exciting team. Morenz picked up twenty points in thirty games. In January the crash came.

Pain forced choking sobs from Howie Morenz. He lay on his back in the dressing room, puffing a cigarette and crying in agony. "I'm all through. This is the finish."

"Damn Siebert," someone near the table said. "Lousy Siebert."

For an instant Morenz regained control. "Don't blame Siebert," he said. "Accident. My skate caught."

Morenz was placed on a stretcher and carried out of the Forum to an ambulance that waited in the street. An off-duty police captain commandeered a squad of men to clear a pathway through the crowd. *"C'est le grand Morenz,"* habitants murmured in shock. As the fans pressed close to the stretcher, Morenz waved. Then he was inside the ambulance. Clem Loughlin, the Black Hawks' general manager, stuck a hand into his pocket. "Hey," he said, pulling out a ten-dollar bill. "Send the kid this much worth of flowers."

Next morning Elmer Ferguson described the clubhouse in his column: "Little Aurel Joliat sat despondently, his chin cupped in his hands, staring at the floor. Beside him was an empty chair, and from the back of it there dangled loosely a tri-colored sweater. As players or visitors brushed past, the sweater would swing a bit, and then you could see that the number on it was 7." No other member of the Canadiens has worn the number 7 since.

Dr. J. A. H. Forgues, the club physician, reported that Morenz would be hospitalized for five weeks and that his leg would remain in a cast for two months. But soon the leg stopped hurting. Howie's hospital room became a mecca. Friends came constantly. There were rules and visiting hours, of course, but what nurse or doctor in Montreal was going to tell a hockey player or a sportsman that he could not visit the great Howie Morenz? Morenz drank with all his visitors. He issued a statement to the press: "I'll be back next year."

In theory he had only to rest, but how could the man rest his thoughts? He had made money swiftly. He had spent it just as swiftly. Little was left. He was broke. There were three children, Donald and Marlene and Howie, Jr. He told reporters he would be back, but inside the cast his leg was stone. It was hard to lie in bed and watch for morning. If he could only walk — not skate, just walk. But he was sentenced to the bed in which he lay.

Late in February Morenz suffered a nervous breakdown. The will that had carried him and the Canadiens so far so swiftly had vanished.

He seemed to be getting better when he died.

1956

The Original
Sugar Ray

People with more expertise than I say that pound for pound Sugar Ray Robinson was the greatest fighter who ever lived. That mixes divisions as well as eras, but many believe it.

As much as the magnificent boxer, I knew a gentleman of style.

T he night before, someone had broken into the bar. "It was what we call person or persons unknown," a policeman said. "They came in the window of the men's room and they broke open the cash register and they cracked the juke box and they even cleaned the dough out of the cigarette machine. But they didn't mess with the stock. They didn't take much of Sugar Ray's liquor."

"What do you do now?" I said.

"Fingerprints," the policeman said. He pronounced it the way Jack Webb might have, very low-key. It was his punch line, and he walked away.

The world headquarters of Ray Robinson Enterprises, Inc., is an old four-story building on upper Seventh Avenue in New York City. A religious revival center stands across the street. Traffic drones past. This is close to the center of Harlem. On one side of the entrance is the barbershop Robinson owns. On the other is a neon sign and the door to Sugar Ray's, his night club. That morning two police cars were double-parked on Seventh Avenue. Like everyone else, the policemen were waiting for the man.

Inside the bar Steve, a short, restless fellow from the Atomic Music Company, said he was going out of his mind. He was looking at the poleaxed juke box and shaking his head. "How am I gonna tell the company about this?" he said.

Butter, a chubby girl who works in the club, looked as if she were about to cry. "Look what they did to the television," she said. "They tore off the *knobs*."

"They were just trying to steal that, too," a white police sergeant said, "but they couldn't get it out of the wall."

"How am I gonna tell them?" Steve said.

Miss Surena, the bookkeeper, laughed a high, tense laugh. "I'm sorry, Steve," she said. "I know it isn't funny. I'm sorry, but you're making me laugh."

It was ten-thirty A.M., the time that Robinson had suggested we meet. "I've spoken to him on the telephone," Miss Surena said, "and he said to tell you this might delay him, but to come into his office and make yourself comfortable."

We walked out of the night club, past Jack Webb and the rest of the policemen, down a long hall that ended at a frosted glass door marked "Ray Robinson, Pres."

"Ray Robinson Enterprises is a corporation," Miss Surena said, "and Mr. R. is the only officer. He more or less tries to keep his hand on top of everything. He has fifteen employees. The pressure and his fighting and everything else . . . well, a weaker man would have been fitted for a straitjacket long ago." Miss Surena offered a cup of coffee and excused herself.

The office of Robinson Enterprises is expansive, perhaps the size of two boxing rings, and is dominated by a photograph of Edna Mae Robinson, Ray's wife, blown up larger than life. A drawn curtain conceals a dressing area in one corner. Plaques and awards, a tiny portion of the champion's collection, decorate the walls. Water colors of a Paris street scene and the Café Moulin

Rouge hang alongside the photograph of Edna Mae. The book-cases, low along one wall, are almost filled. There is an anthology of American Negro poetry, a biography of Booker T. Washington, and a collection of the public papers of Franklin Delano Roosevelt. It is the office of a man with cultivated tastes.

Understandably a bit late, the champion, who was robbed, ambled into the office. He moves with grace as naturally as he breathes. "Sorry, partner," he said. "Sorry I'm late." He was wearing a small smile, but he seemed tired. He had a cold. "They robbed the store," he said. "Last night."

"How much did they get?"

"I'm not sure exactly," Robinson said. "Something like twelve or fifteen hundred."

"You insured?"

"I don't know," Robinson said. "Depends just what they took." He wheeled. "I got to go talk to the police."

He was clad in a jet-black coat tailored to the lines of his lean body. ("The body of an especially muscular black panther," Red Smith wrote.) The coat had no buttons, only a belt wrapped around the waist. It fit perfectly; no buttons were necessary.

Robinson walked into his night club and grinned. Everyone looked up, even Butter brightened.

"Hey, Butter," Robinson said, "we still got a fiver?"

"We got a fiver," Butter said.

"Then we're in business," Robinson said. He turned to the policemen. "Hiya, boys," he said. A fingerprint crew was dusting the cash register.

"You gonna need me?" Robinson said.

"Not now," a plainclothesman said. "Maybe later."

"I got to get downtown, then," Robinson said.

He started out of the bar and paused near the door. "Hey," he called, "be sure and fingerprint all my employees." He laughed and the employees laughed and the policemen laughed. As he left, the robbed tavern was cheerful.

Outside, in a Cadillac convertible he had borrowed from Edna

Mae, Robinson dropped the mask. "Hell," he said. "I got my singing debut on television this week and my music lessons and all that, and now this damn thing." The car raced away from the curb. On the corner of Morningside Avenue and 125th Street, a few blocks distant, he parked. He pointed toward a church called St. Joseph's. "You want to know about anything, partner," Robinson said, "you come here. This is where it all has to start." He ran up the church steps and slipped between heavy wooden doors, a trim, handsome Negro who was alone.

He says it starts in church and maybe it does, and maybe it all started somewhere else. On a corner almost thirty years ago, as a boy named Walker Smith, the man we call Sugar Ray Robinson danced for pennies. He had a good body even then, and he knew it would bring him more than pennies. "Someday, Marie," he told his sister, "I ain't gonna be dancing for pennies on this block. I'm gonna own it." The corner was 124th Street and Seventh Avenue. The champion doesn't own the whole block, just a good part of it.

Or maybe it all started in a ring. Once, when he was training at Greenwood Lake, New York, I saw him walk into a ring by himself. A crowd sat around the gym on little bridge chairs, and when he walked in through the door everybody cheered.

He took off the robe, and there was the fighter's dancing body, stripped except for royal purple trunks. He walked through the ropes and into his fighter's dance. The left hand flicked. "Sss," said Ray Robinson through clenched teeth. The right hand moved hard and straight. "Sss," the fighter said. The hands were moving swiftly, first one, then the other, and each time the hands moved, he hissed. He was alone, fighting only the air. The people couldn't stop cheering.

Or maybe it started on the day he first understood the meaning of the color of his skin. Last year he was talking to reporters, and the conversation, as it does so often before Robinson fights, turned from boxing to money.

"What do you want?" a writer asked.

"Forty-five percent," Robinson said.

"What are they offering?"

"Forty," Robinson said. "There's a difference."

"What do you care," another writer asked, "about the five percent?"

"There's a difference," Robinson repeated. He sensed hostility and smiled. "I suppose you guys figure I'm always thinking about money before I fight."

"Yeah," someone shouted gaily.

"Well," Robinson said, "I'll tell you somebody I'd fight for free."

"Who's that, Ray?" a writer asked.

"Faubus."

"Who?"

"Governor Orval Faubus," Robinson said. [Faubus was fighting school integration in Arkansas.] "I'd like to get into the ring with him. Any ring, and he can name the time."

Or maybe it started with rhythm; rhythm and restlessness and a sense that he could do anything in the world. Watch the champion when he moves to the jazz drums at Sugar Ray's and beats out wild night music. He plays the piano and the saxophone and the organ, but he always comes back to the drums. "When he beats them things like hell," said someone, "it's the only time I see him relaxed and happy."

Maybe it's parts of all these things — the church, the poor days, the ring, the colored skin, the boomlay drums. No one, least of all Robinson, knows. Emotions drive him, and he moves forward without looking back, a versatile, talented man who is proud of each of his talents.

After he left the church, Robinson drove to mid-Manhattan, where the Musicians Union was holding an election. "This is gonna be my new career, partner," he said, as he nosed the Cadillac into Central Park. "I'm gonna work at it like I work at everything." He drove swiftly and well, pushing the big car past taxis, skimming fenders by inches, beating New York's cab drivers at their own hustling game.

At a stop light a cab driver stared and then, recognizing the champion, waved.

"Hi, old buddy," Robinson shouted.

The driver waved again.

"You don't get much privacy," I said.

"Never hurts you to say hello to people," Robinson said. "They appreciate it."

At the union hall Robinson voted and said hello to half a dozen musicians. "I'm the guy that got you into music," a florid-faced man said. "You remember that, Ray, don't you?"

"Sure, I remember," Robinson said.

"You're a great champ," the man said.

Robinson picked up Herman Flintall, his accompanist, and then, fifteen minutes after coming downtown, he started uptown for a singing lesson.

Maestro Jarahal, Robinson's voice coach, is a short, white-haired native of India, whose studios are on a side street in Harlem. "Mr. Robinson is the most remarkable person I've ever worked with," the maestro said, as the fighter loosened up by singing scales. "He can apply himself to most anything."

First Robinson ran through exercises by repeating the sound "la." Jarahal sat at a baby grand piano playing, and Robinson, entirely consumed by what he was doing, sang along. "Throw it out," the maestro said. "Throw out the notes. Don't stop them at the roof of your mouth."

"La," Robinson sang.

"Loosen your lower lip," the maestro said, loosening his own. "La," the maestro sang.

"La," sang Robinson.

"That's it," the maestro said.

"I have a cold," Robinson said.

"I can tell," the maestro said.

"They robbed my tavern last night."

The maestro shook his head. "I can tell your thoughts are wandering," he said. "Concentrate."

After the lesson Robinson mentioned side interests. "Just because I'm a fighter," he said, "doesn't mean I should just stick to fighting. Why should you be confined to one talent? It's how you apply all your talents, not one talent."

The maestro left his studio to accompany Robinson to a loft downtown, where a rehearsal of "The Steve Allen Show" was scheduled for two o'clock. The retinue was growing. There was Herman, the pianist; the maestro; Leon Antoine, the maestro's adopted son; Robinson; and myself. The Cadillac was stowed in a parking lot and we rode downtown in two taxis.

Robinson led the charge upstairs to the loft, where four chorus girls and four chorus boys were working on a makeshift set. "Let me show you the routine," John Butler, the choreographer for the Allen show, said. Butler walked through a routine with the dancers, and Robinson studied him and nodded. Herman sat down at the piano, and Ray started through the routine, singing a song about success. Robinson sang the song correctly and picked up the dance routine immediately. Robinson went through the number twice more, and then Butler called a break. "He's very good on his feet," the dance director said.

Robinson was wearing a light sweatshirt and gray slacks, and you could see the feline slope of his shoulders. "He doesn't look like a fighter," someone said. He didn't, of course. He never does, except in the ring.

The chorus girls gathered near Robinson.

"Do you like fighting?" asked a good-looking blonde in tights.

"It's cruel," Robinson said. "It's barbaric. The only reason I got into it was my sister. She was the best fighter around when we were kids and she got me interested."

"You like to dance?" the blonde asked.

"Yes, I do," Robinson said earnestly. "The rhythm, the movement, I get a kick out of it."

"You dance very well," the blonde said.

"It's important for a man to do a lot of things," he said. "Don't you agree?"

"Yes," said a brunette.

When Butler called Robinson back to work, the brunette turned to the blonde. "I didn't expect a fighter to be like that."

For the rest of the week, Sugar Ray's days were so filled with rehearsals and singing lessons that he had to take time away from his business. Aside from the barbershop and the tavern, there are apartment houses and a real estate brokerage within Ray Robinson Enterprises. "But this singing," the champion said, "is gonna be my new career. I got a hunch it could be bigger than the other."

We got together again on Sunday afternoon when Steve Allen was leading final preparations for the show and making small jokes. "This Norelco," he said, holding up an electric razor. "I never smoke anything else." Something went wrong with one of Robinson's entrances, and Allen said, "Fight called! Check the equipment."

That night Ray sat in dressing room 23 at the Broadway Colonial Theater watching the first part of the show on a small television set. A barber labored over his hair.

"Is this like before a fight?" I asked.

"Hell, no," Robinson said. "You go into a ring, you only got to fight one person. You go out on television, you got to fight millions. This ain't like a fight at all."

The show ran for forty-six minutes before Robinson went on, and he watched the entertainment only casually. Every so often he broke into a passage from one of the songs. He was rehearsing again and again within himself. When the call came, he got up easily.

"Best," I said, and we shook hands.

"Thanks, buddy," the champion said. His hand felt cold to the touch.

Afterward people crowded toward the dressing room, and more people waited near the door. "How was it?" Robinson asked.

"Well, we learned one thing," said Herman, the pianist. "From now on, we take 'em in a higher key."

"It went fine," said Maestro Jarahal. "Didn't you hear them cheering?"

"Were you out there?" Ray asked.

"Yes," the maestro said, "and they were cheering."

Robinson grinned. He was going to Birdland now, and it would take four or five taxis to carry his whole retinue along. He wanted to hear jazz; he thought music would relax him. Then later, when the crowd had cleared, he might go uptown to his tavern and enter, triumphant among his friends. There, if the spirit gripped him, Ray Robinson, the fighter, would slip in among the jazz drums and beat wild rhythms out through the quiet, turbulent Harlem night.

1959

Sugar Ray Robinson died at the age of sixty-seven in 1989, a victim of Alzheimer's disease.

«*Toonder*» on the Right

For whatever it means, there has not been a white heavyweight champion since Ingemar Johansson, out of Göteborg, Sweden. Johansson held the title only until he fought Floyd Patterson the second time. Patterson hit him with a left hook at the Polo Grounds, and Johansson went down for fifteen minutes. His body twitched. No reporters were allowed in the dressing room afterward. Elizabeth Taylor was. Ingo recovered his senses quickly.

Among the issues at stake on that warm wet evening when Ingemar Johansson and Floyd Patterson stepped into a field of light at Yankee Stadium, the heavyweight championship of the world ranked third.

As the startlingly low attendance underscored even before the fight began, the first question was whether boxing could survive in its old manner as a popular carnival of blood. Despite months of competent promotion, fewer than 20,000 customers showed up on a night when television coverage was blacked out within a seventy-five-mile radius of New York City. The night of a heavyweight championship fight traditionally has been the time to see Jim Farley and Tom Dewey and a few eager actresses pushing their way through crowds on the way to ringside. I remember staring up at rows of empty seats at Yankee Stadium and wondering if a big fight could again become an event at which it was fashionable to be seen.

The second issue came down to a struggle for the control of big-time boxing. Patterson is a proud, intelligent, young fighter, but he entrusts all his financial affairs to his busy manager, Constantine (Cus) D'Amato. Grouped against D'Amato, who in certain poses bears a resemblance to Napoleon, are Johansson, independent and wise in the ways of the dollar, and Bill Rosensohn, a Williams College graduate, who promoted the Johansson-Patterson fight and would like to promote all Johansson's future fights.

Until recently, control of boxing was no more in question than control of the telephone lines. The business functioned as pure monopoly. The sponsoring corporation tied up the best arenas so that fighters who wanted bouts in those arenas had to agree to terms set down by the promoting corporation. The title of the corporation has changed each generation, but there is a lineal chain from president Tex Rickard, who promoted fights in the days of Dempsey, to president Mike Jacobs, who promoted fights in the days of Louis, to president Jim Norris, who promoted fights after World War II.

In 1958 the Supreme Court snapped the chain by ruling that promoting fights *and* controlling arenas constituted a violation of antitrust laws. The International Boxing Club, Norris's corporation, deflated with a gurgling rush of air.

Since Yankee Stadium or Madison Square Garden or the Los Angeles Coliseum was now required to open its doors to anyone with rent money, the promoter could no longer rule the ring, and with the ring the fighter.

What this means, in a practical sense, is that the heavyweight champion and his manager can call their shots. After the Supreme Court decision, Cus D'Amato could book Patterson anywhere. Even while the decision was pending, D'Amato played a hunch and refused to do business with Norris's powerful IBC. Instead he matched Patterson, who is Negro, against a white amateur pushed all the way into a Seattle ring by a group of segregationists. Then he matched Patterson against a harmless semiprofessional from Texas. Both fights were dull, although D'Amato insisted he was getting the best possible opposition for his charge. He was getting the best possible paydays without suffering the International Boxing Club.

D'Amato had been a poor man, and there is some suspicion that with the IBC collapsing, he saw in Patterson not just a good ten years but a rich lifetime. By building a stable of champions, starting with the heavyweight, he could inflict fierce terms on promoters. Some might go broke, but as D'Amato once read, there's another one born every minute.

To D'Amato's surprise, Rosensohn, who looks boyish at thirty-nine, decided to gamble against him. After a firm contract for the Johansson-Patterson fight was signed, D'Amato pressed for more money. Rosensohn balked and won a dangerous victory. This minor setback enraged D'Amato, who then hinted that Rosensohn would promote no further Patterson fights. Rosensohn knew that the best way to enlarge the personal fortune he had inherited was to promote not one fight but a series of major fights. He looked miserable but stood his ground. Johansson appeared to like Rosensohn, and as advance sales lagged, Rosensohn rooted quietly and desperately for the challenger.

All this is heady stuff to consider at ringside, and I don't suppose anyone considered it as the sky stopped dripping and the two heavyweights stepped into the ring. Immediately there was a championship to be decided. We knew Patterson, fast of foot and hand and reflex but without great punching power. We had seen him wear down opponents, confident in command, with just a faint tendency to be careless and leave himself open for a right hand.

Johansson was unknown. He brought most of his family and a pretty brunette friend from Sweden when he set up his Norse camp outside of Grossinger's strictly kosher hotel. There is an old rule that fighters should live monastically while training, and, old boxing hands insist, training camp sex is the quintessence of evil. The reasoning holds that a man deprived of sex tends toward surliness and that a good, surly fighter will beat a good, cheerful postorgasmic fighter anytime. While old hands shuddered, Johansson danced frequently with his brunette friend in the grand ballroom at Grossinger's.

He did not throw one right-hand punch in front of newspapermen during seven weeks of training. "Toonder," he said holding the hand high. "There is toonder here." No one heard the thunder. Few believed that it existed.

The fight began with Patterson following a characteristically cautious opening. He moved quickly and lightly, holding his gloves together in front of his chin and studying Johansson. Normally Patterson fights several cautious rounds, trying out his moves before he truly makes them.

Once Johansson threw a right hand. It grazed Patterson's head as he sparred in his conservative way. There was booing after the second round. Nothing had happened.

With twenty seconds gone in the third round, Patterson moved toward Johansson. The challenger poked his left hand at Patterson's right shoulder, and the champion parted raised gloves to block the blow. Then, through an opening scarcely bigger than a fist, Toonder rumbled. Johansson's right caught Patterson squarely on the nose, and the champion fell over backward. Suddenly this proud, intelligent, young man had no idea where he was or who he was fighting or what had happened.

He sat up at six and got to his feet at nine. He was holding one hand to his nose like a little boy who has been hurt and doesn't want to fight anymore. Johansson struck with a left and a right to the head, and Patterson went down again. There were seven knockdowns before the referee stopped the fight and made Johansson heavyweight champion. As he did, Rosensohn raised his own hands in celebration of a personal triumph.

Two moments linger in the mind from Johansson's demonstration. Once, after the fourth or fifth knockdown, as Patterson lifted himself on the ring ropes, his frame shook with a sigh. Then Patterson's mouth tightened, and he turned, a professional, moving forward with all hope of victory fled, to face the blows of a stronger man. At about the same time, Sandra Patterson, Floyd's wife, rushed toward the ring crying, "No, no, no." Each time Johansson drove a punch into her husband, Sandra made a whimpering sound.

These are not things one soon forgets, but, quite coldly, Floyd Patterson warrants no pity. He chose to be a prize fighter voluntarily. Prize fighting has made him wealthy. Statistically, he is safer in the ring than he would be if he played sandlot football. Boxing's harshest critics ignore these points, and they choose to ignore as well the fact that a great fight crams courage and strength, fear and weakness, into a tiny cockpit. That fight at Yankee Stadium might have given even Aristotle catharsis.

The business of boxing is changing, but the heavyweight division still generates the most electric instant in sport, when a great right fist crashes home.

1959

Ingemar Johansson is living in Sweden. He is said, today, to weigh 300 pounds.

The Last Summer of Number 6

The fantasy of Camelot, blacks burning their own neighborhoods, two Kennedys assassinated, and the murder of Martin Luther King. Jackie Robinson supported Richard Nixon in 1960, and radicals had the ignorance to call him Uncle Tom. Robinson simply didn't trust John Kennedy. The fellow here, Stan the Man, seemed always beyond politics. Actually he was a liberal Democrat, eventually a George McGovern man. He may also be the nicest person on Earth.

Disturbing paradoxes surround an aging baseball player. He is old but not gray; tired but not short of breath; slow but not fat as he drives himself down the first base line. Long after the games, when the old ball player thinks seriously, he realizes that he has become obsolete at an age when most men are still moving toward their prime. It is a melancholy thing, geriatrics for a forty-year-old.

To Joe DiMaggio age meant more injuries and deeper silences. To Bob Feller it meant months of forced jokes, with nothing to pitch but batting practice. To more fine ball players than anyone has counted, age has meant Scotch, bourbon, and rye. Athletes seldom bow out gracefully.

Amid the miscellaneous excitements of the current National League pennant race, the most popular ball player of his time is trying desperately to overcome this tradition. Stanley Frank Musial of the St. Louis Cardinals, now thirty-nine and slowed, intends to end his career with dignity and with base hits. Neither comes easily to a ball player several years past his peak, and so to Musial, a man accustomed to ease and to humility, this has been a summer of agony and pride.

Consider one quiet June evening in Milwaukee when Musial walked toward the batting cage to hit with the scrubs, dragging his average (.235) behind him. He had been riding the bench for two weeks.

"Hey, what a funny-looking ball player," called Red Schoendienst of the Braves, who was Musial's roommate on the Cardinals for five years. Musial grinned wide. It was an old joke between friends. Then he stood silently among anonymous second-liners, attempting to act as though he were used to the company.

"Stash," someone said, while George Crowe, a St. Louis pinch hitter was swinging, "did you know that Preacher Roe was using a spitball when he pitched against you?"

The question snapped Musial to life. "Sure," he said enthusiastically. "We had a regular signal for it. One day Preacher goes into his motion, and Terry Moore, who's coaching at third, picks off the spitter and gives me the signal. Preacher knows I've got it, so he doesn't want to throw the spitter. But he's halfway through his wind-up, and all he can change to is a lollipop [a nothing ball]. I hit it into the left-field seats, and I laughed all the way around the bases."

Musial laughed again at the memory, then stepped in to hit. He swung three times but never got the ball past the batting practice pitcher. A knot of Milwaukee fans jeered as Musial stepped out of the cage, and the sound, half boos, half yahs, was harsh. Musial blushed and began talking very quickly about other games against Roe and the old Brooklyn Dodgers. "Yeah, I could really hit those guys," he said. It was strange and a little sad to see so great a figure tapping bouncers to the pitcher and answering boos with remembrances of past home runs.

Why was he doing it, one wondered. He was long since certain of election to the Baseball Hall of Fame. He was wealthy, independent of the game. (One friend estimates that Musial earns $200,000 a year, no more than half of that from the Cardinals.) He was a man who had always conducted himself sensibly. Now here was sensible old Stan Musial reduced to a bench warmer as he waged trench warfare against time.

The answer, of course, is pride: more pride than most of us suspected Musial possessed, more pride than Musial ever displayed when he was Stan the Man, consistent .350 hitter, owner and proprietor of most National League pitching staffs.

The issues in the case of Stan Musial versus time have cleared considerably since his May benching and his dramatic July comeback. He was not through in June, as many suspected but, because Musial is well loved, few put into words. But neither was he the young Musial in July, as many said loudly, and few, I imagine, really believed. Both the benching and the comeback represent skirmishes in the continuing battle Musial joins whenever he puts on a pair of spikes and heads out toward left field, trotting a shade more slowly than he once did.

After a career in which he had never batted lower than .310, Musial hit .255 in 1959. Since he was thirty-eight, the wise conclusion was that he was finished, and most baseball men assumed he would retire. In fact, most hoped he would choose retirement instead of the awkward exit that seemed inevitable if he played this season. "No," Musial insisted during the winter. "I want to go out on a good year. I'm not quitting after a lousy year like that." Athletes, like chorus girls, are usually the last to admit that age has affected them, and Musial appeared to be following the familiar unhappy pattern. His timing seemed gone — change-ups made him look foolish — and he appeared to be the only man who didn't realize it.

During the winter Musial enrolled in a physical education program at St. Louis University. The exercises were orthodox — push-ups and such — but the emphasis was on tumbling.

He arrived at spring training splendidly conditioned, and he hit well, if not sensationally, during exhibition games. For the first three weeks of the regular season he played first base, batted about .300, and fielded poorly. Then his hitting dropped sharply, and for the next three weeks his average drifted toward .200. Finally, on May 27, Solly Hemus, the Cardinal manager, benched Musial. The decision brought pain to Musial and pain to Hemus, too, since what the manager did, after all, was bench a legend.

"He'll be back," Hemus said vaguely. When? Solly wasn't quite sure. "I'll play whenever they want me to," Musial said cheerlessly. But he didn't start another game for almost a month.

Hemus is a conscientious, combative man of thirty-six, who joined the Cardinals in 1949 when Musial was already a star, a factor that later complicated the manager–ball player relationship. "I'd never pulled much," Hemus recalls, "and when I first came up Stan gave me some tips. He told me to concentrate on hitting that right-field screen — it's close — at Busch Stadium. I admired him, and I guess he liked me." It got so that when Stan came home, his daughter, Janet, wouldn't start by asking if he got any hits. First she'd say, "Did Solly get any hits?"

Discussing the Musial benching troubles Hemus. He was buffeted in St. Louis sports pages for the move, and beyond that it strained a friendship. But he talked about the benching at some length and with tremendous earnestness after one recent Cardinal night game.

"What's my obligation as manager?" Hemus said, staring darkly into a glass of light beer. "It's not to a friendship, no matter how much I like a guy. My obligation is to the organization that hired me and to twenty-five ball players. I have to win. Stan was hurting the club. He wasn't hitting, and balls were getting by him at first base. It wasn't something I wanted to do. I had to do it."

For all his attempts to show indifference, Musial hated the bench. He confided to a few friends that he wouldn't mind being traded to a club that would play him every day. Hints appeared in the press that he and Hemus were feuding. They weren't; they were just miserable about the situation. But Musial still says, in the closest he comes to a grumble, "Don't let anyone tell you they were resting me. I was benched."

On June 19, after Musial had spent three weeks in the dugout, Hemus said before a double-header: "Maybe I'll use you in the second game." The Cards won the first. In the clubhouse afterward Hemus announced simply: "Same lineup."

Later Musial, deadly serious, approached him. "There's one thing you shouldn't ever try to do, Solly," he said. "Don't every try to kid me along."

Hemus said nothing. There wasn't anything to say.

"He caught me," the manager remarked over his beer. "He knew me well and he caught me. I was wrong to kid him, but I did."

Hemus paused and gathered his thoughts. "I spent a lot of time, a lot of nights worrying about this thing," he said finally, "and I got to remember the coffin. What does he want to take with him to his coffin? Records. Something that people will remember. As many records as he can. Now what do I want to take to my coffin? Honesty. I always wanted to manage, and I want to know I managed honestly. I was right to bench him when I did, but I was wrong to kid him, and I know it makes me look bad to admit it, but I was wrong."

Hemus never evolved a plan to work Musial back into the lineup. While benched, Musial pinch-hit nine times but batted safely only once. There was no indication he was going to hit any better than he had.

On June 16 Bob Nieman, who had been hitting well, pulled a muscle, and suddenly Hemus needed a left fielder. He alternated Walt Moryn and rookie John Glenn, but neither hit. Then he turned to Musial, hoping for batting but not really confident that he would get it.

What would have happened to Musial if Nieman hadn't been

hurt, or if Glenn or Moryn had started slugging? Again Hemus speaks with frankness. "I really don't know," he says. "I just got no idea."

On June 24 Musial started in left field against the Phils and got one hit in four times at bat. On June 25 he was hitless, but on June 26 he started again and that day took off on a devastating hitting tear (fifteen games, .500 average) that surprised everyone except, possibly, The Man.

What brought Musial back to batting form? "Well, one reason I didn't quit," he says, "is that they weren't throwing the fast one by me. Last year they were giving me changes, and I wasn't going good, so I kept swinging too hard. I figured that one out. Now I'm going to left real good on lots of the change-ups."

Musial has also changed the unique stance that was his trademark. Remember the old crouch? Now Musial stands closer to the plate, a change that gives him better control of fast balls over the outside corner. He still crouches, but less markedly. His stance remains unusual, but it is no longer radical.

He always concentrated when he hit, but Musial's concentration seems to have deepened further. It must make up for what age has taken from his reflexes, and he now plots his swings with great care.

Nobody around the league has an easy explanation of Musial's great hitting in July, because there is no easy way to explain great hitting by a washed-up thirty-nine-year-old ball player. "Hell," Musial himself says, "just use that old line of Bosco Slaughter's. Just say I never been away."

One night before the Cardinals played the Braves, Charlie Dressen, a man who has more explanations than newspapermen have questions, agreed to study the revivified Musial and report on what he saw. Musial lined one of Bob Buhl's inside change-ups high into the right-field bleachers.

"Ah," Dressen said later. "I know how to pitch to him."

"How?"

"Same as always," Dressen said. "Change-ups."

"But he hit the home run off the change."

"Wrong kinda change," Dressen said.

Fred Hutchinson, who manages Cincinnati and once managed the Cardinals, took up the Musial question several days later. "What can you say?" Hutchinson asked, shrugging. "He's hitting like hell, that's all. He's hitting all kinds of pitches, just like he used to."

On the field during workouts, he tries to be as he once was, too, filled with small jokes and with laughter. "Do you know what sex is?" he may ask. "That's what Poles put potatoes into." Then, lest he offend, "You know I'm Polish."

Sometimes, while playing catch, he shows his pitches — he was a pitcher in the low minor leagues twenty-three years ago. "Fork ball," he'll say. "Me and [Elroy] Face. Next time I come back it's gonna be as a pitcher."

But once in a while pride, before now the unseen side of Musial, breaks through. He was chatting at a batting cage recently when Jim Toomey, the Cardinals' publicity man, approached and asked broadly if he was telling the story of his life.

"Yeah," someone said. "He's up to a Donora sandlot game in 1935."

"What did you do," Toomey asked, "get four hits?"

"I'll tell you this, buddy," Musial said, quite loudly. "You can bet I got two."

Since his July blaze, Musial has slipped somewhat. "One thing I know about him now," Hemus says, "is that when he gets real tired, one day's rest isn't enough. If he needs it, he'll get a week off. If he goes real bad, he'll get plenty of time to get strong again."

The old 154-game-a-year Musial has vanished. The swift base runner, whose sloped shoulders suggested the contours of a greyhound, has slowed. The great batter, whose forte was consistency, now hits in spurts. Yet, in sum, this season makes for a glorious exit. Musial wanted to go out with a respectable year, and by concentrating on pitchers and conserving his energies, he seems likely to achieve this.

But ahead lies one more trap — another season. Musial has not formally committed himself to 1961, but informally he drops hints that he may play again. He relishes his life in baseball, and when he hits well he seems to feel that he can go on hitting indefinitely. "Maybe my wheels are gone," he says, "but I'll be able to hit like hell for a long time."

Perhaps, but anyone who watched his prideful struggle this summer must wonder. Time presses. The benchings can only get longer, the comebacks still more labored. He has been a fine and gracious man, Stan Musial. It would be nice to see him say farewell with a wave, a grin, and a double lined up the alley in right center field.

1960

Musial retired in 1963. His lifetime batting average was .331. With his last swing he singled sharply to right and drove home the run that proved decisive in a 3–2 victory for the Cardinals.

Death of a Writer

Probably the most famous sports columnists of the 1950s were Red Smith and Jimmy Cannon. Some thought John Lardner of Newsweek *was better than either.*

T he quiet of Lardner's presence," commented Walt Kelly, the famous cartoonist, "was like the silence of a forest, where lack of noise does not indicate lack of life." Kelly became prosperous with the success of "Pogo" and sometimes, at a bar with Lardner and myself, he grabbed the check, saying, "It's all right. I'm richer than you guys."

One afternoon Lardner looked at Kelly and said, in a not unkindly tone, "Chester Check-Grabber."

After that we did not have to hear again how much more money Kelly had than we did, and everybody bought his round in turn.

This remembrance comes from a book of Lardner's pieces that I edited after he lost his life to a heart attack. When Lardner seemed to expire, his physician, Louis Siltzbach, employed heart massage and John revived. The doctor, who was crying, called out, "John, John. You can't die. You're a noble man."

"Oh, Lou," John said, "that sounds like a quotation."

With that, death came.

On a Vermont hillside, five months after John Lardner died at the age of forty-seven, Robert Frost mentioned Lardner's name and made a request. "When you get back to New York," Frost said, "tell this fellow Lardner that I think he has a very unusual slant on things. Comical. Tell him I like his stuff. But be careful now. Don't embarrass him with praise."

Frost was eighty-five then and still too youthful, too concerned with the issues of life, to devote much time to reading obituaries. I could not bring myself to tell the poet that Lardner was dead. Instead, on that high hill, I thought how much this compliment, from one believer in understatement to another, would have meant to John. It certainly pleased his friends. One, who had been a sportswriter, heard of it and said intensely, "That's the way it should be. Cabbies and fighters liked my stuff. Robert Frost liked his."

Although most perceptive sportswriters accepted him as a master, sportswriting was not the craft of John Lardner. Nor was it profile writing, for *The New Yorker*, or column writing, for *Newsweek*. After the painstaking business of reportage, his craft was purely writing: writing the English sentence, fusing sound and meaning, matching the precision of the word with the rhythm of the phrase. It is a pursuit that is unfailingly demanding, and Lardner met it with unfailing mastery. This is not to bracket him with Sean O'Casey and T. S. Eliot, who also wrote English sentences. John chose his arena, created his world within reasoned limits. I think it is fair to say that within these limits, in his time, he had no equal.

The world of John Lardner was a place of grace and humor, where no one was evil as Iago or virtuous as St. Joan, and where it always seemed that everyone talked softly. Unobtrusively, in a corner near the bar, house rules were posted in small type. They went along these lines: "Living is difficult at times, and three out of three people die, but there is not much sense in railing against either. Deal, drink, or read, but do it quietly." It was a pleasant place, without hot tears or strident laughter.

Heroes in his world were gamblers who fleeced innocents, ball players whose ignorance sang, and prizefighters who attempted to father a large portion of their country. There was no question of these heroes having feet of clay — the clay ran up to the waist.

The villains, at first thought, seemed very much the same, but there was a fine and unwavering difference. Lardner once explained why he liked an avaricious baseball promoter named Branch Rickey and disliked an avaricious baseball promoter named Walter O'Malley. "They do the same things," Lardner said, "but O'Malley won't admit it."

Because the world seen through Lardner's writing was such an enjoyable place, great numbers of people pressed to meet its creator. I don't know what they expected. Possibly Lardner entering with a soft-shoe routine, while the fighter Battling Siki sparred in one wing and the hustler Titanic Thompson booked bets in the other.

What they found was a tall, bespectacled man, black-haired and not comfortable with strangers. Lardner spoke sparely to people he did not know, and it was amusing to watch editors and others cope with silence on first meeting Lardner. Commonly they threw a few of their favorite anecdotes, then slipped into banalities. I can think of several austere types, unused to silence, remarking to Lardner that Mickey Mantle was a good hitter, or that battle tested a man's courage, or that yessir, it certainly had been hot and here it was only June. As I say, it amused me and I imagine it amused John, too, because he listened carefully, solemnly, and kindly. The silence itself was a kindness. John's wit, turned on a cliché, struck sparks.

It was a foolish but understandable error to think one could gain entry into Lardner's world by meeting the man. The world did not exist in the places and things John liked: not in the Artists & Writers Restaurant, where John enjoyed himself standing at the bar sipping Scotch and soda, nor in Saratoga, where he enjoyed himself on those days when his horses won, nor in St. Petersburg, where he enjoyed himself when the springtime sun burned bright. The world existed within Lardner's mind.

This is a point that some find puzzling. I suppose some burst into the Mermaid Tavern looking for Hamlet or Antony and, finding only a bald, bearded playwright, left disappointed. I suppose some asked Herman Melville, "Where do you keep the whale?" A puzzling point, perhaps, but a critical one. For the writer lives in no special physical world. Before him lies only what lies before everyone else. The writer's art begins with his own interpretation and imagination. It is to take the world that has been thrust upon him and from it to create a world beyond, more enticing and more real.

How? Lardner could not have told you, nor could Freud. One knows only that this creation is a private act of the mind. At its highest, it cannot be achieved in editorial meetings or story conferences. It is achieved by one man working alone.

For reasons that he did not bother to make explicit, Lardner never worked for any of Henry Luce's magazines. In the course of earning a living, he worked for several magazines he did not respect or did not take seriously, but always with the proviso that they not be published by Luce. This was an intensely individualistic protest by an intensely individualistic man.

After sparring with Harvard and living in France briefly, he became a reporter on the *New York Herald Tribune*. While still in his mid-twenties, he left the paper to write a syndicated sports column, and presently *Newsweek* hired him to write a sports column once a week. Then came his war correspondence for both *Newsweek* and *The New Yorker*. After that there was scarcely a magazine in the country that did not want Lardner's stories on Lardner's terms. (The reference is to style, not cash.)

It was a memorable career, and at the end Lardner had to beat off editors with bottles of club soda lest he find himself writing stories he didn't like or didn't have time for or couldn't afford. Yet while Lardner grew successful by writing in his own original, individual way, magazines, generally, became less interested in original, individual articles. *Time, Reader's Digest*, even *The New Yorker*, edited up or down to a single level, edited to read as though they had been written by one man, became journalistic giants. At least they made gigantic sums of money.

Like any careful writer, Lardner took editing badly, and when someone changed a word Lardner had struggled to find or a viewpoint he had formed, he burned with enduring rage. Once an editor ordered him to write that Lew Hoad, the Australian tennis player, was as good as Pancho Gonzales, the American. "Grmmmf," Lardner said. He made no further comment until eight months later, when Gonzales had beaten Hoad decisively in a 100-match series. He then spoke of the editor more extensively. "I told the son of a bitch he was wrong eight months ago."

Lardner the journalist moved against the tide of the times and, through something close to genius, triumphed. By not working for Luce, who had popularized group journalism, he was registering a protest on behalf of others swept along by Luce's fad. With the advent of *Sports Illustrated*, which would have allowed him some stylistic range, the protest became costly. Lardner stuck to it as a matter of integrity; he guarded his integrity in a fierce, uncompromising way.

He also stuck to journalism, which troubled some friends. "You ought to write a novel," people told him from time to time. Lardner's answer, when he bothered to make one, was a defense of the essay. One evening three of us argued about the form of writing that is most natural. Two held out for poetry, and having Lardner two to one, we moved in with broad, positive statements. Full-arm blows, fight writers call this sort of attack.

"Let's consider primitives," someone said. "Children are primitives, and what do they respond to? Rhyme and meter."

"All right, consider primitives," Lardner said. "The Rosetta Stone was an essay."

John was an essayist in an era of novel worship, an individual journalist in a time of group journalism. That's two strikes, but until the night he died, no one slipped a third strike past Lardner. In any time, under any rules, his craft would have carried him to a unique and solitary place, just as it did in the difficult times in which he happened to live.

While he enjoyed writing and being read, he could not write easily. It took him a long time to bring each story up to his standard and a longer time to build that standard up to what it was. The night he died, he left five drafts of a good lead scattered about.

Now, of John Lardner, the writer, I think of a few lines, not from an essay, but from a poem.

> The life so short,
> The craft so long to learn . . .

I am not going to tell you where that's from. John would have known, and this piece is for him.

1960

The Press
and Roger Maris

Maris went on to hit home run number sixty-one. But that happened after my deadline.

Someone has described Roger Maris as "the most typical ball player in the world." That summary is glib and incomplete, but it serves as a starter. Beyond anything else, Maris is a professional baseball player. His speech, his mannerisms, his attitudes, derive from the curious society that is a ball club. But into this society he has brought an integrity that is entirely his own, a combative kind of integrity that is unusual in baseball, as it would be unusual anywhere. It is the integrity, and his desperate effort to retain it, that has made the ordeal of Roger Maris compelling and disturbing to behold.

Maris is handsome in an unconventional way. The most arresting feature is his mouth. The points of the upper lip curl toward his nose, creating the effect of a cupid's bow. When one of the blur of photographers covering him orders, "Come on, a nice smile," the response is quick. Then, as soon as the picture is taken, the smile vanishes. It goes to Cheshire. This knack — the forced unforced smile — is common among chorus girls but not among ball players, who, after all, are not in the smiling business. It is the only public relations device that Maris has mastered.

When Maris is angry or annoyed or upset, the mouth changes into a grim slash in a hard face. His nose is somewhat pointed, his cheekbones Slavic high, and the expression under the crew-cut brown hair can become menacing. Since Maris's speech is splattered with expletives, some form an unfortunate first impression. They see a hard-looking, tough-talking man and assume that is all there is to see.

Maris's build bespeaks sports. He was an outstanding right halfback at Shanley High School in Fargo, North Dakota, and he might have played football at Oklahoma "except during the entrance exams I decided not to." He is a strong six-footer of 197 pounds, with muscles that flow rather than bulge. He would be hard to stop on the two-yard line.

At bat he is unobtrusive until he hits the ball. He walks to the plate briskly, pumps his thirty-three-ounce bat once or twice and is ready. He has none of the idiosyncrasies — Musial's hip wiggle, Colavito's shoulder shake — by which fans identify famous sluggers. Nor does he, like Ruth and Mantle, hit home runs 500 feet. By his own estimate, "If I hit it just right, it goes about 450 feet, but they don't give you two homers for hitting one 800 feet, do they?" His swing is controlled, compact. He uppercuts slightly, and his special talent is pulling the ball. Maris can pull any pitch in the strike zone. Only one of his homers has gone to the left of center field.

His personality is unfinished; it is easy to forget that he has just turned twenty-seven and only recently become a star. He may change now, as his life changes, as his world grows larger than a diamond, but at the moment he is impetuous, inclined to gripe harmlessly, and, literally, truthful to a fault.

Recently a reporter preparing an article for high school students asked, "Who's your favorite male singer?"

"Frank Sinatra," Maris said.

"Female singer?"

"I don't have a favorite female singer."

"Well," the reporter said, "would it be all right if I wrote Doris Day?"

"How could you write Doris Day when I tell you I don't have a favorite?" Maris said, mystified by the ways of journalists.

In Chicago someone asked if he really wanted to break Ruth's record. "Damn right," Maris said, neglecting to pay fealty to the Babe.

"What I mean is," the reporter said, "Ruth was a great man."

"Maybe I'm not a great man," Maris said, "but I damn well want to break the record."

This is an era of image makers and small lies, and such candor is rare and apparently confusing. Newspapers have been crowded with headlines beginning MARIS BLASTS, which is a bad phrase. He doesn't blast, he answers questions. Fans, some rooting for Ruth's memory, others responding to the headlines, have booed Maris. "Hey, Maris," someone shouted in Chicago, "the only thing you got in common with Ruth is a belly." In Baltimore fans called, "You'll choke up on your glove."

Every day Maris has been surrounded before and after games by ten or fifteen newspapermen. Necessarily many questions are repeated. Some of Maris's answers are misinterpreted. Occasionally taste vanishes.

"Do you play around on the road?" a writer from *Time* magazine asked.

"I'm a married man," Maris said.

"I'm married myself," the writer said, "but I play around on the road."

"That's your business," Maris said.

A reporter from Texas asked if Maris would rather bat .300 or hit sixty home runs. A reporter in Detroit wanted to know if a right-hander's curve broke in on him. ("I would suppose so," Maris said with controlled sarcasm, "seeing that I bat left.") But aside from such extremes, most of the questions have not been either very good or very bad. What they have been is multitudinous.

Under this pressure, which is both the same as and distinct from the actual pursuit of Ruth, Maris has made four mistakes. A wire service carried a story in late August quoting Maris as saying that he didn't care about the record, that all he wanted was the money sixty-one homers meant. "I don't think I said that," Maris says, "and I know I didn't say it like it came out." Then, in the space of ten September days, he criticized the fans at Yankee Stadium and the calls of umpire Hank Soar and finally, hurt and angry, refused to meet the press after a double-header in Detroit.

"An unfortunate image," comments Hank Greenberg, who as Cleveland general manager signed Maris for a $15,000 bonus in 1952. "I know him, and he's just a boy. They get him talking, and he says things you don't say to reporters. The year I hit fifty-eight [1938] drunks called me Jew bastard and kike, and I'd come in and sound off about the fans. Then the next day I'd meet a kid, all popeyed to be shaking my hand, and I'd know I'd been wrong. But the writers protected me then. Why aren't the writers protecting Maris now?"

Even if they chose to, reporters could not "protect" Maris because Maris is being covered more intensely than any figure in sports history. Not Ruth or Dempsey or Tilden or Jones was ever subjected to such interviewing and shadowing for so sustained a period. No one can protect Maris; he must protect himself. But to do this he would have to duck questions and tell half-truths, and both are contrary to his nature.

Maris talks softly and clearly, but he is not a phrase maker. He is not profound. He is a physical man trying to adjust to a complex psychological situation. This day he is wearing a tomato-colored polo shirt, and he is smoking one of the cigarettes he is paid to endorse.

He is asked what word he would use to describe all the attention he has received. He thinks for a moment and says, "Irritating. I enjoy bull sessions with the guys [reporters]. But this is different, the questions day after day, the big story. I say a guy [umpire Hank Soar] missed a few. I've always said it. Now it's in the papers, and it comes out like I'm asking for favors. I'm saying" — anger colors his voice — "call a strike a strike and call a ball a ball, but in the papers it appears like I'm looking for favors."

About the people he meets?

"Mostly they're inconsiderate. The fans, they really get on me. Rip me, my family, everything. I like to eat in the Stage [a Jewish delicatessen in New York], and it's got so bad I can't eat there. I can't get a mouthful of food down without someone bothering me. They even ask for autographs at Mass."

Now he is talking more easily, going from topic to topic, like this:

Babe Ruth: "Why can't they understand? I don't want to be Babe Ruth. He was a great ball player. I'm not trying to replace him. The record is there, and damn right I want to break it, but that isn't replacing Babe Ruth."

Money: "I want enough for me and my family, but I don't really care that much for money. I want security, but if I really cared about money I'd move to New York this winter, wouldn't I? That's where the real money is, isn't it? But I'm not moving to New York."

Fame: "It's good and it's bad. It's good being famous, but I can't do the things I like anymore. Like bulling with the writers. I like to go out in public and be recognized a little. Hell, I'm proud to be a ball player. But I don't like being busted in on all the time and now, when I go out, I'm busted in on all the time."

Cheers: "I don't tip my cap. I'd be kind of embarrassed to. I figure the fans who cheer me know I appreciate it."

His current plight: "I'm on my own all the way and I'm the same me I was, and Mickey is, too. Once in a while, maybe, it makes me go into a shell, but most of the time" — pride stirs in his voice — "I'm exactly the same as I was."

When the Yankees arrived in Minneapolis late in August, Maris had fifty-one homers and Mantle forty-six. Both were comfortably ahead of Ruth's record pace, and both had to share uncomfortable amounts of attention.

A chartered bus appeared in front of the Hotel Radisson well

in advance of each game to carry the Yankees to Memorial Stadium. The downtown area of Minneapolis is compact, and the bus
served as a signal to hundreds of Minneapolitans. As soon as it
appeared, they herded into the hotel lobby. "Seen Rog?" they
asked. "Where's Mick?" Enterprising children posted a watch on
the eighth floor, where many of the Yankees were quartered. When
Maris or Mantle approached the elevator, a child scout would
sprint down eight flights and shout to the lobby, "Here they
come." The second day, tipped off by a bellman, Maris and Mantle began leaving the elevator on the second floor and taking a
back stairway to the street.

Nothing much happened the first night in Minneapolis, except
that Camilo Pascual of the Minnesota Twins became the father of
a son and pitched a four-hit shutout. But a day later Mantle hit his
forty-seventh, lifting a slow curve over the left-field fence, and the
following day he hit number forty-eight in the fourth inning.
Maris did nothing.

The Yankees flew to New York, where they settled the pennant
race by sweeping a three-game series from Detroit. They beat Don
Mossi 1–0 in the first game on Bill Skowron's single in the ninth
inning. Maris and Mantle were hitless but still attracted the largest
crowds in the clubhouse.

"Mossi had good stuff," Mantle said of his own effort.

"When you're going lousy, you're lousy," Maris said of his.

The next day Maris hit two home runs, numbers fifty-two and
fifty-three, but Mantle pulled a muscle checking a swing. "I'll take
you out," Houk told Mantle on the bench. "I'll help," Mantle
said. "I'll bunt, I'll field, I'll get on." Mantle stayed in the lineup,
and a day later he hit two, his forty-ninth and fiftieth. The Tigers
never recovered, and now, with the Yankees certain to win the
pennant, fans, reporters, and photographers turned all their attention to Maris and Mantle. Newspapers started guessing games,
with cash prizes for those who forecast how many homers the two
would hit. A stripper playing a burlesque circuit adopted the name
Mickey Maris. A Japanese sports editor sent eighteen questions to

the Associated Press in New York, requesting that Maris and Mantle answer all.

After hearing five, Maris said to the AP reporter, "This is driving me nuts."

"That's my next question," the reporter shouted. "They want to know how you're reacting to all this."

During the following week at Yankee Stadium, Maris hit number fifty-four, a fierce liner to right center off Tom Cheney of Washington; fifty-five, a high drive into the bleachers off Dick Stigman of Cleveland; and fifty-six, another drive into the bleachers, off Mudcat Grant, another Indian. Mantle also hit three, and this week, which ended on September 10, was the last in which Mantle fully shared the pre- and postgame pressures.

As a young ball player, Mantle had been almost mute in the presence of interviewers. "Yup" was a long answer; "maybe" was an oration. But over the years he developed a noncommital glibness and a fair touch with a light line. "When I hit forty-eight," he told a group one day, "I said to Rog, 'I got my man. The pressure's off.'" (The year Ruth hit sixty, Lou Gehrig hit forty-seven.) Such comments kept Mantle's press relations reasonably relaxed, but Maris, three years younger than Mantle, ten years younger as a star, had to labor. Maris insists that such laborings had no effect on his play, but others close to him are not so sure. Two days before the Yankee home stand ended, a reporter asked Maris about the fans behind him in right field. "Terrible," Maris said. "Maybe the worst in the league." He recounted remarks that had been shouted at him and, under consistent prodding, ran down the stadium customers for ten or fifteen minutes. The next day, after reading the papers, he said to me, "That's it. I been trying to be a good guy to the writers, but I quit. You heard me talking. Did I sound like the papers made it look?"

"No."

"Well, from now on I'll tell the writers what pitch I hit, but no more big spiels."

"Because one or two reporters roughed you, are you going to take it out on everybody?"

Maris looked uncomfortable. "Listen," he said, "I like a lot of the writers. But even so, they are number two. Number one is myself, I got to look out for myself. If it hurts someone else, damn it, I'm sorry, but I got to look out for myself more than I have."

Maris hit no homers in the double-header that concluded the home stand and afterward committed the only truly graceless act of his ordeal. "Well?" a reporter said to Maris, whose locker adjoins Elston Howard's.

"He hit a homer, not me," Maris said, gesturing toward Howard. "Mr. Howard, tell these gentlemen how you did it."

"If I had fifty-five homers, I'd be glad to tell the gentlemen," Howard said pleasantly. "Fifty-six," Maris snapped at his team mate. "What are you trying to do? Shortchange me?" Then he marched into the players' lounge to watch television.

A fringe of Hurricane Carla arrived in Chicago on Tuesday the twelfth, shortly after the Yankees. The game had to be called in the bottom of the sixth, when a downpour hit Comiskey Park. Maris had come to bat four times and hit no homers. Reporters asked if he'd had good pitches to hit.

"I didn't get too many strikes," Maris said. "But they were called strikes. Soar had me swinging in self-defense."

The next day's newspapers headlined that casual, typical ball player's gripe. Maris was shocked. Until that moment he had not fully realized the impact his sentences now carried. He had not fully realized the price one pays for being a hero. He was disturbed, upset, withdrawn. Tortured would be too strong a word, but only slightly. He showed his hurt by saying little; his mouth appeared permanently set in its hard line. He hit no home runs in Chicago, and when the Yankees moved on to Detroit he hit none in a double-header.

That was the night he declined to meet the press. His brother, Rudy, a mechanical engineer, had driven from his home in Cincinnati to see the games, and later Roger and Rudy sat in the trainer's room, from which reporters are barred. "Get him out," a reporter told Bob Fishel, the Yankees' publicity director.

Fishel talked briefly to Maris. "He says he's not coming out,"

Fishel announced. "He says he's been ripped in every city he's been in, and he's not coming out."

Eventually Maris reconsidered, relaxed, and emerged.

"Any complaints about the umpiring tonight?" a Detroit newspaperman asked.

"Nope," Maris said, "and you got me wrong. I don't complain about umpiring."

When the reporters left, Mantle walked over to Maris. "Mick, it's driving me nuts, I'm telling you," Maris said.

"And I'm telling you, you got to get used to it," Mantle said.

The next night Maris hit number fifty-seven, and a day later, after missing a home run by a foot, he won the game for the Yankees in the twelfth inning with number fifty-eight, a drive into the upper deck in right center field.

As the ball carried high and far, the Yankee dugout erupted in excitement. "Attaboy, Rog!" the most sophisticated players in the major leagues shouted, and "Yea" and "Attababy."

"It was one of the warmest things I've seen all year," said Bob Cerv, the outfielder. "We all know how tough it's been for Rog, and I guess we all decided right then, all at once, that we wanted him to know how much we were for him."

The team went to Baltimore by train. Maris had hit and lost a homer there on July 17, when rain stopped a game in the fifth inning. He had hit no other homers in the Orioles' park. If he was going to catch Ruth in 154, he would have to hit two there in two games.

He hit none the first night, dragging through a double-header. Now, in addition to hoots from the stands, he was getting hoots by mail (two dozen letters) and wire (six telegrams). "A lot of people in this country must think it's a crime to have anyone break Ruth's record," he said.

The second night, in the Yankees' 154th game, Mantle, who had long since left center stage, vanished into the wings with a cold.

No one who saw game 154, who beheld Maris's response to the challenge, is likely to forget it. His play was as brave and as moving and as thrilling as a baseball player's can be. There were more reporters and photographers around him now than ever before. Newsmen swelled the Yankee party, which normally numbers forty-five, to seventy-one. This was the town where Babe Ruth was born, and the crowd had not come to cheer Maris.

The first time up, Maris shot a line drive to Earl Robinson in right field. He had overpowered Milt Pappas's pitch, but he had not gotten under the ball quite enough. An eighth of an inch on the bat was all that kept the drive from sailing higher and farther.

In the third inning Maris took a ball, a breaking pitch inside, swung and missed, took another ball and then hit number fifty-nine, a 390-foot line drive that maybe broke a seat in the bleachers. Three more at bats and one home run to tie.

When he came up again, Dick Hall was pitching. Maris took two strikes and cracked a liner, deep but foul, to right. Then he struck out. When Maris came to bat again in the seventh inning, the players in the Yankee bullpen, behind the fence in right center, rose and walked to the fence. "Come on, Roger, baby, hit it to me," shouted Jim Coates. "If I have to go fifteen rows into the stands, I'll catch that number sixty for you."

"You know," said Whitey Ford, "I'm really nervous."

Maris took a strike, then whaled a tremendous drive to right field. Again he had overpowered the ball and again he had hit a foul. Then he lifted a long fly to right center. There was that eighth of an inch again. An eighth of an inch lower on the bat, and the long fly might have been a home run — *the* home run.

Hoyt Wilhelm was pitching in the ninth. He threw Maris a low knuckle ball, and Maris, checking his swing, fouled it back. Wilhelm threw another knuckler, and Maris moved his body but not his bat. The knuckler, veering abruptly, hit the bat, and the ball rolled back to Wilhelm, who tagged Maris near first base.

"I'm just sorry I didn't go out with a real good swing," Maris said. "But that Wilhelm." He shook his head. He had overpowered pitches in four of his five times at bat and had gotten only one home run. "Like they say," he said, "you got to be lucky."

Robert Reitz, an unemployed Baltimorean, retrieved number fifty-nine and announced that the ball was worth $2,500. "I'd like to have it," said Maris, "but I'm not looking to get rid of that kind of money."

The Yankees won the 154th game, 4–2, and with it clinched the American League pennant. Maris wore a gray sweater at the victory party, and someone remarked that in gray and with his crew cut, he looked like a West Point football player. One remembered then how young he is, and how he believes in honesty, as youth does.

"The big thing with you," I said to him, "is you tell the truth and don't go phony."

"That's all I know," Roger Maris said. "That's the only way I know how to be. That's the way I'm gonna stay."

1961

The next spring, after he had read this story, Maris sought me out. "Hey," he said, "of all the horseshit that got written, yours was the best."

Maris died of lymphatic cancer in 1985 at the age of fifty-one. He remained a private person till his end.

$$C = \frac{(Frank\ Ryan)}{2}$$

I am no longer certain what this title means. Otto Friedrich, a gloriously gifted editor, who devised it, can be reached at Time *magazine, where he now writes, for amplification.*

I am sure *that the subject was an ambulatory Greek Ideal.*

The two worlds of Dr. Frank Ryan meet in infinity. It confuses him sometimes, going from one to the other. He is upset when athletes or sportswriters misstate his work in mathematics. He is startled that mathematicians allow themselves to envy his skills as a quarterback. After a while spent at the side of Frank Ryan, a proud and humble and sensitive man, one comes to recognize his confusion and its symptoms: disgust, annoyance, anger. One recognizes the confusion, and then one is left to marvel that Ryan can alternate between his worlds at all.

For approximately six months and approximately $40,000, Ryan plays quarterback for the defending champions of the National Football League. For the balance of the year, and for perhaps $4,000, he lectures and undertakes research in advanced mathematics at Rice University, where he earned his Ph.D. last June.

He likes football, likes to win, is proud of victory and embarrassed by defeat. On the field he possesses a ferocious kind of courage. He likes football, but he loves math. "To me," Dr. Ryan says, his solemn young face shining, "it's like a painting must be to the artist. Other people can observe the painting, but nobody else can feel what the artist felt when he made it."

People always want him to explain. "Hey, Frank," a Rotarian asks at a Cleveland Browns football luncheon, "just what is that thesis of yours about, anyway?"

"I was wondering, Frank," asks an academic colleague in Houston, "just what kind of person is this Jimmy Brown?"

No comprehensible answer is possible to the first question. No simple answer is possible to the second. Thus Ryan's worlds, like parallel lines, meet only in infinity.

"He is certainly a promising mathematician," reports Dr. B. Frank Jones, Jr., once a roommate of Ryan's at Rice and now a member of the Institute for Advanced Studies at Princeton. "The Ph.D. is not in itself significant. Very few of your Ph.D.'s are good. But he has excellent potential, although football obviously has held him up."

"Ryan," says Jimmy Brown, greatest of running backs, "is the quarterback who makes our ball club move. Frankly, I don't know why. He is not a natural. He just has this ability to move the club, particularly in the clutch."

"There seems to be an impression," says Professor A. J. Lohwater, formerly of Rice and now with Case Institute, "that Ryan was handed his doctorate on a platter. Nothing could be less correct. That man worked hard for his degree. He worked for seven postgraduate years under Dr. G. R. MacLane, one of the best geometric-function theorists and a man of uncompromising standards. Frank wrote an excellent paper as well."

"As a quarterback," says Blanton Collier, head coach of the Browns, "Frank seems to have mastered the ability to concentrate on detail, which psychologists tell me is an acquired characteristic."

A theory, popular with people who know less math than Dr. Lohwater and less football than Coach Collier, suggests that a mathematical mind helps a man play quarterback in the National Football League. Although Ryan regards the theory with professorial scorn, its origins are understandable.

Leaders of the NFL, unhappy with the image of football players as mindless muscle, pretend that only the highly intelligent make good football players. The league is rich, and its image makers are skillful. Word is current that defensive tackles have to be literate, which is false, and that quarterbacks have to be scholars, which is absurd. "An *analytical* mind certainly can help a quarterback," Ryan says, "but people who say that a mathematical mind is important are just not very well informed about mathematics. What I do at the university has nothing at all to do with what I do on the field. Nothing. Nothing at all."

"He is always about five jumps ahead of you with that mind," says Gary Collins, the Browns' gritty flanker, "but last year we were playing the Giants at Yankee Stadium, and he got down on his knees right out there in front of all those people, and he drew his play in the dirt like you do when you're a kid. I thought it was funny, drawing in the dirt, him being a doctor and all. But I ran the pattern he drew, and we scored."

It is true that football plays are numbered, for purposes of classification and brevity. "Eighty-one fullback flare screen," is a satisfactorily terse way of saying, "OK, Jimmy. You go out toward the sideline over there, and I'll hit you with a short one, and you big guys kind of drift over, will you, and get in front of Jimmy and give him a little blocking, OK?"

It is true, too, that quarterbacks are expected to execute detailed game plans based on sequences and variations of more than a hundred different plays. The work is neither simple nor scholarly. The mental process involved is akin to playing bridge in competent company, except that the quarterback, unlike Goren, may be dismembered at any time.

But to suggest that the interesting business of playing quarterback is related to Dr. Ryan's life work is not true. It offends Dr. Ryan, and it offends a number of his teammates, who feel that quarterbacking is good honest work, vastly superior to "something flaky like that math."

High mathematics is an area of pure abstraction, exotic symbolism, and shapes that may not actually exist. Imagine infinity, Dr.

Ryan suggests. Now imagine an infinite collection of infinities. The idea takes considerable grasping. "For every infinite collection," Dr. Ryan proceeds, "you can find a greater collection of infinities, which is a pretty crude way of expressing something basic."

"I am sure Ryan will be glad to talk to you," Harold Sauerbrei, a former sportswriter who is general manager of the Browns, said in early autumn. "But that doesn't mean you'll know what the hell he's talking about."

"I keep the title of Frank's thesis on a piece of paper in my wallet," Nate Wallack, the team's public relations director said. "I don't feel I should be expected to remember it." The title is "A Characterization of the Set of Asymptotic Values of a Function Holomorphic in the Unit Disc."

"You will find him a little far out," a newspaperman advised. "I mean, like one time we had photographers out at the Browns' training camp, and Ryan threw left-handed all day. What a damn time at the office. We thought every negative had been reversed."

Ryan is very deep rather than far out, and he is intelligible to anyone who takes the trouble to listen. He is lean, tall — six feet three — and his hair is turning gray. His eyes are deep-set, withdrawn; often his mouth seems on the verge of a grin. "About the time you threw left-handed," an interviewer asked him recently.

"Oh, uh, that," Ryan said, and there was the grin. "Actually, it was Ninowski who started throwing left-handed, but I kept it up, and all the pictures were wrong. But that isn't the point. Wouldn't you think the photographers would have noticed? The point is that a professional photographer, assigned to spend a day taking pictures, should make it his business to prepare himself, to find out whether his subject throws left or right."

Ryan was approaching Higbee's, a big Cleveland department store, where he was going to autograph copies of a new book about the Browns. No one recognized him in the street. It was early in the season, a gray, cheerless day.

He traveled to the signing by escalator, riding up the five floors to the book department with a pleased, embarrassed smile. Ryan likes escalators. He was less sure about the rest. It was not merely that he would have to write his name nonstop for two hours. He had not read the book. "I don't read as much as I should," he said, "and I probably don't read the right things, but damn, I should have read this one. Now I don't know if what I'm signing is any good."

Paul Warfield, a slim, unwrinkled pass catcher, was there ahead of him, sitting at a table, signing. At a second table sat Galen Fiss, a large, hearty man from Kansas who plays linebacker for the Browns and sells insurance in the off-season. "Good of you to show up," Fiss said amiably.

Ryan nodded and slipped into a chair beside Warfield, and nearby salesladies swooped.

"Oh, you're the one with all the degrees."

"Yes, ma'am."

"I suppose we *should* call you doctor."

The grin became resolute. A compulsory grin. "How many books are you going to want me to sign?" Dr. Ryan asked.

"About a thousand," said a saleslady.

"Um," Dr. Ryan said. "A thousand books. Two hours. Eight times one twenty is nine sixty. Eight and a third books a minute, or, ah, uh, seven and one half seconds per book."

He lifted a copy from the pile in front of him. *Return to Glory*, the jacket announced in black and white and orange. *The Story of the Cleveland Browns* by Bill Levy. Ryan stretched his left arm, exposing his watch, and wrote his name in the flyleaf.

"Three seconds," Ryan said. Then, smiling to himself, "I get a four-and-a-half-second break every time."

The signing process, all but automatic, gave Ryan something to do with his hands while he talked to the interviewer. "I hope you can make clear," he said, "that I don't consider myself a competent mathematician yet. My thesis is addressed to an individual problem, and a mathematician is something more than someone who can relate to an individual problem and get it done."

"What is the problem you take up?"

"Nothing you can understand," Ryan said. "If I were in chemical engineering or in physics, and I wrote, say, a thesis on the bombardment of an isotope of boron with neutrons, I could tell you. But mathematics isn't like that at all."

"That Gary Collins really likes the way you throw, doesn't he?" a sharp-faced teenager said across the table.

"To begin to understand my thesis, you would have to have at least three very basic understandings," Ryan said to the interviewer. He gave the teenager a fast little grin. "You'd have to understand a complex plane. You'd need to understand a holomorphic function. You'd have to understand the limits at the boundary of the unit disc in the complex plane.

"There are a lot of inadequacies that have to be corrected in my mathematical makeup," Ryan said, "but I think my degree of capability is of a high level." Excitement suddenly charged his voice. "There is so much in mathematics that is fantastically interesting that I could learn and do."

He stopped signing books and quickly wrote a paradox evolved, to the general frustration of mathematicians, by Lord Bertrand Russell, the philosopher and pacifist. Lord Russell's paradox involves sets. In mathematics, sets are collections of objects that are grouped together according to a rule or, for that matter, a set of rules. A standard example of a mathematical set is the set of all positive integers — in laymen's terms, all whole numbers, but not the fractions, 8 but not $8^1/_2$, between zero and infinity.

Obviously, mathematicians point out, a set can contain elements that are themselves sets. The set of all *positive* integers, 8 but not $8^1/_2$, contains the set of all even integers, 8 but not 7 or 9. Further, it is possible for a set to contain itself as one of its elements.

Lord Russell's famous paradox proceeds enthusiastically from this point. Sets that contain themselves are classified as "extraordinary." Those that do not contain themselves are ordinary. "Here," Ryan said, showing a piece of paper on which he had written: $C =$ the set of all ordinary sets. "Now," he said, compressing the paradox to a question, "is C itself ordinary or extraordinary?

"Look," Dr. Ryan said, placing two blue ballpoint pens together. "That's a nice set of blue pens. That's something you can see. People like things that they can see. But lurking in the grass are snakes like this." He gesticulated angrily toward the paper on which he had written the statement of Russell's paradox.

"I want to learn Russian," Dr. Ryan said. "My French and German are fine, but I do have to get with Russian. The Russians are doing a tremendous lot academically. Anyway, another reason for learning Russian is that it means learning new symbols, and mathematicians are always in need of new symbols." Ryan grimaced slightly. "You, uh, understand," he said, "that last is sort of a joke."

Ryan's humor has a special academic dryness. Joan Busby Ryan, an English major, was actually able to find a joke in his doctoral thesis. "The work deals in part with things that Frank calls necks," Mrs. Ryan says. "These necks intersect with other things that he calls laces. Well, the intersection, when he diagrams it, has a shape something like a diamond. You see? Diamond. Neck. Lace. That really broke them up in the math department at Rice. Frank likes to joke, but he has his moods."

"What do you think of Y. A. Tittle?" asked the persistent fan at Higbee's.

Ryan was getting tired. His mouth, which grins so easily, curled downward at the corners. The fan and a saleslady beat retreats.

"He's moody, all right," says Gary Collins, who caught three of Ryan's passes for touchdowns in last season's play-off game. "I mean you can never be sure whether he'll say 'good morning' or 'go to hell.'"

Early this season the Browns played the Redskins in 100-degree heat at Washington, and although they won they did not win as handily as they should have, and Ryan was not satisfied with his performance. Immediately after the game a perspiring reporter charged up to Ryan in the clubhouse. "On the play when Collins was free way downfield, and you threw short —" the reporter began.

"Do I know you?" Ryan asked.

The reporter said a name, impatiently. "Anyway, on that pass —"

"Have we met?" Ryan persisted.

"I'm with UPI," the reporter said.

"Yes," Ryan said. "Well, I saw Gary out there, and I decided to get a pass out to him, even if it was an imperfect pass. Just get the ball downfield." He smiled warmly. "After all," he said, "I am an imperfect passer."

A few weeks after the Washington game the Browns defeated the Eagles in Philadelphia although Ryan was confined to the bench with a sore foot.

"How did it feel to sit one out?" another sportswriter asked afterward.

It had not felt very good, but what was the point of saying so? Disinclined to lie, Ryan elected not to answer. He turned away.

"Just because you've gone to school five years longer than the rest of us," the reporter said, "don't think you're too good to talk to me."

"Get your face out of mine," Dr. Ryan cried. "Get your face out of mine and get away from me." His tones carried over the buzz of a victorious clubhouse, and long afterward he was embarrassed. Some of the scorn he had felt for a reporter now spilled over onto himself. He, a mathematician, a Ph.D., had let a boor wound him in front of everyone.

He lives very hard and very deeply, committed to integrity, which is not the easiest of ways to do it. He cannot insinuate, flatter, bend the knee. He tries to insulate himself against cliché and compromise, the way good academicians do, but just when he is happy with the insulation someone tells him over a light Irish whiskey and soda, "That math must really help you out there on the field." Then the mouth moves painfully from open grin to scowl, and he is caught between his separate worlds.

Probably Ryan has always lived hard. His family was successful and social in Fort Worth. His grandfather on his mother's side, Dr. Frank Beall, was a surgeon and a scholar. On his father's side there was a heritage of blue. "I believe I am the first Ryan in three generations not to attend Yale," he says. But the social, successful home where he was reared knew trouble. His parents eventually were divorced.

He was an intense boy who loved physics. He was not outstanding at baseball or basketball, but he could throw a football with superb skill. "Fifty yards," a high school physics teacher once told him, "is as far as anyone can throw the thing, Frank. I've made certain calculations, taken into account the shape of the ball, and that is the top distance it can be thrown."

Ryan took the teacher to a field. There he threw the ball as hard as he could. They measured the distance. Frank had thrown seventy-three yards on the fly.

He was not certain about college except that he did not want to go to Yale. He had been a good but not remarkable high school football player, and Rice was interested in him. But some of the people at Rice had a hard time understanding that he wanted to major in physics. That was a pretty stiff course, they felt, for an athlete. After a while they stopped arguing, and he matriculated.

Ryan did not dominate football at Rice. King Hill, now a quarterback with the Philadelphia Eagles, was the star. Ryan was a spot performer, a substitute. He was amazed when the Los Angeles Rams drafted him.

Several of his professors at Rice, including Dr. MacLane, had urged Ryan to abandon physics for mathematics in his senior year. His mind seemed better oriented toward pure math, they felt. Before the Rams chose Ryan in 1958, he had been accepted by both UCLA and Berkeley for graduate work. With his blond, perceptive bride, he worked out a sensible future. He would play football for the Rams and study at UCLA. This future seemed more than sensible. It seemed perfect.

Joan Ryan remembers the years in Los Angeles with the detailed horror that nightmares inflict on memory. "In that first year," she says, "Frank played a total of nineteen minutes. Not only that, the next season he was always being humiliated. If he made a mistake, he was taken out at once. The Los Angeles football team is influenced by Hollywood. Click fast. Razzle-dazzle. Make it big or out you go.

"Our third year in L.A. we knew it wasn't working out," Joan Ryan says. "By then we had children, and we had moved to Burbank, where there was a big apartment complex, a *lanai*. We had a view of the Burbank Flood Control. That is California for 'ditch.' When it rained, the torrent amused the children. When it was dry, they threw their toys into the ditch. Frank was away a lot, and when the kids threw their toys, I'd have to hire teenagers to climb down into the Burbank Flood Control and retrieve them."

In 1962 the Rams dealt Ryan to the Browns for a tackle and no sensible reason, except that the Los Angeles football team has a penchant for trading away championship players. Playing quarterback for the Browns in 1962 was preferable to attending kindergarten, but the intellectual difference was not easily discernible. Paul Brown, who had invented the team in the heady days that followed World War II, would not let quarterbacks call plays. Paul Brown called plays himself.

Not only was the Cleveland quarterback treated like a dunce by his coach, he was also the number two man in the backfield. Number one was the big fellow, Jim Brown, who didn't fake much and who wouldn't block and who was the best running back on earth. The Browns did not win under Paul Brown, or with Jimmy Brown, partly because the pass is mightier than the run. But they made it close. It was thrilling to watch them lose to the Giants and the Eagles and the Steelers. The big fellow made great yardage while they lost.

Ryan was hired in Cleveland neither to think nor to play. He was employed to spell Jim Ninowski, a quarterback of fine physical attributes who has seldom won in the National Football League. Only when Ninowski suffered a broken shoulder halfway through the 1962 season did Ryan become the Brown's first-string quarterback. He was twenty-six years old, and it was the first time he had been a first-string quarterback since high school. Soon afterward, pressing, he threw an interception. With an ultimate effort Ryan managed to tackle the interceptor just before he crossed the goal line. Frank trotted off with the relieved feeling of one who has erred and atoned.

"Why?" screamed Paul Brown. "Why, why, why?"

"Why what?" Ryan asked.

"Why did you throw that interception at a time like this?"

Paul Brown was later fired by Arthur Modell, the young president of the Browns, for a complex of reasons, and now resides in La Jolla, California, where he is paid twice Ryan's salary, some $80,000 a year, not to coach.

Brown's replacement, Blanton Collier, is cordial, pedantic, and hard of hearing. "The first thing I did," Collier says, "was make Ryan the first-string quarterback. He's done well. You can accomplish anything you want as long as you don't care who gets the credit."

Perhaps, as he credits himself, Collier did install Ryan as his number-one quarterback. But all through the exhibition games before the 1963 season Ryan had to alternate with Jim Ninowski. A year ago Frank won notice with a series of scrambling come-from-behind victories. But it may be no more than a modest exaggeration to assert that he finally won his job on Sunday, December 27, 1964, when he moved the Browns from a scoreless first half to a 27–0 victory over the Baltimore Colts and a championship against John Unitas, the nonmathematician whom many regard as the finest of modern quarterbacks.

To some outsiders Dr. Ryan would seem to have solved the business of living. He has his math and his three sons and his football. Joan, attractive, gracious, and intense, writes a column for the Cleveland *Plain Dealer* called "Back-Seat Brownie." Frank is the hero more often than not. He has the respect of Jim Brown and A. J. Lohwater. Blanton Collier takes him seriously. Last October, with forty-nine seconds left and the team two points behind Pittsburgh, he was able to talk Collier out of ordering a field goal try. Then, on the next play, he hit Gary Collins with the pass that won the game.

But to someone as sensitive as Frank Beall Ryan, the business of living, like Russell's paradox, resists solution. "I want to accomplish fantastic things myself," Ryan says. He is concerned that he does not read more. He wants to learn music. He should read modern poetry. Unitas throws better. Others have achieved more in mathematics. The restless mind quests and finds no peace.

1965

Frank Ryan is vice president of Rice University.

The Game
Without the Ball

People trusted Lyndon Johnson enough to elect him in the 1964 landslide, when he ran as the candidate for peace. Then came Vietnam.

During that war professional football invented the Superbowl and drew ahead of baseball in television ratings. Coaches talked about linebackers on a "blitz" and began describing the long forward pass as a "bomb."

Games and life, like the war, went on.

The idea to watch a football game from the point of view of a tackle rather than a quarterback was suggested by Gordon Manning when we both worked at Newsweek *during the late 1950s. I tried it there, but I couldn't get enough space really to make it work.*

For this one I knelt on the sidelines, moving up and down with the Rams' defensive unit, throughout a warm afternoon. Merlin Olsen, incidentally, went on to earn a master's degree in economics. Was I becoming a specialist in scholar athletes?

Impossible. There weren't enough of them.

Tuesday is a rotten day for tackles. A hip or thigh or shoulder still aches from Sunday's game, and another Sunday distantly approaches. Tuesdays mix old pain with impending demands, a trying circumstance.

"You have to forget what was," Merlin Olsen is saying in the den of his weathered-shingle home in South Pasadena, California. "We worked hard in Baltimore last Sunday, and we got a tie. You know what a tie is. It's like kissing an *ugly* sister. But you discipline yourself, forget it, and point for the next one."

Olsen is a gigantic man, six feet five inches tall, with a hard, supple body and a great, blond head. He weighs 276 pounds. As the defensive left tackle for the Los Angeles Rams, he overwhelms guards, tramples centers, runs down halfbacks and, perhaps most important, charges and crushes quarterbacks as they try to pass. Coaches say he is as good at all these deeds as any tackle in professional football.

"People have the impression," Olsen says, "that tackles have to be violent, hostile people. That isn't so. That isn't true at all. If it were true, every quarterback in the NFL would have had his legs broken many times."

The speaking voice of Merlin Olsen is deep, modulated, and manly. Listening, one envisions microphones in his future. *Good morning, Lilliputians. Welcome to the Merlin Olsen Show.*

"I know I'm not weak," Olsen says easily, "and there have been dozens of times when I could have broken a quarterback's legs. Nothing could be further from my nature.

"When I'm working, my responsibility as tackle calls for me to stack into a quarterback. Grab his passing arm. Bowl him over. Let him know that I'm around. Teach him that my footsteps promise trouble, and make him strain to hear them. But that's not hostility. That's my job." Susan Olsen, fair, petite, and quiet, is curled on the couch. Around her Merlin's trophies sit on shelves close to her volumes of Voltaire and his books, which range from T. E. Lawrence to a graduate textbook called *Administrative Control and Executive Action*.

"Tackles have a second-class image," Olsen says. "Hostile and dumb. Well, on the Rams we have eight or nine basic defensive alignments, with ten to fifteen variations on each, which have to be

memorized, and which Maxie Baughan, who calls defensive signals, can change by calling any one of ninety audibles just before
the snap. A rockhead at tackle couldn't do the job."

"People don't know how complicated his work is," Suzy says.

"People don't really watch tackles," Olsen says, "any more than
the camera does."

"When I'm watching I get heartburn," Suzy says.

"There are two games out there," Merlin says. "The one that
gets televised is the game with the ball. I may not play in that at all.
Where I'm working all afternoon is somewhere else. I'm playing
where the ball is not." He shrugs briefly as a pinched nerve stabs
him.

"I start getting nervous along about now, on Tuesday," Suzy
Olsen says. "It builds from here."

"How nervous?"

"It depends on Merlin."

"How nervous does Merlin seem?"

"I just can't say for sure," Suzy Olsen says. "He's never played
against Sonny Jurgensen before."

The game will be the twelfth of twenty to twenty-four, depending on the final standing of the clubs, that tackle Merlin Olsen is
going to play this season. It matches the Rams against the Washington Redskins, an inconsistent team, and presents a special
appeal to the game's theorists. The Ram's Front Four — Olsen,
David Jones, Lamar Lundy, and Roger Brown — weigh 1,096
pounds, or slightly more than a white rhinoceros (*Ceratotherium
simus*), a beast that untracks locomotives with its charge. The four
are accepted as the best defensive line extant. Christian Adolph
(Sonny) Jurgensen, Jr., the Washington quarterback, is the National League's master at frustrating linemen. Last season he was
thrown only once for every twenty-seven times he dropped back to
pass. The question, then: what happens when the best of lines
rushes the most elusive passer?

Now it is Wednesday, and coach George Allen has finished the
morning session in the locker rooms at Blair Field, Long Beach.
He has run films of Redskins, and he has lectured. "Watch that

Jurgensen. Time him. Clock him. He releases in one and a half seconds on that short one." The films are over, and his men have taken the field, bending and stretching and grunting under a smog-gray sky.

Coach Allen is striding toward his men. "What somebody should write about Olsen," he says as he walks, "is that he possesses qualities of leadership and that he's a student of the game." Allen is forty-five, black-haired and sturdy without great size. "You know a problem on any team is the early workouts. The men are pros, and they like to coast a little early. Olsen works as hard today or yesterday as he does on Friday. That sets an example; it's important."

In the corner of the field Olsen and his colleagues on the Four are working to perfect their charge. His shoulder pads make him look even huger than he did the night before, but it is not difficult to associate Olsen on the field with the poised and orotund speaker of last evening. He concentrates on what he does or says. He is concentrating now.

Marion Campbell, one of Allen's assistants, is playing the role of Jurgensen. While reserve linemen crouch, Campbell barks briskly, "Ninety-six, fourteen. Set." He pauses. All the linemen freeze. "Hut."

The Four charge. What is astonishing about Olsen is his speed. At the word "hut," he bursts out of his frozen posture like a sprinter. Like a big sprinter. Like the biggest sprinter anyone ever saw.

"We use a variety of charges," Olsen has said. "There are four of us, and the Redskins are going to have six, or maybe seven, protecting Jurgensen. We could crash, four against seven, dead ahead like your rhinoceros, and because we're strong maybe get away with it. But not for very long. A period at most. The men who're trying to keep us out aren't pygmies."

"Set," commands Marion Campbell in the smog.

"Brown," announces Merlin Olsen.

"Hut," Campbell cries.

The word "brown" was a signal, charting a path for all four men. Now, at "hut," Olsen springs not forward but to his left. David Jones, six feet five and a svelte 260, serves inside. Neither man is rushing as a defender would anticipate. A guard trying to fire out — block straight ahead — would hit air.

"Each of us," Olsen likes to explain, "has a specific basic technique for attacking the man across from us. We use strength, quickness, and deception. To understand it, think of basketball. Each of us is driving toward a basket, which is the quarterback. Unfortunately, this particular basket can move, and besides, we can't just drive right in, knowing that the rules are with us. In football there's nothing against decking an oncoming man."

"Stunting" is what the pros call changing patterns. A lineman stunts when, with premeditation, he switches the path of his rush in concert with another lineman, or with a linebacker, who assumes responsibility for any gap that is created. "There's where the rhinoceros image breaks down," Olsen suggests. "No one has ever yet seen four rhinos stunt."

A siren wails to change the drills. After half an hour of unrelieved crouch, spring, charge, Olsen is allowed a breather on the sidelines. Nearby he sees Chuck Lamson, a defensive back, who went to the University of Wyoming.

"The Wyoming cowboy," Olsen says, adding a dash of syrup to his voice.

Lamson, a lean six-footer, looks ahead. "I was one of the real great ones," he says.

"Yes, sir," Olsen says, in perfect sportscasting tones. "One of the all-time greats. We'll never forget him. There he is, our very good friend, ol' What's-his-name."

Lamson grins thinly, and Olsen stares at the field. Humor comes hard. Mostly, in practice, the men are working and studying and trying to breathe deeply.

"You get a feeling for each other, a sense of warmth and pride," Olsen insists. "I happen to be the only white guy in the line. But these people I've played alongside for so long get close to you.

Everybody pulls for everybody else. Once I told some stupid joke involving a Negro stereotype. For a week I worried if David Jones had overheard me. It was callous of me and offensive. We kid each other about color now."

After the workout the Four are peeling off pads and jerseys next to each other. David Jones, a large, pointed-faced man from Florida, feels the closest to Olsen. "We came into the league about the same time. We've done our learning together side by side. He's an aggressive-type tackle, and I'm an aggressive-type end. We know how to work together and help each other real good."

Lamar Lundy, tallest and leanest of the linemen, at six feet seven and 260 pounds, is a poised, confident man from Indiana. With Eddie Meador, a free safety, he is a defensive co-captain. "We've become a reading line," Lundy says. "We read from the other man's moves what the play will be. We begin by playing for a pass; we look for a pass on every down. And we understand each other. Oley does a lot of code-calling at the line, but you know your own moves and how they work with somebody else's. I like the slap-by. Hit the other man's helmet with both hands. He blinks. You're by him."

"Hey," Merlin Olsen says. "Believe nothing this man tells you."

Roger Brown, the other tackle, is still an outsider. The Rams acquired him from the Detroit Lions two months ago after Roosevelt Grier suffered a severed Achilles tendon in an exhibition game against Kansas City. "I can't tell you much about him yet," Brown says, "and that shouldn't matter much anyway. You're writing a story about him, not about me."

"You have to work to develop relationships," Olsen says later. "Things don't come easy, or right away."

It is early afternoon on Saturday, still smoggy. "Just can't get to that man in one and a half seconds, Coach, maybe even if no one's blocking me," Olsen says.

"That's right," George Allen says, "but tomorrow there's just one thing we want to take away from Jurgensen. That's the long pass. We want to take away the bomb."

"Ban the bomb!" Merlin Olsen shouts fiercely.

Late Saturday is a time for recollections. Olsen comes from Logan, Utah, two ridges and eighty miles north of Salt Lake City. He was the eldest of nine children, reared and still being reared by Merle B. Olsen, a schoolteacher, and Lynn J. Olsen, a "graduate expert on the nature of local soil." To the child of a Merle and a Lynn, the first name came without magic. The family, pioneers in the area, is staunchly Mormon.

There is a modest park across the street from the white frame house in Logan. There Merlin played football with older boys, and skated and roughhoused. He doesn't remember ever being afraid. The challenge of playing with older boys subdued the fear. He went to Utah State on a scholarship and graduated as an All-American, and he had the second-highest average of anyone in the business administration program, 3.69 out of a possible 4.0. He accepted $50,000 to sign with the Rams and began work on his master's thesis, still incomplete. Its title is "The Coming World Crisis in Sugar."

Now, six years later, as he is about to go forth against a good quarterback playing with an ordinary team, Olsen has discovered that he is less certain than ever of what he wants to do. He and his wife have a daughter of two, Kelly, and another child due early next year, and they have left small-town Utah for Los Angeles.

"I like it out here," Merlin says. "The question is, how will the future be. I may never finish my master's. I love playing tackle, but that isn't going to last. I work as a special representative for Allied Chemical, but you know that's tied to football. To tell you the truth, with everything, good marks, all-pro, I have no idea what ultimately I want to do."

"It isn't only football, is it?" Suzy Olsen says. "The whole country, everybody in business, is moving around. We're all having to get used to the fact that these days almost nobody is able to plant roots."

After a week of tearless toil and sweat, nothing on Sunday necessarily relates to what has gone before. Two nearly equal machines are meeting. If Merlin Olsen has been considering Jurgensen's release, Jurgensen has been measuring Olsen's charge. If

Olsen is bright enough to plot devious rushes, his opponent, Vince Promuto, is smart enough to plot counters. Promuto is a graduate of American University's law school.

Sunday is hazy and warm. Olsen parks his Ford LTD at the Coliseum at eleven o'clock. At the same time the Washington Redskins are climbing into a bus outside the Sheraton-West Hotel. Joe DiMaggio is riding along as a guest; he knows Edward Bennett Williams, the Redskins' president. The few people watching the Redskins gape at DiMaggio. Someone recognizes Jurgensen, and someone else spots Bobby Mitchell, a speedy back and pass catcher. But nobody notices Vince Promuto, 245 pounds, who soon will take the bar exam and who now plays guard.

The game is on. Olsen rushes onto the field. Jurgensen barks his signals clearly. At the snap Vince Promuto leaps backward, more agilely than Olsen had expected. As Merlin charges, Promuto fires into him low. The men hit hard. Somewhere else the pass is incomplete.

In the huddle Maxie Baughan calls for a zone defense. Olsen claps hands as the huddle breaks. "Let's hit."

"Gold," he says at the line as Sonny Jurgensen calls numbers. Olsen feints Vince Promuto, drives past him, and Jurgensen throws in haste to halfback A. D. Whitfield. David Jones was charging very wide. He spins and runs down Whitfield, who has made six yards. Third down and four, the game's first significant play.

"Eight, seventeen. Set. Hut, hut, hut."

The Front Four crash straight in as Jurgensen sprints back. They hold their arms high and, throwing above six or eight huge hands, Jurgensen overshoots a receiver far downfield. "Attaway," Merlin Olsen says. "Good going, guys."

The 'Skins get the ball next on their own forty-seven. Bobby Mitchell tries the center, but Olsen, slammed by Promuto and Len Hauss, the Washington center, holds his ground and slaps an arm at Mitchell's middle. The runner spins around, and David Jones completes the tackle after a three-yard gain.

The Rams watch for a pass. "Set," Jurgensen is calling. "Hut." As the ball is snapped, Vince Promuto pulls out of the line and begins running toward the left sideline. *Sweep,* Olsen thinks automatically. He runs wide, 276 pounds of effort in one short burst, and overtakes Mitchell five yards behind the line. When he comes out, Olsen takes a salt capsule, washed down with an elixir for quick energy.

"He's moving back and firing out, Oley," says Roosevelt Grier, who has been watching Promuto closely.

"Right," Olsen says. The Ram offense has moved and stalled. Another punt gives Washington the ball on its own fourteen. The defensive pressure is beginning to work. "Dig in, dig in, fire out," Olsen says at the line. The Four rush straight, and Jurgensen's pass sails near nobody but a Ram defensive back.

In each huddle Maxie Baughan is calling overall patterns, varying zone defenses and man-to-man. Olsen is talking at the line, calling the charge. "Set," cries Jurgensen. "Hut, hut, hut." Now Brown and Olsen twist. Brown shifts to the left in front of Olsen and turns in to charge. Olsen moves laterally before he starts his rush. Lamar Lundy, the right end, moves in and tries to burst up through the middle. As Jurgensen flees backward, David Jones, running an inside route, is almost on him. The Redskin blockers have picked up Olsen and stalled him. Jones is on top of Jurgensen, and Lundy is closing, as the right arm flashes and the ball sails out of the melee.

Damn, Olsen says to himself, stopping his charge. Damn.

They have done their job, kept the fierce pressure on, but not quite made the tackle. Fifty yards upfield the pass descends into the large, sure hands of Charley Taylor, who has outrun Clancy Williams and Eddie Meador. He makes the catch on the Ram forty-seven and sprints the rest of the way with smooth, enormous strides. The touchdown play has covered eighty-six yards. Almost a hundred yards away, Merlin Olsen shakes his head.

It is not going to be an easy day. As the Rams walk upfield, they talk about putting on more pressure. But Jurgensen has passed for a score under extreme pressure. Great individual effort defies a week of plans.

Midway into the second period, Roman Gabriel organizes one

scoring march and soon afterward strikes on a sixty-one-yard play to end Jack Snow. But Jurgensen manages to complete a long pass to the Rams' twenty-five. The Front Four are driving now, annoyed. Twice, on twists, they make Jurgensen get rid of the ball for no gain. On third down they go to straight power.

"Brown," Olsen calls. At the snap David Jones veers, and Olsen begins to storm inside. Shoving against Promuto, he makes progress with an intense effort.

Jones closes in on Jurgensen, who looks to step up, dodging. But Olsen rises in front of him. Jurgensen has nowhere to go but down, under David Jones's 260 pounds, eleven yards behind the line of scrimmage.

The 'Skins are far short with a field goal, and the Front Four trot off. "You feel good," Merlin Olsen says, "when you've done your job."

"Attaway, you guys. Attaway, Merlin," Coach Allen says.

Later they put on the pressure again. "Hut, hut," Jurgensen calls. He runs back, fleeing before Olsen's driving charge. He cocks his arm, and Olsen thinks, *I can't get to him.* Merlin raises both hands and leaps. He leaps again, hands almost ten feet in the air. Jurgensen sails the ball up, out toward the end zone. There the football drops, a high pop fly falling into the grasp of tight end Jerry Smith.

After one half, Washington has not shown very much. Jurgensen has been harried. The running attack is negative — in all, a total of four yards lost. But twice Sonny Jurgensen has contrived to throw the long scoring pass.

"Damn," Olsen says to David Jones, on the way to the locker room. "We took away everything but the bomb."

There is nothing coach Allen has to change, nothing wrong with the strategy. Jurgensen has simply been too good. Suddenly, halfway through the third period, Jurgensen completes four short passes. Going for five, from the Rams' thirty-seven, he looks for a receiver. But as he does, Olsen, who has charged dead ahead, is looming in front of him. Jurgensen does not *throw* the ball; he *discards* it as Olsen's fearsome charge bowls him over.

The Redskins have a second down and ten. Olsen calls, "Red." Again he fires straight ahead. This time Promuto is ready, plus the center and one of the halfbacks. The three men stop him. One lineman should be free, but Roger Brown fails to penetrate. Jurgensen finds Smith in the end zone, and the Rams are behind again. The quarter is almost over before the offense can mount an eighty-yard drive to tie the score.

The fourth period is going to be the game. "We got to keep that pressure up," Olsen says on the sideline. He has taken more salt tablets. He does not feel fatigue. A drive ends with a missed field goal. The Four throttle the Redskins. A Los Angeles drive stalls. Jon Kilgore punts a line drive, and Rickie Harris of the Redskins scampers fifty-one yards for a first down on the Los Angeles thirty-nine.

The Rams may lose. "Tight zone," Maxie Baughan says in the huddle.

"Gold," Merlin Olsen says. A full-power drive.

It falls to Merlin. He crashes in. Promuto springs back, sets, and tries to hold him. It is enough. Olsen realizes that he will not reach Jurgensen in time.

He leaps, reaching for air, exposing his underbelly. Promuto is rising as he does. The guard lifts Merlin higher, flipping him into the air. The great hands flap toward the ball and then sharply, rudely, Olsen turns upside down and crashes to the ground. He has fallen on his back from a height of six feet. For an instant he lies silent, stunned.

Noise reaches his ears. It is more noise than usual. That is his first thought. Something has happened that is either very good or very bad.

His back hurts. Something stings him in the neck.

Did he block the pass? Merlin Olsen wonders.

And then he knows. He did not block the pass. The crowd is making noise because Jerry Smith caught it for a touchdown. A hard late drive by Gabriel manages to save a tie for the Rams.

Afterward he has poise left, but very little. He is undressing alongside Roman Gabriel, his friend.

"Goddamn, I played a bad game," Gabriel says.

"You did not," Olsen says. "You threw good."

"My calls," Gabriel says.

"They were OK."

"They were erratic."

"Look," Merlin Olsen says, in pain and distress, "any game on this club where the offense scores twenty-one points or more we ought to win. Gabe, I want to apologize to you on behalf of the defense. We didn't do our job."

"Another tie," Gabriel says in disgust.

"Last year we were losing this kind of game. We're a coming team. We're getting better. Sure, I know about a tie. It's like kissing your ugly sister."

"And two ties in a row," Roman Gabriel says, "is like kissing your brother."

Olsen smiles thinly. It has not gone the way he meant. His neck hurts, but not as badly as the disappointment. He is spent. His body is worn, beyond the redemption of salt pills and sugared drinks. Looking at his face, one knows at once that it would not take much to make big Merlin Olsen cry. And there is tomorrow. He will have to talk for Allied Chemical, answering people who want to know something he himself does not know. Why didn't the Rams win the game?

Maybe after that he'll look at films.

Then will come Tuesday, and Tuesday is a rotten day for tackles.

1967

Thanks to the mellifluous voice and CBS, Merlin Olsen has become a nationwide institution.

An Hour or So
of Hell

*After assignments writing politics — few people have disturbed me
as much as Lyndon Johnson during Vietnam — I wanted to turn
to something honorable. I thought of a hockey goalie. There is
nothing duplicitous in stopping a puck moving at 120 mph.*

*I asked about Ed Giacomin in New York, but John Halligan of
the Rangers reported that the coach was afraid I'd make Giacomin
more nervous than he already was. "I have another good one for
you," Halligan said. So he did. The story won me my third Dutton
Prize.*

The night before their All-Star game in Toronto, the world's
best hockey players were assaulting Canadian beef and listening to speeches that all seemed to begin: "Hockey benefits a man
mentally, physically, and spiritually." Then, in a ballroom of the
Royal York Hotel, a comedian rose and the mood brightened.

The Toronto Maple Leafs had gotten so old, said Johnny
Wayne, the comic, that their team physician was a prostate specialist. One goalie Wayne knew was so erratic that he made a great
save on television but missed the same shot on an instant replay.
People wanted to get rich in hockey, but the only way to make a
small fortune was to begin with a large fortune and buy a team.

The big room rang with laughter, but directly under Wayne's gesticulating left hand, Glenn Hall, the All-Star goaltender, sat dourly.

"Didn't you like the jokes?" someone asked.

"Ooh, yes," Hall said, in the brogue of western Canada. "Wayne is one of our best comedians."

"You weren't laughing."

"Ooh, I chuckled once or twice," Hall said, "but you want to be careful. Mind you, you don't want to give too much away."

His chubby face appeared merry, but Hall was serious. At thirty-six, Glenn Henry Hall, of the National Hockey League All-Star Team and the St. Louis Blues, is a complex athlete, fond of poetry and farm journals, solitude and manly companionship. But through all his moods there runs a theme of thrift. It is an asset for a goalie to give nothing away, and Hall comes by his penury naturally. He grew up in a cold country during the Depression.

"The truth is I don't like to play hockey anymore. Aiyee," he says, making the pronoun a sound of pain, "don't like it, but it is a marvelous sport. I like the people, the talk, even the dinners. I love everything about hockey except the games."

His distaste for play is overwhelming. Invariably, as Hall is about to leave the clubhouse to guard the six-by-four-foot entrance to the goal, nausea seizes him. Often he loses the lunch devoured six hours earlier. "Hall's bucket," one of his old teammates suggests, "belongs in the Hockey Hall of Fame."

Still, Hall cannot retire. He has tried, but reality brings him back. In Stoney Plain, Alberta, where Hall lives, he has never been able to find a job that pays as much as $100 a week. For goaltending in St. Louis this season, Glenn Hall, the man of thrift, is earning $47,500.

It is an odd story, really, and touching. Here is a man whose boyhood was filled with a dream. He wanted to be a hockey player. By ten or twelve his dream became specific. He would become one of the six men who played goal in the National Hockey League. With manhood his wildest hope came true. Hall became not just a goalie, he became the best of goalies: Mister Goalie, sportswriters called him. But under the whistling pucks, the hurtling bodies, the beating sticks, the slashing skates — the thousand natural shocks that he fell heir to — Hall came to hate and fear his work. The process was inexorable and irreversible. Now being a goaltender disturbs his sleep, upsets his stomach, lays him low. "Every game I have to play these days," says Glenn Hall, "is an hour or so of hell."

As a result of goaltending injuries, Hall has endured 250 to 300 stitches, 75 of them around the mouth, almost all in emergencies, when there was no time for Novocain. "I don't like needles," Hall says, "and I don't like pain."

Techniques of scoring goals have been evolving with a terrifying swiftness. Once most of the scoring came on short, accurate wrist shots. That was before hockey discovered its home run. The slap shot, a full, prodigious swipe, propels the puck, a six-ounce disk of frozen rubber, at speeds as fast as 120 miles an hour.

Still, goaltenders, with their instant reflexes and Martian padding, can handle pucks moving at two miles a minute except under certain handicaps. These handicaps are critical to the modern goalie. When a fine marksman — Bobby Hull, Gordie Howe, Rod Gilbert — winds up to shoot, his teammates promptly scramble toward the goal. One tries to block the goalie's vision. Another may extend his stick to deflect the speeding puck, to alter the angle of its flight at the last millisecond. The crouching goalie becomes both blind and helpless.

In self-defense, many goalies have started wearing masks, and every NHL team now uses two goalies, to spread the shell shock, so to speak. Hall is happy that a thirty-four-year-old rookie named Seth Martin frequently relieves him, but he cannot bring himself to wear a mask. "What worries you most is the eyes," he says, "and a mask may not help there. You wouldn't want to go stopping a puck with an eye, even if you were wearing the mask. But there's something else. A mask might throw me off. You don't want to look the fool out there, out in front of all these people."

Hockey men agree that goaltenders are a species apart, difficult, indeed unfathomable. They are not even precisely sure what makes some great. After listing a variety of attributes — reflexes, hands, vision, ability to anticipate — Hector (Toe) Blake, who coaches the Montreal Canadiens, shakes his head and says, "With great ones, like Hall, it's something else. You get four goals off them, or five, but the goal you've got to have to win, somehow the great ones don't let you get it." The sense of thrift is always recurring.

Hall was in his team's training room when I met him. He lay on a table, wearing a towel and a frown. One of his knees ached; it bore a circular purple scar. "Cartilage?" I asked.

"Noo. A skate. The cut is from a long time ago."

It was the day of a game, when Hall is most tense. "You have to respect those feelings," his wife, Pauline, had said. "But don't be afraid of Glenn. He's not an ogre."

He knew what I wanted and got up from the table and asked if William (Scotty) Bowman, the Blues' astute young coach, was using his dressing room. Bowman was not, and we walked into the room, a windowless, sealed cubicle. "It should be quiet here," Hall said, and it was, except when other players beat hockey sticks on the steel door in high good humor.

"What can you do about slap shots?" I asked.

"Well, you don't want to get hit with one," Hall said. "You watch the puck. You never let the puck out of your sight. But your eyes take in other things. You notice where the forwards are stationing themselves. You calculate the caroms."

"Sheer speed, then, is not a problem?"

Hall blinked. "Huh?" he said. "Speed *ought* to bother you. Bobby Hull — he has by far the hardest shot I've ever seen — can hit you in the chest and knock you over. You've made the save, but I guarantee you don't feel good about it."

"Do you do anything special for your reflexes?"

"I like Ping-Pong. I like to get up very close and have a big fellow slam at me harder and harder. I keep moving in against his slams. I know the Ping-Pong ball won't hurt me, and I'm trying to make a habit of moving in."

He seemed intense but poised. No, he had not slept well the night before. He never slept much the night before a game. The New York Rangers, whom he would play, were a good, hard-working team. He was going to eat soft food at two o'clock, then try to sleep. As Hall left, he even managed a wry joke. "If you don't think I'm familiar with that puck," he said, "let me tell you exactly what's written on it: 'Art Ross, patent number 2226516.'" He half smiled and was gone.

That night, at seven-thirty, the last of the Blues on the ice was a transmogrified Hall. Under his forty pounds of equipment he skated without effort. That was his body. His face was something else. The lips were tightly pressed and very pale. At the corners the rigid mouth turned down. The brown eyes were furtive. They gazed downward and darted. Hall looked frightened, unhappy, and nauseated.

The game began at eight. Hall bent in the net, nervously scraping invisible ice shavings with his stick. On his left hand he wore a huge mitt, something like a first baseman's glove. It is called a trapper. The right hand, also gloved, held the thick stick. On the back of the right glove was a large flat leather pad to deflect shots up and away.

The Rangers won the face-off, and soon Phil Goyette, their center, was digging hard toward Hall. Al Arbour, a bespectacled St. Louis defenseman, moved with Goyette, but the Ranger slammed a swift, low slap shot from forty feet away. Hall lowered his stick, but a speeding puck, like a speeding baseball, curves or dips or sails. At the last instant Goyette's low shot dipped still lower. It slipped under Hall's stick, and at 8:29 Hall found himself beaten. He grimaced. He was embarrassed. Then he told himself there was no going back. He still had plenty to worry about.

The Blues are not a strong shooting team, and they have trouble coming from behind. Hall played superbly for the balance of the period, making a lunging save and blocking two successive rebounds. Under pressure he dropped both knees to the ice, his lower legs fanning wide. That way he was covered on low shots; for high ones he dug his skate toes into the ice and bounced to his full height. Hall is the inventor of this technique, which young goalies copy. Still, at the end of the period the Rangers led, 1–0.

They were not going to be caught. A defenseman's mistake hung Hall in the second period, and he was screened on a slap shot in the third. The final score was 3–1, but he still was bothered by the opening goal. "A knuckle ball," he said. "He beat me with a flicking knuckle ball. It dipped."

We were riding out to the airport in Al Arbour's car for a midnight flight to Chicago, where Hall had once played for the Black Hawks. It was snowing very hard.

"Wonder if they'll be flying?" Arbour said.

"A knuckle ball," Hall said.

"Look at this snow," Arbour said. "When I came here to St. Louis, they promised me golf every day, all winter."

In the airplane Hall began to relax. "Did it drop straight down?" I said.

"Straight down."

He did not play in Chicago. Considering his knee and his general tension, Scotty Bowman decided to rest him. Hall spent ten years with the Black Hawks, and I asked if he was going to give pointers to Seth Martin. "Ooh, you tell him to watch Ken Wharram on breakaways," he said. "One or two things, but not too much. You want to be careful. It may not come out the way you say."

The Chicago fans applauded when Hall skated onto the rink, but he responded with a look of deep discomfort. Even before a game in which he would not have to play, he looked miserable. The game ended in a tie, and I asked him afterward how he could get himself so worked up for an evening on the bench. "You *have* to be nervous," Hall insisted, "if you consider all the possibilities. Seth could be hurt. Then I'd have to play, wouldn't I?"

We flew to Toronto the next morning, where Hall was the only St. Louis player among the All-Stars. He was going to work the third and final period of the game against Toronto, which last year won the Stanley Cup. Ed Giacomin of the Rangers, a Hall disciple, would play goalie first. Terry Sawchuk of Los Angeles would follow.

"Aren't you fellows nervous?" Hall asked in the dressing room.

"It's just an All-Star game," Sawchuk said.

"I never get that tense," Giacomin said. Still, the Rangers rarely play Giacomin against Chicago, because Hull's slap shot seems to paralyze him.

While the All-Stars warmed up, driving shots at Giacomin in practiced patterns, anyone behind the goal could witness hockey's strongest shots in safety. The boards in Maple Leaf Gardens are topped with high panels of a transparent plastic called Herculite. According to its manufacturer, Herculite is bulletproof.

On the ice Detroit's Howe, balding, muscular, and fierce, was slashing a shot with his great wrists. The puck flew past the cage, a few inches off the ice, and boomed into the boards. Next Hull, broad and powerful, unloaded. Giacomin caught the puck but looked awkward as he kept his body out of the way. Norm Ullman of Detroit shot — "not a hard shooter," Hall was to insist — and the puck sailed over the goal and slammed into the Herculite directly before my face.

What happens with these shots is that they leap. Americans, used to catching baseballs or bullet passes or returning tennis serves, have never seen anything like the approach of a well-stroked hockey shot. The puck starts small, then seems to gain momentum, and in the last few feet of flight the thing explodes. A hard crack against the Herculite. That was all there was. One routine shot. One brief encounter. Facing a firing squad is a brief encounter too.

Although some All-Star games are passionless, this one was close and included a fight (Howe vs. Mike Walton of Toronto to no decision). The Stars were beaten, 4–3, but the game provided a fine sample of Hall's skill.

Midway through the final period Toronto's center, swift and wily Dave Keon, stole the puck and broke alone toward Hall.

Keon skated toward the right corner of the net, moving his stick from side to side, shifting the puck. Hall crouched low, considering skater and puck approaching at twenty-five miles an hour.

Abruptly, through instinct or memory of other situations or both, Hall charged. That is, he skated directly at Dave Keon.

Keon stopped dead. Ice sprayed as he dug in his skate blades. He hooked left in a swift semicircle. Hall dropped back and covered the new move. Keon faked at the left corner of the goal, but Hall read the fake. When Keon drilled a hard, low shot diagonally to the right, Hall was there. He caught it in his trapper.

"Nice," I said afterward in the dressing room.

"I was jerky," Hall said. "Not fluid enough."

"That guy," Ed Giacomin said, pointing at Hall, "is unbelievable. It's his hands. It's his reactions. He's the greatest."

Hall still was tense. With the dressing room emptying, he bent toward his bag, packed with forty pounds of gear. We each grabbed a strap and made our way by subway to a downtown restaurant.

Hall ate lightly with Lou Angotti, an All-Star from Philadelphia who played two seasons with Hall in Chicago. "They tell you," Angotti said, "no one can say a word to the man here before a game. Even a sneeze, and he has to use the bucket. But I'd talk to him. I'd walk right up and tell him, 'You better be sick, Hall. They're gonna take *sixty* shots at you tonight.'"

Hall almost laughed. "Whenever *you* were in there, Louie, they would."

I said I'd see them in Philadelphia, where that weekend the Blues would play the Flyers, who were leading the Western Division of the league. St. Louis was moving up. "That looks like a big game," I said.

"They're all big games," Hall said. "Either you need it for a spot in the play-offs, or when you've clinched a spot you need it to maintain momentum, or you need it to improve or to keep sharp. In the fifteen years I've been in this league, I've never played a game that wasn't big."

Hall comes out of Humboldt, Saskatchewan, the son of a prairie railroad man, who died of cancer on Christmas Day, 1967. Glenn was born in 1931 and remembers that there were always groceries for the table. "Maybe there wasn't much behind that, but Dad always made sure we had groceries."

Glenn could do well at schoolwork anytime he tried, but he felt that his life, his real life, began in the outdoors on biting winter afternoons. The game was shinny. It is an informal game with varying rules, akin to hockey the way stickball is to baseball. In Humboldt thirty years ago the schoolboys tramped down the snow and formed two goals and raced up and down in street shoes. They played for hours, chasing a rolling puck, perhaps cardboard, perhaps frozen horse dung, and batted it toward handmade goals.

Hall learned to ice-skate soon after he learned to walk. He liked playing wing, but after assessing his own ability, he decided that if he had any chance at all of cracking the National Hockey League, he would have to make it as a goalie.

He worked his way up slowly through juvenile leagues until he was old enough for amateur leagues. (Canadian amateurs, unlike American amateurs, are paid by daylight.) "What first attracted me to him," says Pauline Patrick Hall, the nurse Glenn married in 1949, "was not Glenn so much as his car. Not many had cars around Humboldt in those days. We girls knew that a young fellow with his own car was someone substantial."

Hall signed with the Detroit farm system, and in 1956, his first full season with the Red Wings, he turned in twelve shutouts, one shy of the modern record. He allowed only 2.11 goals a game (any average under three is very good) and was the National League's rookie of the year. For this the Red Wings paid him $6,000.

At the end of Hall's second season (2.24 average), the Red Wings opened the play-offs against Boston. Late in the game Vic Stasiuk of the Bruins slammed a hard shot at Hall, and as he did, another Bruin skated across the goal mouth. Hall's vision was blocked. He had lost the puck. "When that happens," Hall says, "you make yourself as big as possible, trying to cover the greatest area." He was making himself big when he saw the puck again. It was five feet in front of him, mouth high, traveling ninety miles an hour.

Hall regained consciousness in the Detroit dressing room with a physician bending over him. His eyes were going black, and his mouth was messy. "How many will it take?" he mumbled.

"A few," the surgeon said. "You really caught one this time."

"Well, let's get it over with," Hall said.

Half an hour later he skated back on the ice. Twenty-three stitches held his mouth together. He finished the game. Boston won, 3–1.

He was not outstanding thereafter, and when the Red Wings lost the series to the Bruins, Detroit decided to dump Hall, although he had played in seventy consecutive complete games. He lacked courage, someone suggested. That July he was traded to Chicago, where he ran his streak to 502 games.

This season the National Hockey League, traditionally a profitable monopoly, has submitted to a semirevolution. As if to make up for years of lost expansion, the league doubled in size, going from six teams to a dozen. A complex draft helped stock the new franchises, and each of the old clubs was required to relinquish two goalies. The Black Hawks let Hall go because he was over thirty-five.

The splendid veteran found himself suddenly assigned to a new city and an unknown club. He would have to leave old Chicago friends, find a winter house in St. Louis, place four children in new schools and, most important, play goal for a team whose ability to provide minimal protection was questionable.

Uncertain and unhappy, he was considering retirement when two Blues executives, Lynn Patrick and Sid Salomon III, took a private jet to Edmonton to make an intensive pitch. They offered him $47,500, by far the highest salary paid to any goalie since the dawn of ice, and Hall nodded with joyless resignation. He would play.

He now owns 475 acres, twenty miles from Edmonton, on which he grows barley. He has put in 250 pines, spruces, and poplars near the site where he intends to build a house. "A huge fireplace is what we want most," Pauline Hall says, "where we can sit and enjoy its warmth with friends."

"But I couldn't keep everybody eating on what I've got," Hall says. Each save, then, is helping to buy the farm.

In Philadelphia on the weekend, the hockey game was rough and ragged. Hall played well, and with about eight minutes to play, he was clinging to a 2–1 lead. Then Forbes Kennedy of the Flyers skated into the Blues' zone. He drove for the goal, was blocked, and had to go behind the right side of the cage. He passed, fell, and lay prone.

The puck moved to the left side, and Hall followed it. Philadelphia forwards were scrimmaging dangerously close. As he shifted to the left, Hall surveyed the right side with a swift peripheral glance. The right was clear. He saw no trouble. He had missed Kennedy, still prone.

Then Kennedy scrambled up, dashed in front of the net, took a quick pass and tipped it toward the goal. Hall's left skate was a blur. The puck was faster. The point-blank shot tied the game, which stayed that way.

Afterward Hall was furious. He wants to win, not tie. The tying goal was scored not only because Kennedy lay prone at a key instant but also because a St. Louis defenseman neglected to cover him when he got up.

"You know," Hall said as we sat in a little restaurant, "I used to live for winter. Now I never get to spend a winter at home."

"How many games do you have left?"

"Thirty-one."

"Did you ever think of trying tranquilizers?"

"I did," he said. "I got relaxed, and I played relaxed too."

"TV announcers always talk about the pro football teams fighting nervousness by praying."

"In times like these," Hall said, "I'd think God would have something more important to worry about than football or a hockey game."

"Well, it isn't all bad, and you'll miss a lot of it when you're through."

"Oooh, I know that," Hall said. "The fellowship. Where can

you find fellowship like in hockey? But I like my land and the way the hills roll, and the fields and the space and all that privacy all day and every day." Then he recited:

> West wind blow from your prairie nest,
> Blow from the mountains,
> Blow from the west . . .

"You're a country man," I said.

"You're trying to tell me I'm a farmer."

He was as relaxed as I had seen him. "The team's picking up, and you're going well," I said. "There's no reason why you can't keep on making the money and playing five more years."

He looked at me, hurt, and then he looked away. He was contemplating five more years of slap shots. The color slipped from his face, and his lips pressed tight together, and right before my eyes Glenn Hall, the greatest of modern goalies, thought about his work and turned pale green.

1968

Glenn Hall resides in Stoney Plain, Alberta. He reads poetry, works his land, paints barns.

Kareem Arrives

Al Silverman, editing this story, was distressed by my use of the word "nigger." He was concerned that readers might misinterpret. But Silverman, a more secure editor than most, thought the matter through and came up agreeing with me. The word was essential.

I know one reader who did not misinterpret. Lew Alcindor, now Kareem Abdul-Jabbar, mentioned in an interview with TV Guide *two years ago that I had been honest and supportive when he was starting.*

He did not mention an error. I wrote that he might play for fifteen years. He came closer to twenty.

The motel was called Quality Court, which meant this was no Plaza Suite, and the black man lying under the brown blanket seemed endless, and you had to wonder what was going to happen when he stood up. Would there be room for all of him under that low plasterboard ceiling?

"I have a hyperactive mind," the black man said. He threw his head from one side to another, as though in pain. "I have to clear my mind to play basketball, see? I can't have it all cluttered, man. That's why I look relaxed, but I'm not relaxed." He paused. His moments are full of silences. Then, "I'm all worked up, man, deep down inside."

The tall and troubled black was Ferdinand Lewis Alcindor, Jr. It had been difficult to get an appointment to see him. His employers at the Milwaukee Bucks appeared cowed, as well they might. The personage of Lew Alcindor may be more consequential than the Milwaukee basketball franchise. Certain press reports described Alcindor as mercenary, rude, possibly antiwhite. Finally, he had an unnerving recent record of aggressiveness toward opponents: one broken jaw, one knockout, and one foiled attack in a few months. You go into this kind of interview carefully, preparing all the questions, gauging your subject, wondering about your own jaw.

That was how it had been, but now it wasn't that way at all. Now I was sitting in this dreary room in St. Louis with a bright, sensitive, aesthetic young man, wondering if he was going to bump his head and wondering, too, about the rest of us and the society that had made him both millionaire and nigger.

Alcindor gazed at the wall. It was four o'clock in the afternoon of a game; the drapes were drawn, and the only light came from a reading lamp on the night table. He was lying on his side, the great legs bent under the brown blanket, and the upper part of his body supported by an elbow. His body was curled so that he could lie with his head on the pillow and stare at the wall.

"How do you see your role in the black movement?" He blinked. No other sign or motion.

"When Jackie Robinson broke in," I said, "it was enough, it was significant, for him to get base hits. That was enough."

Only his mouth moving, Alcindor said, "Because white people thought he wasn't good enough to do it."

"But it isn't enough anymore. Black intellectuals don't want black athletes for leaders. They feel there've been enough famous blacks in sports and jazz."

Alcindor made a spasmodic nod. "I know that," he said. He lunged from the bed and began to stride. He bent slightly at the waist. There was room between his head and the ceiling, but he had better not jump.

"I'm figuring it out," Alcindor said, pacing, towering. "It's fragmented, man. Some go to church. Some go to school. Some do nothing. Some want revolt."

The black community at large. That was what he had decided to talk about. "Where do you stand?" I said.

"Try to get change as quickly and painlessly as possible." Alcindor returned to the bed. "Try to stand for something positive. Be something positive."

"What about violence?"

The body shifted under the blanket. Alcindor resumed considering the wall.

"What about violence on the basketball court?"

"You want to know what happened in Seattle. Someone hit me couple times. Bob Rule got a finger in my eye. Man, I went for Rule. And I spit. And a kid, some big-mouthed teenager, I gave him a shove. And I want to stand for something positive, and I managed to have everyone in the whole arena dislike me. I was a protagonist." Alcindor shook his head. I thought he might spring up again. "These things you want me to talk about," he said. "They're hard to put into words." He smiled and scowled, as though in a private dialogue. I wondered if violence was something he disliked.

"Lew. When you went for Bob Rule, did you mean to hurt him or just give him a shove?"

Alcindor turned and looked directly at me and said, quite evenly, "When I went for Rule there was murder in my heart."

It is not going to add up. Of that you can be assured. In a society that does not add up, the Lew Alcindor phenomenon, frozen in full flow, which is what we are trying to do, is not going to provide one of those comfortable *Reader's Digest* pieces with smooth beginning, anesthetic middle, tidy end. The Alcindor phenomenon is a mix of rough edges and incompleteness and immaturity and wisdom and misinterpretations and rages and regrets. It makes Ray Patterson, president of the Bucks, discuss dimensions of maturity; and John Erickson, the general manager, speak of uneven development; and Larry Costello, the coach, long for days that may never have been, when professional basketball players concerned themselves only with professional basketball.

These things are important, but important, too, is what Guy Rodgers had to say. "Lew is a very nice guy, with a fine sense of humor, a terrific person."

We were sitting over steak in a Milwaukee restaurant late at night. Rodgers, at thirty-four, had played a brilliant game against Los Angeles, and his young wife, Lita, had just learned that their seven-month-old baby, who has an eye disorder, was not going to need an operation. It was a cheerful time.

"Lew is your teammate," I said. "Suppose you didn't think much of him? What would you tell me then?"

Rodgers was wearing steel-framed spectacles and an ascot. "You didn't know me in Philadelphia," he told me.

"I was wondering," Lita said, "why we're having dinner with him, if the story he's doing is about Lew."

Rodgers winced slightly.

"I wanted to have this dinner," Rodgers said, "because there are a couple of things people ought to get straight.

"Ask anyone who really knew me in Philadelphia, and they'll tell you I'm a pretty honest guy. If I didn't like Lew, maybe I wouldn't knock him to you, but you can bet we wouldn't be having dinner right now. What I'm trying to say is that this is a special kind of kid, and I played with Wilt in the beginning and I've been in this league for a long time. Believe me, this kid is a rare human being."

That is something to remember as we work our way across the jagged edges. Alcindor, at twenty-two, has won the warmth and admiration and friendship of a fine old professional.

I had heard of Alcindor a long time ago, a gifted black from Inwood, which is a hilly section of Manhattan, far north of Harlem, with trees and grass and integration, to which vanguards of the black middle class escaped during the 1950s. He was Roman Catholic, or his parents were, and he burst upon us, a gloriously gifted young giant, at Power Memorial Academy, a Catholic prep, accompanied always by a white man, his coach, Jack Donohue. The coach hid Alcindor from the press and seemed to be his closest adviser, and right or wrong, the word was that Jack Donohue was going to hang on to Alcindor's Achilles tendons and follow him to a college job. The recruiting of Alcindor — he could have gone anywhere — produced at least one charge that Donohue was writing himself into the letter of intent. But then, to general surprise, Alcindor fled to UCLA, far from his old schoolyard, far from Donohue, and far from his parents, who had moved to Queens.

The Alcindor era was the finest in UCLA basketball annals. The Bruins pivoting around him were chronic national champions. After that the only question was where he would play professionally and for how much. He was fortunate to graduate at a time when two leagues were battling. The Milwaukee Bucks, for the NBA, and the New York Nets, for the American Basketball Association, made offers. Alcindor settled on Milwaukee, a lovely city in many ways and in many ways a backwater, for a supposed $1.4 million. That is roughly $200,000 per foot and also, when you consider it, possibly more than the owners of a new and rather modest NBA franchise carry in a checking account. Then Alcindor began playing, with enough potential to draw this from Bob Cousy: "Alcindor is the only man I've seen with the possibility of combining Bill Russell's mental concentration with Wilt Chamberlain's physical dominance."

Later Alcindor crashed into print, selling three installments worth of memoirs to *Sports Illustrated* for a reported $20,000, or about a dollar a word. The memoir paired Alcindor with a talented, busy author named Jack Olsen, and offered us this quite early:

> I'm going to tell you my life story . . . and if you think that it takes a lot of conceit for a 22-year-old basketball player to tell his life story, then that's your hang-up. The way things are in America today — and have been for 200 years — the story of any black man has meaning, even if he's a shoeshine "boy" or porter or your friendly neighborhood Uncle Tom.

That was the tone. The story described how being called "nigger" had wounded Alcindor; friendly neighborhood coach Donohue had told him once, "You're acting just like a nigger." It presented background and outlook and anecdote, but always with a kind of insolence, which, I would learn, was not entirely fair. It is a weakness of the genre, the collaborative form, never to be wholly true to either party. Two egos are working and sometimes clashing. When one man is white and the other black, the conflict becomes more complex, and when both are working to provide a black life for a magazine that caters to affluent whites, the impure art form must be discolored. What we have is not pure Alcindor and not pure Olsen. Instead we have a hybrid: Olsendor.

On the telephone John Erickson would not comment on the stories. "As general manager," he said, "it's my job to be concerned about Lew on the court. I make it a point not to interfere with other matters. He had every right to do those stories, and he has every right to see or not see whom he pleases."

I was making a pro forma call before flying to Milwaukee. It is always a sound idea to check in with management; professional athletes are busy people, not always punctual or even reliable, and it can be helpful to have management arrange introductions.

"When can you get us together?" I asked Erickson.

"I can't get you together."

"But you're the Bucks."

"That's right, but as I say, aside from what goes on during the games, Alcindor is on his own."

I telephoned a newspaperman who had been covering Alcindor. "He can be very difficult," the newspaperman reported. "Says very little. Gets into fights. Not always cooperative."

After two more calls to the Bucks, one to the commissioner of the NBA, and two to a California stockbroker who was supposed to be Alcindor's confidant, I mounted the jet to Milwaukee. There was not going to be any trouble seeing him, I was assured. And sure enough, when I went to the Milwaukee Arena there he was, in a sweat suit of forest green and white, practicing lay-up shots —

swish, swish, slam. The Bucks were going to play the Cincinnati Royals, who offer Oscar Robertson and an interesting supporting cast, with Connie Dierking, a somewhat fleshy six ten, playing center.

Alcindor seemed listless during the warm-up. His face was expressionless. Often he stood by himself. There was no enthusiasm to his moves, no adventure. He does not go out of his way to stuff shots, and several times I had to remind myself of Cousy's quote and of another observer's remark: Alcindor possessed so much ability that he is a basketball third force all by himself.

Alcindor won the tap, but the Royals stole the ball. Robertson dribbled, jumped, and scored. Then the Bucks drove. Alcindor, moving slowly, trailed everyone else. A shot missed. The Royals stormed. There were two fast passes. Suddenly Johnny Green laid up an easy shot. Where was Alcindor?

Two minutes into the game, Lew put in a pretty hook, spinning toward the center from a post on the left. Quickly Tom Van Arsdale hit a jump, and Robertson drove, faked, fed to Dierking, who sank a lay-up. Alcindor looked confused. At the end of the quarter, Cincinnati led, 33–20. Rodgers stirred the Bucks in the opening minutes of the next period, but Dierking hit from the circle, then with a hook, then with a running lay-up. Alcindor still trailed plays, got himself boxed out, seemed out of things. Halfway through the second quarter, he *was* out of things. Larry Costello sat him down in favor of Dick Cunningham.

Alcindor returned for the second half, and the Royals, more or less ignoring his presence, ran five straight baskets. Connie Dierking was dominating underneath. He scored at the rate of a basket a minute until, four minutes into the half, Costello yanked Alcindor again. The Royals walked in that night 129–104.

It is difficult to describe this late November performance except in terms of negatives. Alcindor did not often get position for rebounds, and when he did, he would not fight for the ball. The statistician credited him with five rebounds for the first half, when the issue was in doubt, while Rodgers, more than a foot shorter, grabbed six. Overall, Alcindor took thirteen shots, several from underneath, and sank five. He scored just thirteen points. He was not a third force or any force at all. He was a cipher.

The Bucks' dressing room is closed for a time after each game, but on the other side, Coach Cousy was smiling and relaxed and smoking a large cigar. "It isn't fair to comment on Alcindor's play tonight," Cousy said, making a comment. "He's a rookie and he's having troubles. It's hardest for rookies at center. But everything I said about his potential still goes."

The Bucks dress in cramped quarters; when I got there Larry Costello was obviously upset. "What is there to say about something like this?" he told Bob Wolf of the *Milwaukee Journal* and Lou Chapman of the *Sentinel*. "They didn't come to play."

"*Anything* good tonight, Coach?" Chapman said.

Costello made a little laugh. "In a game like that?"

"Rodgers," Chapman prompted.

"That's right," Costello said. "Guy did a good job."

I wandered toward Alcindor, who was dressing quickly, silently. He was neither friendly nor hostile. He was civil. "How's four-thirty tomorrow?" he said.

"Fine."

I returned to Costello, who was becoming more upset. The performance was disturbing him slowly but surely, like a bad clam. "I don't understand some of these guys," he said. "Here they play a terrible game like this, and now they're taking off, going their separate ways. It wasn't that way when I was playing." Costello gulped a soft drink from the bottle. He has a flat, pleasant, tough Irish face. "If we played one like this, we'd want to sit around for a long time and talk, talk among ourselves." At that moment, not twenty feet away, Alcindor slipped out of the dressing room alone.

"So many outside interests," Costello said. "So many things on the side."

"What about all that money?" a reporter said.

"Look, the more money a guy can get, the more power to him. And everybody on the team feels the same way. I'm just saying when it goes bad, sit around and talk. Stick around. Hang together like a team."

"You speaking of anyone in particular?" a reporter said.

Costello blinked. "Nah," he said. "Nobody in particular. I'm talking about the whole team."

The situation was charged in a community with an unhappy recent sports history. Milwaukee tried to support professional basketball in the early 1950s — Ben Kerner's Hawks. The community failed, and the Hawks moved on to St. Louis, where they prospered until hockey swept down the Mississippi.

Enter the Bucks, organized by a Milwaukee syndicate that includes Wes Pavalon, a man of means and a goatee, who rides chauffeured limousines, thanks to his invention, Career Academy, a chain of trade schools. The new spirit has moved someone to song:

> Milwaukee Bucks! That's the name of our team,
> And they will win, with an effort supreme.
> Milwaukee Bucks! How they handle the ball,
> And they break great, whether they're short or tall.

They did not break great a year ago. The Bucks won twenty-seven games, finished last in the East, and the NBA guide spelled their name Milwuakee. At about this time, when the rustlings of spring 1969 stirred, the downbeat Milwaukee trail and the upbeat road of Lew Alcindor intersected.

The NBA operated with a draft, and since Milwaukee and Phoenix, last in each division, were expansion teams, Commissioner Walter Kennedy drew cards to see who would have the first pick, then the call. The card came up Phoenix. The call was heads. The coin came up tails. Milwaukee had won.

"Whooop!" cried Wes Pavalon, embracing John Erickson and burning one of Erickson's ears with his cigarette. That was the beginning of Milwaukee's Alcindor ambiguities.

In Encino, a San Fernando Valley city where Alcindor had holed up with a friend, Lew was aware that a fortune awaited. But he was conscious too that blacks were once peddled from the slaver's block. He didn't want that; it had been humiliating. Paul Robeson used to sing: "No more auction block for me." "There won't be any bidding for me," Alcindor decided. "Each team [Milwaukee and the New York Nets of the American Basketball Association] can make one offer. Then I'll pick the one I like."

Everyone, from Pavalon to Alcindor, promised that the Milwaukee offer would be kept secret. The figure of $1.4 million comes from an excellent source, but that source can provide no detailed breakdown. "Probably it will be spread at about $300,000 a year." Suffice it, then, that Alcindor appears to have been paid three and a half times what Joe Namath appeared to have been paid to become a professional athlete.

Lew talked to Milwaukee on a Monday and to the New York Nets on a Tuesday. He decided quickly for the Bucks. "All things being equal, it would have been easier to play in New York, but things were not equal."

When his decision became known, an ABA spokesman made the doomsday bid. To play for the Nets, Alcindor could have a $500,000 cash bonus, five years each at $200,000 salary, an annuity of $62,500 a year for twenty years starting at age forty-one, ten percent of a proposed ABA television contract, and five percent of the Nets franchise. Alcindor declined. "I told each of them," he said, "to make one offer. I'm sticking to that. I'm going to Milwaukee."

Pat Boone, the singer, is one of the ABA's backers. "Our negotiator blew it," Boone announced in California. Lawyers for the ABA brought an action against the NBA, charging that the teams in the older league "conspired to jointly purchase a superstar through the use of defendant's combined powers." What that means, aside from the point that lawyers split infinitives, is that the ABA did not believe Messrs. Pavalon et al. carried a spare $1.4 million. Instead, the ABA was asserting, there had been a kind of subscription throughout the NBA to finance the Milwaukee bid and thus keep Alcindor out of the new league. This litigation may be one reason why not Erickson nor Alcindor nor Pavalon will disclose the terms of the signing.

At any rate, on Wednesday, April 3, Alcindor affixed his Ferdinand Lewis to a Bucks contract. "It's a dream come true," Pavalon said. John Erickson said he was thrilled, not only because of Alcindor's skill but "because of the quality of the person. He carried on his contract talks with the greatest trust and integrity I've been a part of." Larry Costello said he expected to play Lew at both a high and a low post. "Lew has the talent to shoot from outside," he said, "but since he's seven four, I'd rather have him under the basket."

Officially Alcindor was, and is, seven feet one and three-eights inches. Had Costello let something slip? One more mystery. Erickson moved to the microphone and said smoothly, "Lew appears to have grown today because he has entered the business world."

Alcindor then answered a few dozen questions courteously and for the most part well. Yes, the ABA actually had made that $3.25 million offer, but only after it appeared in the newspapers. Yes, he thought the ABA had demeaned itself. Yes, he did look forward to dunking again because it would be good playing basketball the way it was meant to be played. Yes, he had a boyhood idol, Jackie Robinson. Yes, he'd had some bad experiences with the press, but eighty-five percent of the experiences were good. No, he couldn't describe his impressions of Milwaukee. He hadn't really seen it yet. The Milwaukee press was delighted, and after touching base with his parents in New York, he flew back to California, a dignified, literate, and now wealthy man who had only "a few inconsequential courses" to complete for his degree and who had earned a little time for quiet breathing.

Trouble shattered the quiet in June. Playing what is described as a pick-up game at a Los Angeles high school, presumably for fun, Alcindor suddenly lost control of himself. According to one witness, Alcindor's team was taking the ball out of bounds when "Lew turned and threw a punch and walked off the court and left the gym." There is enormous leverage in those lank arms: Alcindor's punch struck the jaw of one Dennis Grey, six eight and 215 pounds. The jaw was fractured, and surgeons at Hollywood Presbyterian Hospital had to wire it together.

Grey was under contract to the Los Angeles Stars of the ABA. A teammate, Warren Davis, said, "There was the usual shoving that occurs when guys are tired, but Dennis couldn't understand why Lew hit him." Grey consulted a lawyer and presently sued Alcindor for $750,000. "Frankly," said Grey's lawyer, Paul Caruso, "the injury may have ruined Dennis's basketball career."

The suit was still pending when Alcindor joined the Bucks, and despite a sprained ankle, he worked out impressively. The Bucks were not simply a changed team. They were a new team, capable on any night of defeating anyone. They would not be last, and although they would not win, they were certain of reaching the NBA play-offs. Lew could drive and dribble as no big man before him. He had a remarkable eye. He had speed and quickness, which are different things, and grace and intelligence, and he was tough.

On October 31 the Bucks defeated the Philadelphia 76ers for the first time, and that night Alcindor's temper burst again. It was rough under the boards. Darrall Imhoff, who is shorter than Alcindor but just as heavy, had been shoving and elbowing underneath. Suddenly, in the second quarter, Alcindor swung his right elbow full force into the back of Imhoff's neck. Imhoff fell forward onto all fours, the way fighters sometimes do, and stayed there on knees and elbows, too dazed to move. Alcindor walked to midcourt. He placed both hands on his hips and watched impassively. Imhoff could not play again until the second half.

The Philadelphia crowd began to hoot. When Alcindor fouled out late in the game, he responded smartly to the boos. He gave a "V" sign — victory and peace. The boos continued. Alcindor clenched a fist and held it high. Black Power.

"I have no comment," he said in the dressing room.

A Philadelphia sportswriter said, "Could it be that you wanted to hit Imhoff, but not around the head?"

"I have no comment," Alcindor repeated.

But Luke Jackson, six nine and 240, had a comment from the other side. "That was dirty," he said. "Deliberate and malicious. If I'd had an opening later, I would have nailed him."

Trouble with the Milwaukee press flowered the next month. In Milwaukee nearly everyone reads the *Journal*, a fine, fat afternoon and Sunday paper. Each weekend the *Journal* carries a slick, nicely written magazine section called *Insight*. Because Alcindor was important autumn news, George Lockwood, who edits *Insight*, assigned a writer named Evans Kirkby to prepare a feature. The story was cast as a visit, a rather easygoing account of a reporter's adventures and impressions as he calls on a celebrity. Conversation gives a "visit" thrust; the subject, ideally, is voluble.

Whatever Alcindor's natural inclinations, he had already made his $20,000 arrangement with *Sports Illustrated*. For the money he had to promise not only his life story but also exclusivity. In effect, until the *S.I.* series appeared, he could grant interviews only if they were dull.

Trying to be true to his word to the national magazine, Alcindor antagonized the man from the local paper. "My first attempt to meet Alcindor," Kirkby began, "had been a social and professional failure." He found the rookie "aloof in speech and habit." Alcindor was brusque and late. "When the photographer said he thought he had what he wanted," Kirkby wrote, "Alcindor turned, a West Pointer doing an about-face, and strode off to change his clothes. He did not say goodbye." Kirkby called his article "A Short Visit with Lew Alcindor." It's a fact that getting a bad press feeds itself. If one experience is sour, why try to make the next sweet? Damn 'em all.

In Detroit, Alcindor walked into a press conference arranged for him by the Pistons and, according to *Detroit Free Press* columnist Joe Falls, "Never have I seen such a discourteous display." By Falls's account, Alcindor refused to answer questions or made one-word answers or simply grunted. "Farewell, Alcindorella," Falls began an ensuing column. Alcindor, he added, "is one of the smallest men I have ever met."

Finally, at about the time I was asking Erickson about arranging an appointment, came the Seattle blowup. The Bucks held a three-point lead before 13,000 at the Seattle Center Coliseum, with fifteen seconds to play. Alcindor held the ball near a foul line, looking to pass. Then Bob Rule tied him up. The referee called a jump. In abrupt fury Alcindor lunged at Rule. All four teammates grabbed him. The Bucks called time.

As the team huddled, Larry Costello said, "Let them shoot. We've got three points. Just don't foul. We don't want to give them a three-point play."

When action resumed, Alcindor lost the jump. Three seconds later he fouled Lucius Allen, an old UCLA teammate, as Allen took a short shot. Costello gazed in agony. The ball dipped into the basket and spun out. No three-point play. Still, Allen would have three chances to make two free throws.

That was Alcindor's sixth foul, and as he walked off, fans jeered. He responded by spitting on the court. Allen made only one of three, the Bucks won by two points, and as they started toward the dressing room, a teenager ran toward Alcindor, shouting, "You big bum." One sweep of the giant arm and the teenager was knocked to the floor.

In the dressing room a reporter said, "Were they too rough out there?" "Yeah," Alcindor said. He picked up his suitcase and stormed out.

Greg Smith, a young Milwaukee forward, stood nearby. "Look," he said to the reporter. "This is not a good time for him."

Costello was less charitable. "This is a game where there is a lot of contact. Guys are bumping you all the time. If Lew ever gets mad like that at the beginning of a game, he might ruin his whole game."

So there we were, a few days later, in the motel room in St. Louis, Alcindor and I trying to understand what was happening.

"It gets me," he said from under the brown blanket, "the way people say now you've got the money, you've got contentment. The money makes for a stability, but there are pressures, man. Out there you're a vector for all the hostility in the stands. It all comes and they're shouting that I'm not hustling and that I stink and I'm a bum. Maybe there are some bad calls; the refs miss some or call something they shouldn't. And all that's happening, you know, and you're trying to be positive and you know if you let all this upset you, you can lose your mind. Sometimes I think about what Wilt said in the beginning. Turn on. Tune in. Get out."

He talked about his background after that. He has traced his family back to the Caribbean through a great aunt, and he has heard of a forebear who stood almost six ten. "I don't know how well he moved. They say he had flat feet. The name Alcindor is originally Moorish," he said.

"I know *al* means 'the.' What about the rest?"

"The firebird," he said. "You know, the bird that rises from its own ashes. That's what Alcindor means."

His father, a trombone player, attended Juilliard, one of the finest classical music schools on earth, but because classical music organizations retain frightful prejudices, he had to go to work for the New York subway. Imagine years spent studying Brahms and Berlioz and Beethoven, great longings expressed in exquisite sound, and then, because of the color of your skin, having to listen every day to the subway's atonal, grinding roar.

"I don't turn on to Beethoven myself," Alcindor said. "I don't know why. A Miles [Davis] record was fine, but not the classical stuff. My Dad, he's the expert in that area."

Growing, Alcindor went from six three to six eleven in two and a half years, between the seventh and the ninth grade. He was a good all-round athlete, swimming, running track, playing baseball, and he says he did not mind the tremendous rate of growth, although for a while his knees hurt constantly. He always wanted to win in whatever he did; he took pride in winning.

"What about your temper?" I said. "Has that always been a problem?"

He sat up in the bed. "It was when I was very small, until about the sixth grade. Then I got it under control, and I thought I had it under control until this year."

Bob Rule is black; Alcindor has gone after blacks and whites with impartiality. Still I wondered about the fan in Seattle.

"There was nothing racial there," Alcindor said. "I just didn't like what he said. I shouldn't have spit and I should have ignored the kid."

"Do you get much racial needling? Does that trigger things?"

He shook his head. "I don't hear any of that; just once in a while in the mail I get a letter that calls me a no-good nigger."

We talked about Jackie Robinson, and how Jack had heard "nigger" almost daily in the beginning, and how Eddie Stanky once held up a pair of shoes in the St. Louis dugout and screamed at Robinson, "Hey, porter. Shine these."

Alcindor seemed surprised. "Stanky did that? What did Robinson do?"

"He took it; he had to take it. Maybe he stole an extra base."

We considered the press. Alcindor insisted that he would never give up his right to privacy. It was very difficult in Milwaukee. "I like to walk, and I could walk in California, but in Milwaukee as soon as I step outside I get mobbed." He had been interviewed while at UCLA, but that was nothing like what was going on now, when the press wanted him all the time, it seemed.

"You better get used to it," I said.

He turned and gazed.

"You're going to play for a while, maybe fifteen years. Well, you better be ready for fifteen years of interviewing. That's part of what all the money is for."

"I don't have to give up my privacy," Alcindor said. "I'm not peddling that."

I remembered Roger Maris and the year of his sixty-one home runs; troops of journalists attached themselves to the Yankees and put questions to him day after day. The same faces asking the same questions.

Alcindor grimaced.

"He got good questions," I said, "and stupid questions and rude questions. He handled all the questions pretty well."

"What bothers me," Alcindor said, "are stupid questions. Somebody asks a stupid question, man, I think why are you taking up my time?"

Sometimes a seemingly stupid question is a reporter's way of starting a subject talking. (Other times, to be sure, it is simply a stupid question.) But what seemed to me to be the point for Alcindor was that he accept the questions with grace. Like jump shots, they are a part of his professional life.

He mentioned feeling good about his past. He had left the Catholic church to become an orthodox Muslim because that was his true heritage. The book that had influenced him the most was *The Autobiography of Malcolm X*. He speaks a number of languages, including Yoruba, a West Nigerian dialect. At length in the motel, he seemed to enjoy talking; seemed happy to be able to describe himself and his heritage; seemed relieved to be able to say that yes, the press versus personal privacy was a problem; seemed unburdened to review the story events of Seattle and to concede that he, proud Lew Alcindor, had been wrong. His movements became less spasmodic. He talked in longer sentences. He listened hard. When Flynn Robinson, his roommate for this trip, walked in and began to dab at his hair, Alcindor said amiably, "That won't help. They'll still see your bald spot."

I rose to go. Alcindor stood and from his great height extended a hand. "Good luck, tonight," I told him.

"I'll need it," Alcindor said. Then, quite warmly, "If you think we ought to talk some more, I'm available. Just get me the word."

We were a short walk from the restaurant Stan Musial runs. The Bucks were going to play Atlanta that night in the St. Louis Arena. Ben Kerner had arranged the game, which would benefit a local charity and honor a number of old stars from the St. Louis Hawks. I went to the arena on foot, the better to think, and passing Musial's, the contrast was almost too pat. Stan had answered questions with grace and charmed the press (and kept his private life private) with the same ease he displayed when he clubbed a curve. Now here was Alcindor, to whom everything, except perhaps the $1.4 million, was coming so hard.

Traffic was filling the St. Louis street. There was going to be a crowd at the arena. I had been here often for hockey, but tonight was basketball, and as cars turned by me toward the parking lot, more Negroes were coming than I had ever seen come here to watch the Blues.

It was foolish then to contrast Alcindor with Musial. Alcindor, to you and me, may be one of the great athletes of the era; to himself he is one of the significant *black* athletes. He carries all that heritage within him, a sense of black aristocracy and black dignity and how the Moors were warriors and how his uprooted family was supposedly free, in a society that condemned a Juilliard man to work in subways.

Then it was game time.

Milwaukee won, 130–115. "We were collapsing on Alcindor all night," complained Richie Guerin, the Hawks' coach, "but we were collapsing stupid."

Alcindor had confused or panicked the Hawks. That changed the game. He finished with thirty-three points, six assists, and thirteen rebounds, but the numbers don't tell it. He dominated. "How do you feel?" I said in the dressing room.

"Redemption time," he said, and grinned.

The next night, back in Milwaukee, he played another splendid game, but my eye was caught by Rodgers, who in a few spurts moved the ball beautifully and drilled passes through openings that had not seemed to exist. That was the evening Rodgers and I were to go out. I stopped at Alcindor's locker and told him how much I'd liked Rodgers's passing.

"I liked it, too," Alcindor said. He looked relaxed. "Hey," he said. "Rodgers could get the ball to Jimmy Hoffa, and he's in jail."

It was my turn to grin and thank him. He was doing one of the kinder things an athlete can do for a writer; he was throwing me a line.

What surely can we take from these few days in the life of Lew Alcindor? Something about the man and something about the times in which we live.

The pressure is enormous. He generates a good deal himself with inner drives, but much of it hangs ominously, there, always there, never dissipating. He is potentially *the* black athlete of this era, as Jackie Robinson was the black athlete of another. His role is not more difficult than Robinson's — after all, the Klan is not threatening to shoot Alcindor for what he did to the Atlanta team. But it may be more complex. The black movement has become more complex.

He is no racist; most of his closest advisers are white. Nor is he militant in the sense that Stokely Carmichael is. But he is more militant than, say, Willie Mays, and this goes hard with some.

He accepts advice from others on income spreading and such; one suspects that the lawyers who read the *Sports Illustrated* contract for him advised him badly. Starting in a new city $1.4 million ahead, what should have come first was new relationships, not additional cash. By allowing one magazine to dictate his relationships to all magazines and newspapers and television stations, the lawyers did him no favor. He could have demanded less restrictive terms from *Sports Illustrated* or simply put off composing his autobiography until he reached the advanced age of twenty-three. By then, working relationships in Milwaukee and around the league would have been established. He feels enough pressure this first year on the basketball court without a sideshow of fencing with the press.

But he is a great athlete and a strong man and to me a winning person. At twenty-two this proud, intense black has magnificent moments and dreadful ones, which, if memory serves, is what being twenty-two is like. It is going to be a pleasure to watch his poise and understanding grow — almost as much of a pleasure as it will be to watch him play basketball as no one ever has for the next ten or fifteen years.

1970

The Mick

He hit the ball harder, higher, and farther than anyone I have seen. When he joined the New York Yankees at the age of nineteen, Mickey Mantle was unprepared for the New York press. So he didn't say much. Some reporters concluded that he was sullen, dumb, or both. He is neither.

It all passed so swiftly for Mickey Mantle, the vaulting home runs, cheers like thunder, and the dark devil's wine of fame, that he cannot believe it is done. But it will not come again, even in dreams. "At night," he says, "my knee can hurt so bad it wakes me up. But first I dream. I'm playing in the stadium and I can't make it. My leg is gone. I'm in to hit and I can't take my good swing. I strike out and that's when it wakes me. Then I know it's really over."

He is thirty-nine now and so enormously powerful that he can drive a golf ball 400 yards. But baseball begins with a man's legs, and Mickey Mantle's right knee is grotesque. Four injuries and two operations have left the joint without supportive structure. It flexes outward as well as in, bone grinding on bone, and there is nothing more that surgery can do. "A flail knee," doctors say, and make analogies to a floppy rag doll. So, still sandy-haired, still young, but no longer able to play ball, Mantle sits in Dallas, living hard, dabbling at business, working at golf, cheerful, to be sure, but missing major league baseball more than he ever thought he would.

"I loved it," he says, his voice throbbing. "Nobody could have loved playing ball as much as me, when I wasn't hurt. I must have fifty scrapbooks. People sent 'em to me. Sometimes after breakfast, when the boys get off to school, I sit by myself and take a scrapbook and just turn the pages. The hair comes up on the back of my neck. I get goose bumps. And I remember how it was and how I used to think that it would always be that way."

For two decades Mickey Charles Mantle of Commerce, Oklahoma, Yankee Stadium, New York, and Dallas, Texas, bestrode the world of baseball. He could throw and he could run down fly balls. Someone with a stopwatch timed him from batter's box to first base in 3.1 seconds. No ball player has yet matched that speed. He drove home runs for shattering distances: 450 feet, 500, 565. With any swing he could make a ball park seem too small. Sometimes when Mantle connected, the big number 7 stirring as he whipped his bat around, it seemed that a grown man was playing in a park designed for Little Leaguers.

Center field at Yankee Stadium stretches toward monuments and flagpoles and a high bleacher wall, 461 feet from home plate. People talk about prodigious outs stroked there by Hank Greenberg and Joe DiMaggio. But one summer night not so very long ago, Mantle stepped up and swung, and everyone watching knew this drive would not be caught. It climbed farther and higher than seemed possible, carrying over the center fielder, soaring over the flagpoles, finally crashing into a bench halfway up the bleachers. Briefly the crowd sat silent. You *couldn't* hit a baseball that far. Then came a swelling roar. "Make it an even five hundred feet," called a newspaperman, one hand to his face in amazement, "give or take a couple of miles."

I don't remember whether Mantle hit that home run batting right-handed or left-handed. He hit the 565-footer batting right-handed in Washington. Batting left-handed, he hit a line drive that was still rising when it hit the roof of the third tier, 108 feet high in right field at the stadium. "The guys I played with," he says, "figure that was my best shot."

Mantle is not very big — about five eleven and 185 pounds at his playing prime — but there is no mystery to all that power. In the great years, his frame was fashioned of thick, supple muscle. For all his strength, there was no stiffness, no weight lifter's rigidity. "The body of a god," said Gerry Coleman, a teammate. "Only Mantle's legs are mortal."

He ran as if pursued. He cocked each swing for distance, and when he missed, the exertion drew a grunt. Watching him one could see a man driving himself harder than human sinew could endure, until at last, too soon, the body yielded. Mantle disagrees with that view. He traces his physical problems to a single injury suffered in 1951. Whatever, with the exertion and the power and the pain, there was no sense of ease to Micky Mantle.

He did not court the press. Even when relaxed, he tends to limit himself to short comments and dry one-liners. Interviews discomforted him, and in time he developed a special response to questions he did not want to answer. It was a baleful, withering look, scorn all the more startling on the open country face. As he saw it, his job began and ended on the field. For fun he'd run with Whitey Ford or Billy Martin. Answering all those reporters — What did you hit, Mick? Where was the pitch? — was bullshit. Where was the pitch, Mick? Hell, in the upper stands in left.

Elvin "Mutt" Mantle, an Oklahoma lead miner, trained his oldest son to be a ball player. As Mickey remembers it, he began learning baseball in 1937 when he was five years old. It was a familiar American scene, the father pitching relentlessly in the hope that the son might someday hit well enough to make the major leagues and carry the family out of a depleting existence. Not one boy in ten thousand is signed to a professional contract; no more than one in twenty-five professionals is good enough to play in the major leagues. "But I got an idea," Mutt Mantle said. "A time is coming when ball players will be platooned. A boy who can switch-hit will have a real advantage."

When a right-handed batter faces a right-handed pitcher, the ball seems to be coming toward his ear. Then, as the batter fights a reflex to duck, the curve breaks down and across the plate. The batter sets himself and digs his heel spikes into the ground. Now the pitcher throws a fast ball at the chin. In this frightening game, the pitcher holds the wild cards. But when a left-handed batter stands in against the right-hander, the balance turns. The ball seems to be coming from the outside. "You see it real good out there," hitters say. A curve breaking inward can be a fine pitch, but the illusion of impending concussion is lost. Everybody hits better from the opposite side, left against right and vice versa. The switch-hitter always bats that way.

Against both percentages and logic, Mutt Mantle's ambitious dream came true. The Yankees signed Mickey at seventeen. Two years later, when Mickey became a major leaguer, Casey Stengel was introducing platoons in Yankee Stadium, just as Mutt had foretold in Oklahoma fourteen years before.

Cancer invaded the Mantles' happiness. The Yankees won the pennant in Mickey's rookie season, but by World Series time, October 1951, Mutt lay in a New York hospital, dying at thirty-nine. In the fifth inning of the second Series game, Willie Mays lifted a looping fly to right center field. Mickey sprinted toward the ball; he had a chance to make a backhand catch. "I got it," called Joe DiMaggio from center. Mantle braked. His right spikes cut through turf and slammed against a hard rubber tube, part of the sprinkler system. His leg jammed and he fell heavily. As the ball was dropping out of DiMaggio's reach, Mantle lay in motionless agony, knee ligaments terribly torn.

He was bedridden now like Mutt, and by the time the father died, a somber identification had occurred. Mantle believed that an early cancer awaited him. When players discussed pensions at a clubhouse meeting once, he said, "That's for you guys to worry about. I won't be around." When someone made the remark that cancer was not purely hereditary, Mantle said, "Sure. And it killed my uncle, too."

His career mixed glory and pain. He was the hinge on which the Yankees wheeled to eight pennants in a decade. In 1956 he led the league in batting, runs batted in, and home runs. In 1957 he batted .365. In 1961 he hit fifty-four home runs. Through all these seasons injuries nagged him. With the bad right knee, he was forever straining muscles. As he was running to first in 1962, a right hamstring tore. He pitched forward and crashed heavily on the left knee, the good knee. It was not a good knee after that. A year later he broke a foot. Throwing hard, he chipped a bone fragment in his shoulder. He kept playing, but the bone sliver worked its way into sinew, giving him a chronic sore arm. By 1965 Mantle, then thirty-three, could not play every day or hit .300. The Yankees have not since won a pennant.

He liked good living, but off the field he shied at crowds. The New York pace excited him. But country stayed strong in Mantle. "I don't want no fuss," he said, "no big deals." If Babe Ruth's image shows an ultimate libertine, and Leo Durocher is the corner crapshooter, Mantle by contrast has been a shadowy bucolic.

Last summer Jim Bouton's unfortunate *Ball Four* pried into the Mantle mystique. Bouton drew Mantle as a voyeur, as a grouch who disliked autographing baseballs, and as a hedonist whose training habits were less Spartan than, say, Jim Bouton's.

With his mustachioed ghost, Leonard Shecter, Bouton wrote: "I ached with Mantle when he had one of his numerous and extremely painful injuries." And to show the full measure of their hurt, Bouton-Shecter added, "I often wondered, though, if he might have healed quicker if he'd been sleeping more and loosening up with the boys at the bar less."

"What did you think of Jim Bouton's book?" someone asked. Mantle stared. Then he said, "Jim *who*?"

*　　*　　*

Dallas was warm and windy, and Mantle said he was going to play some golf and make a talk, and why didn't he start by showing me where he lived. He wore blue slacks and a blue shirt when he picked me up at a motel. He was slightly heavier than when he played, but still boyish. He hadn't read Bouton's book, he said, just a chunk in some magazine. "Anybody," he said, "who's been on the road can write a book with sex in it. You could, I could. But I wouldn't do it. Why do you suppose the sons of bitches picked on me?"

"It was a commercial effort," I said, "and you're box office."

"Roger Maris hated Bouton. He always wanted to belt the bastard. Is the book rough on Maris?"

"He's hardly in it."

"The other guy, Shecter, was an agitator. I didn't speak to him for the last four years at the stadium. I'd just give him the stare. Do you think maybe the son of a bitch was trying to get even?"

"Yes."

"Do you think maybe the book ought to read: by Shecter, edited by Bouton?"

"For lots of it, sure."

"Only thing that really bothered me was the stuff about autographs. New York was my town, but for all those years I couldn't walk a block without getting stopped. I wouldn't sign? Hell, I've signed maybe a million." Mantle shook his head. "Well, come in and have a cup of coffee."

Mantle lives in a rambling buff ranch house, set on a cul-de-sac on the north side of Dallas. His wife, Merlyn, has decorated the den into a shrine. One wall shows twelve framed magazine covers of Mantle batting, running, smiling, glaring. Another is crowded with pictures of the Mantles and famous men, Babe Ruth and Bobby Kennedy. Locked behind glass are the jewels of a great career: the silver bat he won as batting champion; his last glove, bronzed like baby shoes; three plaques celebrating the seasons in which he was most valuable player in the American League; a baseball signed by Mays, Mantle, Ed Mathews, Henry Aaron, and

Ted Williams, an aristocracy in which everyone has hit five hundred home runs. Mantle stood in the den, shifting his weight from side to side.

Preston Trail Golf Club, limited to 250 members, no pool, no tennis, spreads over rolling acreage twenty miles north of Dallas. Under the clear wide sky, city towers shape a fringe of horizon. "Good weather here," Mantle said, "but sometimes it turns. It's warm and then the wind shifts — a norther they call it — and the sky gets blue as a marble and you have to hurry to the clubhouse. It gets cold." He walked out to practice putting, and Gene Shields, the house professional, described Mantle's game. "Swing is a little flat, like all ball players, but he's the longest hitter around. Our tenth hole runs 495 yards, and last October, with a little wind, he drove to within 70 yards of the green. Ed Hoffman saw it, and no matter how you figure that, he drove, counting roll and all, 425 yards."

Mantle played in a fivesome of serious, laconic Texas golfers, who bet as they rode along in golf carts. Mantle's cart made the best time. He whipped up knolls and spun around turns, the first to reach each tee. "You know the old rule," he said. "He who have fastest cart never have to play bad lie."

The wind gusted, eased, and gusted, disturbing the precision of everyone's game. Mantle smacked enormous, low drives, and his chatter was easy and professional. Landing behind a tree, he said, "Well, I can make a fine golf shot from here." On the eighth hole, hitting into a quartering wind, he drove an astounding 300 yards. He waited impatiently for the others to make their second shots, then found his ball dead center in the fairway. "You sometimes give up distance for accuracy," he said.

As he roared toward the clubhouse in the cart, someone drove up, bellowing, "Mantle, Mantle. Goddamnit. Gimme your spare putter."

"Another club in the water?"

"Never mind. Just gimme your spare putter."

Mantle obliged with a small grin. "I got some clubs in the water myself."

The wind hoisted scores, and Mantle's eighty-two was good enough to win his bets. "Double J.D. and Seven-Up," he ordered in the locker room and insisted on taking the check. His limp was worse. "With the cart it's not so bad," he said, "but without it, I can just about make eighteen holes. That's all the leg has left."

He spoke at a banquet in Fort Worth that night. "They say I was a hitter," he began, "but I struck out around seventeen hundred times. Then I walked around eighteen hundred. Figure that out, and it comes to five years I came up to the plate and never hit the ball." Three other major leaguers sat on the dais. Mantle was the star. Afterward he had to sign programs and baseballs for forty minutes.

We went to a Dallas club for a nightcap, and at one point rock musicians made it difficult to talk. "The question," Mantle said, "is not, is the piccolo player a son of a bitch? The question is, is the son of a bitch a piccolo player?"

"You want to manage?" I asked when it was quiet.

"If they got a major league team in Dallas. I had good managers. Casey gave me my chance. Ralph Houk kept saying as Mantle goes, so go the Yankees. He's the leader. Like that. It gave me confidence. I wouldn't want to manage outside of Dallas. I wouldn't want all that time on the road."

"What's tomorrow?"

"More golf. Talk with my lawyer, Roy True. We got things going. The employment agency with Namath. Some other things. I stay in touch."

"You bored?"

"Hell, no. I enjoy what I'm doing. I miss baseball, but I like to play golf. There's nothing bored about me, nothing sad. My health's good, 'cept for the knee. I'm not worried any more than anybody else."

He grabbed for the tab and said, "You got enough to write?" and when I nodded he started out of the club toward his car, still looking like a kid from Oklahoma but limping from the agony that baseball has left him, along with scrapbooks and memories that give him chills.

1971

Mantle has re-emerged as a superstar at baseball card shows. Every few years he hires a ghost to help him write a book. The last two, about as literary as third base, have become best sellers.

Jack Roosevelt Robinson

There were no blacks in the neighborhoods where I grew up, none in the schools. Segregation was not a monopoly of the South. I was someone who disapproved of segregation intellectually. Then I met Jackie Robinson.

It is now almost a year since Jackie Robinson broke a dinner date for the most pardonable and least acceptable of reasons. He fell dead.

It was planned to be an evening of warmth, six of us seated around the stone fireplace in our living room, with banter of politics, psychology, and power. Robinson was fifty-three then, but already almost blind, and we had picked the extra couple with care. Dr. Jacob Goldman is a vice president of Xerox, and Robinson, as a successful man, liked being with other successful men. Besides, Goldman's rank commands chauffeured limousines. That evening could be tuned to the clink of friendly glasses without concern about someone later hurtling off a highway into a New England stone wall.

During his last days Robinson was fired with an idea. Use black capital to finance new homes in the black ghettos. "Private-sector stuff," he said, in the political cliché that colored some of his conversation. Then he was off, explaining financial maneuverings and cures for trade union racism with all the enthusiasm he offered friends twenty years earlier, when they asked just how he knew when to steal home against an obscure knuckle-ball pitcher called Willie Ramsdell.

Yet he was dying, and he knew that he was dying. "He suffered through a year of premonition," his wife, Rachel, said after the interment. And he was dying a bad death. Not the cancerous agony of *Cries and Whispers* nor the slobbering senility of Winston Churchill. Rather, his death was a kind of inversion of the conceptual process itself.

During the last spring of World War I, two impoverished southern blacks embraced in a weathered cabin. Embryo grew into child, and the child, Jack Roosevelt Robinson, who never knew his father, matured into a perfect athlete. By young manhood he had mastered all the games we play save swimming. He set long-jump records, burst from scrimmage like a bolt, starred as a corner man for the UCLA basketball team, played varsity shortstop and, literally, was unbeatable at table tennis.

Then God or nature, having created perfection with such care, set about slowly to destroy it. At forty Robinson was stricken with diabetes. Soon after, he developed high blood pressure. Diabetes weakens the small arteries, and now, strained by elevated blood pressure, the arteries began to rupture and heal, rupture and heal, but never healing fully.

That brought on the blindness. Capillaries burst in both retinas. A limp, which romantically I interpreted as the result of too many hard slides home, was simply another symptom of the affliction. Tiny blood vessels were forever bursting in the stout legs and in the kidneys and about the heart.

He accepted the blindness and the limping with great courage. At an old-timers' game last season in Los Angeles, someone threw a baseball at him from the grandstands, ordering, "Hey, Robinson. Sign this." The unseen baseball struck his forehead. He signed it. At the 1972 World Series, where he accepted tokenistic honors from baseball officials, he barely discerned the stance of Bobby Tolan, who holds his bat high, as Robinson did. "Never hit major league pitching like that," Jack said, and smiled.

Late in the afternoon of October 23, while he sat at his desk in the Jackie Robinson Construction Company, an attack of retinal bleeding struck behind the left eye, the clearer one. The remaining vision blurred. Blood oozed into his throat. He could taste the blood on the back of his tongue. Tearlessly, with unutterable despair, Robinson closed his eyes, placed both fists against his brow, and shook his head.

At a hospital doctors sealed off the capillaries with laser beams. "The standard procedure," one physician tells me, "and a good one, except once in a while it throws off a clot." Next day, as he was preparing for a morning trip to Washington, something, perhaps a clot, stopped Jackie's heart.

Dr. Joseph Wilder, professor of surgery and an intense, emotional man, telephoned me late that night. "Goddamnit," Joe stormed, "you know where we stand in medicine today. We've got a condition and we've got a label. Psychosomatic. Mind and body. But a label doesn't mean we're within a hundred years of understanding anything. I don't care what a thousand other doctors say, you can't tell me that on that moment when he hemorrhaged and shook his head and closed his eyes, Jackie Robinson didn't say to himself, 'The hell with it. I can't take any more.'

"And that's what killed him."

I loved Jackie Robinson well enough not to have to deify him. Politically he was an infant. Successively Richard Nixon conned him and Nelson Rockefeller bent him to the expediencies of his will. A tough businessman hired Robinson as a company union man. A talented, sometimes petty newspaperman reduced him to the sewers of his own pettiness by baiting him with wisecracks. Jack was no philosopher, no reader, and if he knew that a man named Franz Schubert ever lived, he kept it a secret, at least from me.

He was called, not entirely willingly, to puncture baseball's cotton curtain. His conservative sponsor, Branch Rickey, president of the Brooklyn Dodgers, shone with a flawed brilliance. Rickey was stingy, and he crammed more theory into baseball than the game allows.

Robinson played first at Montreal, which was then a minor league city and safely extraterritorial from American racism. To prepare the liberal Democratic borough of Brooklyn for Robinson's coming in 1947, Rickey mouthed scores of speeches at black churchmen. Their parishoners, he said, should not bring zip guns, switchblades, or whiskey into Ebbets Field. "Not merely Robinson, but all black society is on trial," Rickey maintained.

White society, which was *really* on trial, passed narrowly. A few good reporters made bearable a generally patronizing press. Various player protests failed. And against beanballs, spikes, and a cesspool of epithets, Robinson succeeded magnificently. I cannot describe him more forcefully than I did once before:

> Robinson could hit and bunt and steal and run. He had intimidating skills and he burned with a dark fire. He wanted passionately to win. He charged at ball games. He calculated his rivals' weaknesses and measured his own strengths and knew — as only a very few have ever known — the precise move to make at precisely the moment of maximum effect. He bore the burden of a pioneer, and the weight made him more strong. If one can be certain of any tomorrows, baseball shall not look upon his like again."

We first met indirectly through a radio program called *Information, Please!*, which employed my father. The idea was to challenge a panel of witty and erudite men with questions that were submitted by listeners and asked by the witty and erudite Clifton P. Fadiman. Guest fees ran to $1,000, and the man who owned the show, an abrasive former union organizer named Dan Golenpaul, abhorred paying $1,000 for thirty minutes of radio silence. Questions were tailored to guests' special areas of knowledge. My father took unto himself the Robinson pre-show interview.

"Any special interests?" Gordon Kahn asked.

"Sports."

"Do you have a hero?"

"Lincoln."

"Since you went to UCLA, I assume you must have certain areas of scholarship."

"Look, Mr. Kahn," Robinson said, "to protect my *athletic* scholarship I had to play baseball, basketball, football, and run track. I got C's, and I was damn lucky to get them."

As I recall the program, Robinson identified the author of the Emancipation Proclamation and distinguished among hook shot, hooked drive, and hook slide.

Something more serious happened two years later. Paul Robeson, *the* prophetic Negro, observed that if the United States and the Soviet Union made war, no American Negro would willingly fight because, in effect, he had nothing to fight for. According to Howard Fast, an affluent radical, one year Robeson earned $250,000 through concerts. Then the noose of anticommunism tightened. "A year later," Fast insists, as he sits beside his lavish free-form swimming pool, "Paul made nothing. Not a dime. The bastards wiped him out." Defiantly, Howard lifts a glass of clear soda water in memory of another man's ordeal, met without compromise.

In July 1949 a Georgia Democrat named John Wood invited Robinson to refute Robeson before the House Un-American Activities Committee. Jackie Robinson was raised to fear God and worship American institutions. He felt flattered, but he could not write his own speech. Branch Rickey tried and floundered. Finally Lester Grainger, president of the Urban League, was enlisted, and the three collaborated on a touching, naive statement.

"I don't pretend to be an expert on communism or any other kind of political 'ism,' " Robinson said, "but I am an expert on being a colored American, having had thirty years of experience at it." He then made a passable case that Communists were stirring

Negroes to protest "for selfish political reasons." Unfortunately Robinson was blind to larger issues. After a docile century, it was surely time for some group, *any* group, to rouse the blacks. And by attacking Paul Robeson for HUAC in 1949, he was helping launch the most dreadful period of political repression in American history.

On the ball fields he increasingly rebutted racists with his quick bat and quicker tongue.

"Alligator bait!"

"Shit, an alligator looking at you would throw up."

What few of us recognized at the time was that he resented slurs purely emotionally, not recognizing that racism is complex, historically rightist, and a world movement. Indeed, when Alan Paton visited Ebbets Field, Robinson wondered, "Who's that guy?" He had never heard of *Cry, the Beloved Country*.

In 1957, with his legs gone and his bat slowed, he signed for about $50,000 plus stock benefits with a chain of Manhattan lunch counters, Chock Full o'Nuts. Virtually everyone working beneath him was black.

"You see," Jack explained at a luncheon, "these people all have a good deal. The president of the company is a fine man. And now some of them want to start a union. That doesn't make sense with things being as good as they are." A more sophisticated black subsequently described Chock Full o'Nuts as "Jackie's Plantation."

In 1960 Robinson went calling on John Kennedy, who said (Robinson reported to me), "I haven't known too many Negroes, Mr. Robinson, being from New England." Robinson next called on Richard Nixon, who spoke of "my own and the Republican Party's historic concern for Negroes and the wrongs done them."

"So I'm for Nixon," Robinson said. "Any senator, like Kennedy, should make it his business to know Negroes, no matter where he's from."

"But can you accept Nixon's sincerity?"

"On this one issue, yes."

Robinson stayed out of the Goldwater-Johnson disaster, but in the late 1960s he performed a variety of functions for Nelson

Rockefeller: assistant commissioner of boxing, special assistant assigned to keep Harlem tempers cool. (Rockefeller rewarded him by neglecting to appear at the funeral of Jackie Robinson, Jr.)

"What are your thoughts on McCarthy?" Jack asked me during the 1970 primaries. Since Gene McCarthy had written a glowing prologue to my book *The Battle for Morningside Heights,* my response was enthusiastic.

"But how can you be for him?" Robinson said. "The Communists are threatening Czechoslovakia, and McCarthy says it's not worth World War III to lose that city there."

"Prague."

"Yeah."

"And it isn't. I wouldn't even argue that losing Brooklyn would be worth World War III."

He stared, then turned away.

Toward the end, as we argued politics, he said, "Don't get on my ass to be for McGovern."

"But I am on your ass to be for McGovern."

"Well, so are my wife and kids and I don't need you."

"And I'm on your ass to dump Nixon."

"Well, I'll admit this. Supporting him against Kennedy was not my most brilliant play."

He spent some of his last year dictating an autobiography called *I Never Had It Made.* It is not a book so much as a tract, dry for long passages, wanting in poetry, and moving in its impassioned honesty.

He now said that he would not have testified against Robeson had he understood the black condition truly. He could reconcile himself to such men as Dick Young, the gifted, ego-ridden newspaperman I described earlier. He was rethinking his approach to politics, to life.

I have many memories. I remember standing alone at first base — the only black man on the field. I had to deny my true fighting spirit so that the noble experiment could succeed. I have always fought for what I believed in. I have had a great deal of support. . . . However there is one irrefutable fact of my life which has determined much of what happened to me: I was a black man in a white world. *I never had it made.*

At last his intellect was catching up to his accomplishment. And then, before the two could join, death interceded.

1973

Sportswriters

John R. Tunis, Paul Gallico, and Jimmy Cannon. Jerome Holtzman of Chicago caught them late in life with their memories intact.

Somewhere Ring Lardner is supposed to have offered, among wry sours, "There isn't anything on earth as depressing as an old sportswriter." Nothing in my first encounter with the breed refuted the great sportswriter, who himself did not live to be old.

There was a man on the *New York Post* who drank three meals a day, deified Leo Durocher, cadged money from anyone who moved, and used to fall asleep while smoking. He started several hotel fires and became a professional joke until he set fire to the bed in his apartment. Most of his body was charred, but the man required no anesthetic for hours. Alcohol had immunized him from pain, although not from death. Three days after his admission to a hospital, the sportswriter died, stone sober for the first time in years.

The *Brooklyn Eagle* had a writer past seventy who dragged after young athletes, barely able to tote his typewriter, loathing the work but having nothing else to sustain his life. "They'll break you, kid," he said. "I used to write short stories, but they broke me, and you'll get broken, too." He tripped over a small step in a hotel lobby, fractured a hip, and died on the road.

Some old writers felt trapped by the insignificance of what they were reporting. During World War II one complained, "The world is blowing up and what do I write? Zeke Bonura got two hits today. That's no work for a grown man, is it?"

Others reacted to the trivia of games by taking unshakable, mindless postures on more important things. "Anyone who sympathized with the Loyalists during the Spanish Civil War," an old *New York Times* man told me, "was a fool."

"Well, Ernest Hemingway supported the Loyalists," I said.

"Means nothing," the reporter insisted. "A man can be a great writer and still be a fool."

Back of the dining room at Vero Beach, Florida, the old sportswriters sat in wicker chairs and played poker with baseball officials who were earning five times as much as they. Betting their rent against someone else's tip money, the writers were constantly bluffed out of pots, forever defeated.

One writer tried to recoup by drinking brandy supplied by the ball club. In a desperate reach toward elegance, he ordered ponies of Courvoisier, dipped his cigar in the drink, lit it, threw out the brandy, and ordered a fresh shot. "Goddamnit," said Buzzy Bavasi of the Dodgers. "Do you think that hundred-fifty-dollar-a-week slob does that at home?"

Without lusting to find out personally, I suppose that everyone's later years are sapped endurance, uncertain sleep, and failing memory. It was Yeats who complained, "What shall I do with this absurdity . . . decrepit age that has been tied to me as to a dog's tail." But old poets — Frost, Masefield, Sandburg — achieve the blessing of patriarchy. Old physicians, who may still believe in leeches, perfect an authoritative look, practice less, and charge more. Old lawyers — well I've heard of one in Bridgeport who has just married seventy-five and is moving toward his second million.

The old sportswriters I knew drew no rewards for vintage. They still had to meet the guillotine of deadlines. They had to argue with room clerks, struggle with baggage, and climb the interminable steps at Princeton that lead to a press box called Thrombosis Terrace. The athletes, young and intolerant, laughed at the sportswriters' salaries. It was said that a football player on a good Big Ten scholarship earned more than a crack reporter for United Press.

Finally, the writers were constantly instructed on their unimportance. A generation of editors preached anti-ego sermons. Nobody cares about you, your ulcer, your bent dreams. Write about hook slides. Indeed, the protean sports editor Stanley Woodward, explaining why a prospect failed, observed, "He single-spaces his copy and he uses the first person." Not a happy group, I thought, on many nights, hearing old sportswriters tell flat stories in a prolix way.

A few years ago Jerry Holtzman, a Chicago baseball writer in middle years, mentioned an idea for a book. He wanted to record the reminiscences of old sportswriters, he said, and did I think he'd be able to find a publisher.

"A dumb one," I said.

"What do you mean?"

"Well, most of these people are going to be dull."

Holtzman, a stocky, intense man, nodded, but I could see from his eyes that he intended to go on. Now, forty-four interviews later, his publisher, Holt, Rinehart and Winston (smart enough, incidentally, to hold the rights to Frost's poems), has sent me *No Cheering in the Press Box*. The finished product staggers and corrects me. *No Cheering in the Press Box* is a splendid work of oral history, on a par with Lawrence Ritter's *The Glory of Their Times*.

Out of the forty-four men he interviewed, Holtzman prints the memoirs of eighteen. (When last we met, he was concerned that he might be making twenty-six enemies.) By rejecting what is maundering, he gives us a book of pace, interest, and even a certain consistency. These old journalists, mean age seventy-five, appear to have come to terms with the toughness of life. It wasn't easy, it isn't easy, and it won't become easy. Yet as Faulkner said, one tries to prevail. That is the sense of the book. Have you ever heard of a man called Richards Vidmer? He wrote a sports column in the *New York Herald Tribune* called "Down Front," which he abandoned to marry a rajah's daughter. They traveled, lived in Barbados, played golf. But Vidmer had a need to work. The rajah's daughter disapproved. Holtzman found him in Orlando, Florida, still handsome, married for a third time and newly philosophical. "Two people, you and I as young men, go into business together and we hit it off fine. We are twenty-one. But when we're thirty-five, your life has changed and my life has changed and we're not good business partners anymore. That's what happens to marriages."

John R. Tunis, eighty-four, has composed a score of books on young athletes struggling and winning. A sample title is *The Kid Comes Back*. In Essex, Connecticut, Tunis says, "I've written what I wanted and tried to explain there is more to life than throwing a football. You can say my books have been read, but only by kids. Nobody has paid any attention. Still my books are the most important thing I did. Damn right. I just sent back the proofs on my latest, *The Grand National*. I doubt I'll do another one. I've always been busy, and this is the first time I haven't another book to begin. Now I may have time to read Flaubert."

Fred Lieb, eighty-six, says he was "in the foremost freshman class that ever broke into the New York press box." That was in 1911, and the other rookies were Grantland Rice, Damon Runyon, Heywood Broun. Lieb talks about his friendship with Lou Gehrig and Gehrig's wife and about "a falling out after Lou died. I found that Lou's grave — he's buried in Westchester County — was very much neglected, a lot of weeds, bird shit all over it." After Lieb complained to a third party, Mrs. Gehrig called him one three A.M. Apparently the two no longer speak.

The most prosperous of Holtzman's writers is Paul Gallico, whom Holtzman traces to a 450-year-old house in Antibes. During the 1920s Gallico suggested to Jack Dempsey that they spar.

"What's the matter, son," the champion said. "Don't your editor like you no more?"

Jack Kearns, who managed Dempsey, protested. "Listen. You don't know this kid. He might be a ringer."

Dempsey said, "Well, I promised the kid and I don't break a promise."

"All right, but don't be a fool," Kearns said. "Get him quick." Dempsey threw a left hook and Gallico went down. He heard Kearns saying six, seven, eight. "Like a goddamn fool, I got up. By then Dempsey knew I was a bum. He whispered, 'Hang on, kid, till your head clears.' But he couldn't stop. He hit me with six straight rabbit punches on the neck, and the next thing I knew, Kearns was saying, 'Thirty-eight, thirty-nine, forty.' A half hour later I was writing my story."

Gallico still fences, enjoys a solitary life with his fourth wife, and relishes Antibes, which he says is a working town, not like Cannes and Nice. "We're sort of locals. We live a very quiet life. You have to concentrate to write. You can't be disturbed. You can't do a lot of running around. You can't stay up too late at night. You can't drink too much. I'm seventy-six, but I don't feel old. I'll write as long as my brain is able to put together two sentences."

Red Smith, now sixty-nine, meditates on glory. "When you go through Westminster Abbey, you find that excepting for that little Poets' Corner, almost all the statues are of killers. Of generals and admirals whose specialty was human slaughter. I don't think they're such glorious heroes. I've tried not to exaggerate the glory of athletes."

Finally, Holtzman gives us Jimmy Cannon, just before Cannon died at sixty-three. I remember Cannon on a night in The Little Club when he was dating Judy Garland. I can't recall what anybody said, but everyone kept talking. As Cannon spoke, Miss Garland's eyes glazed. When Judy spoke, Cannon fumbled for his cigarettes. Cannon's own epitaph makes me wish I'd watched the self-involvement less and listened more.

Sitting in a wheelchair, where a stroke prisoned him, Cannon is hard, exciting, brave. He says, "Sportswriting has survived because of the guys who don't cheer." He would rather have been with Hemingway than with Babe Ruth. He feels that "the great athletes are fortunate that they met me." The best newspaper writers were Ben Hecht, Westbrook Pegler, Damon Runyon. The most neglected writer in America is Nelson Algren. He "wrote better about Chicago than anybody — including Carl Sandburg." Cannon can't stand politicians. "They lie more than football coaches." At the end, crippled and solitary, Cannon sums up his life, this book:

"I've had a great life. I sat at glad events. And I've liked some of the people. My two favorite people in sports were Joe Louis and Joe DiMaggio. They were my friends and I think explaining friendship is like explaining pain. It's impossible after it's subsided. I have terrible pain right now." But what a legacy.

1974

Cheer, Cheer
for Old Ezra Pound

Richard Nixon unhappily led a retreat from Southeast Asia, and Communists marched over South Vietnam. That mattered less to most than an end to the terrible daily lists of North Vietnamese bodies counted and American servicemen wounded and killed.

Baseball came back with perhaps the most exciting of all World Series when the Cincinnati Reds defeated the Boston Red Sox, four games to three, in 1975.

With the return of peace, Pete Rozelle, commissioner of the National Football League, said football was not a violent sport. "War is violent. Football is contact."

Ask any quarterback who doesn't limp.

Is it possible to visit Notre Dame and not interview the football coach? Yes, it is.

The Notre Dame a man can admire these days is not merely the football capital of the Roman Catholic church. It is that, to be sure, because most autumn Saturdays the head coach, an Armenian Presbyterian named Ara Parseghian, works ecumenical miracles with his team. But after wandering the Indiana campus, with its great-rooted trees, its shrines, and its grotto, one comes away with mostly a sense of church in change, of foment, even crisis.

"Slough of unamiable liars,/bog of stupidities," runs a passage from Pound's *Canto XIV*. "Dead maggots begetting live maggots, /Slum owners, usurers squeezing crab lice." Joe Duffy — Professor Joseph M. Duffy of the Notre Dame English Department — employed the passage as the theme of an essay on Nixon and Nixon's accomplices. He published the essay during the 1972 campaign, before Watergate slime surfaced.

"There was some displeasure," Professor Duffy said, in his office at Memorial Library, "but I wasn't muzzled and I didn't lose my job."

"What about football?" I said.

"What about football?" Duffy said.

He is a tall, graying, soft-voiced man in his mid-forties. "Football is simply irrelevant to my life at Notre Dame. I don't own a television. I simply leave the campus on Fridays and come back on Mondays. I've seen one game in twenty years. I'm not sure who won. I remember being awfully cold."

The tradition of powerhouse football at Notre Dame traces at least to 1905, when the Irish eased past American Medical College, 142–0. Notre Dame scored twenty-seven touchdowns but missed twenty extra points. Knute Rockne became head coach in 1918, and during his thirteen seasons Notre Dame, playing the roughest competition, won 105 games and lost 12.

Breathes there a fan with soul so dead that he has never heard, "Win one for the Gipper"? George Gipp, a magnificent halfback, died of a strep throat at the age of twenty-five, and on his deathbed, so Knute Rockne claimed, Gipp made a stirring plea. "Someday, when the going is tough and a big game is hanging in the balance, ask the team to win one for the Gipper."

Rockne's fight speeches on recordings still raise the hair on one's neck. In 1924 he played his trump and told the Gipp story to an undermanned team that was meeting Army in New York. When Rockne finished, there were only two dry eyes in the dressing room. These were Rockne's. The old man was a pragmatist. Notre

Dame's football players choked down their sobs and defeated Army, 13–7.

This is the kind of romanticism that rang through sports in the 1920s, and specifically it is the kind of thing that transformed Notre Dame from a relatively obscure institution to the most famous Catholic college in the country. Football, along with daily Mass ("We pray that nobody gets hurt"), lay at the core of Notre Dame then. It was the tool that ambitious educators used to attract endowments, to make money, and to grow.

Today Notre Dame is fully grown. A huge mosaic on the library tower depicts Christ with both arms in the air. "Touchdown Jesus" the students call it. A statue of Moses points one finger toward an opening in the Red Sea. The students call that "We're-Number-One Moses." Most faculty and trustees are laymen now. The nuns one sees on the campus wear short habits, showing calves. Women are admitted as undergraduates. Considering liberal Notre Dame today, Knute Rockne would have blanched. George Gipp, who lived hard, would have blinked.

But football remains a big part of the place, and I think it is fair to wonder why a university as vital as Notre Dame stays in the football business. It is equally fair to wonder the same thing of Harvard, Princeton, and Southern California, but Notre Dame, at the top, is a place to start.

The Notre Dame athletic program provides for about 30 football scholarships a year, giving Parseghian 120 candidates for his squad. A football player at Notre Dame is not treated like everyone else. An engineering professor named Mike DeCicco supervises the tutoring of athletes. DeCicco is a broad, powerful, forceful man who reminds you of Vince Lombardi. He works closely with Parseghian in the struggle to keep athletes' grades satisfactory.

Certain professors resent what they interpret as the athletic department's intervention in classwork. "I am regularly requested to keep certain people informed on the marks of every athlete I teach," one told me. "I refuse. If I report that an athlete is doing poorly, platoons of tutors will descend on him like locusts, tutors I have not selected myself. If anyone in my class is having trouble, I'm more than happy to tutor him myself, but I insist that all my students be treated equally. That's what I do."

Aside from such intramural tensions, larger football questions arise. More and more, American sport tends toward professionalism. Sport is entertainment. Is it rational for Notre Dame or Harvard to compete for entertainment dollars against the Chicago Bears or the New England Patriots? Beyond that, universities like to describe themselves as places of rational discourse, education, research. What are these places doing in the sports business anyway?

"You may have heard talk that football molds character," associate professor Les Martin of the Notre Dame English Department remarked in his office at the library. He is a dark-haired man who specializes in eighteenth-century drama. "I don't think that position can be defended. Once I gave a particularly strong orientation lecture for a survey course, suggesting that everyone would have to learn some Middle English. The three football players in attendance dropped out right then. Once I flunked two football players. I didn't see another athlete in my class for years."

Martin sat behind a small desk, one hand resting on a dissertation paper. "It is awfully complicated," he said. "Football put this place on the map. Then there came a time in the late 1950s when we ceased to need it. It might have been prudent then to de-emphasize. Now one wonders if we could afford to de-emphasize if the powers that be wanted to."

"Do you find football disruptive to your teaching?" I said.

"I try not to let it be," Martin said, "but before a football Saturday there is a cicadalike nuance in my classroom. The air begins to vibrate. It is disruptive, yes. I try to combat that with humor of a sort. I suggest that football is a prolongation of a pubic rite, a sort of fertility rite, really. The opposing team's end zone is the sacred grove where, in this rite, one attempts to bury the head of the god."

Martin paused. "Look," he said, "football can be justified as a business enterprise. This university has a number of business enterprises, including a television station and a football team. Football gives pleasure, and it can be justified on that basis, too. But as for character building . . . well, one of the rituals of football here is drinking, and on Sunday morning after a big game the campus is stained with the residue of retching.

"It gives me a certain pleasure to announce when the season is over, 'Football has ended. It's Chaucer time again.'"

The old Irish guard was shocked, or at least surprised, when Notre Dame announced last summer that six football players, including four starters, were being suspended for a "breach of university rules." Indeed, the breach was wide. All six were alleged to have had intercourse — sequentially — with the same eighteen-year-old woman in a third-floor room of Stanford Hall, a campus dormitory.

Here the story clouds. The young woman claimed that she was raped. The football players insisted that she was having the time of her life.

Whatever, the six are out for this season, and the New York *Daily News* was able to run the headline: SEX SCANDAL OUSTS SIX NOTRE DAME GRIDDERS.

"This," suggested Father Ed Joyce, "is the worst thing that has happened in my twenty-three years at Notre Dame."

"If what the men say is true," I said, "it's pretty much what happens on campuses all over."

Joyce's face showed pain. "But not here," he said.

The Reverend Edmund P. Joyce, executive vice president of Notre Dame, is a handsome, graying man, a conservative by his own account, who is the chief financial officer of the university. His office is in the Administration Building, a landmark topped by a golden dome that towers above the campus and sparkles in sunlight.

"Why football?" Father Joyce said. "Well, it was significant in my coming here in the first place. I grew up in South Carolina, and there aren't too many Catholics in South Carolina. As a boy I heard Notre Dame games on the radio and I wanted to come here. Otherwise?" He shrugs expressively. "I might have gone to West Point."

"How much does football earn for Notre Dame?"

"Football covers the cost of our entire athletic program. That is, football profits support our fencing team and the rest. After all that, it nets us between two and three hundred thousand dollars a year."

"Can you measure," I said, "how much football brings you in endowments?"

"That's difficult," Father Joyce said. "In the bad years, when we had losing teams before Ara came, there was no falloff in gifts. But certainly football plays a role. We've had a rather happy instance where a benefactor named I. A. O'Shaughnessy, who was first attracted by our football, ended up giving millions for our library. Our endowment is now about ninety million dollars. That's several times the endowment of any other Catholic college, although not much compared to Harvard."

"Do you still need football?" I said.

"I think it's useful," Joyce said. "Most of the students love it. The fall hysteria is a good way for everyone to let off steam. And the point is that we keep the football program controlled.

"Right now the question of football ties into a larger one. Our costs continue to rise and rise. We've had to increase tuition again this year, and I wonder how much longer we can keep doing that, how long it will be before the middle class or the upper middle class, which is our constituency, simply can't afford us anymore and has to send the young people to state schools.

"That's my largest concern. Will any private education continue to exist in America in ten or fifteen years?"

Notre Dame State? A constitutional question exists there, just as it does with Joe Duffy's slough of unamiable liars. Meanwhile, you can cheer, cheer for Ara Parseghian's warriors, while your operative, who prefers pro football anyway, will reserve his highest Notre Dame enthusiasm for English professors who risked distinguished careers to say things that had to be said about Richard Nixon.

1974

The six football players accused of sexual misconduct were suspended from the university for one year. No criminal charges were filed. The woman's name has never been disclosed.

The Shrine

That is the land of lost content,
  I see it shining plain,
The happy highways where I went
  And cannot come again.

A. E. Housman

It was too small. The public urinals were fetid troughs. Its architecture suggested a mail-order tool shed, and every August the grass began to die. Then work crews had to spray the outfield with green paint. There weren't enough seats, and the parking was impossible, and worst of all it had been designed in days when a baseball possessed the resiliency of a rolled sock. Later the ball would leap from bats, and pitchers working there developed sore arms, Jell-O hearts, shell shock. Ebbets Field, 1913–1957. RIP.

Now, having made this obeisance to truth, we may perhaps begin? It was a ball park. Not a stadium or a superdome or a multisport arena. A ball park, bad for football, unsuitable for concerts, unthinkable for track. You scrambled to get there, riding a subway or a trolley car, and you fought for a ticket and you walked steep runways with a loping gait. Two runways and a quick, sharp turn, and there the diamond lay, so close you felt you could reach it in ten strides. There were the Dodgers, gabbling through infield drill, wearing white and blue, standing so near that you could almost hear their chatter.

In 1951, the year of Bobby Thomson, a stately English literary critic named J. Isaac asked me to take him to Ebbets Field. We rode the BMT to Prospect Park, Professor Isaac bristling with concern that he might show enthusiasm. "Promised some people a book," he said. "American mores. Need to see baseball. Ebbets Field. Waste of time."

We climbed from the subway, and Ebbets Field loomed, gray and dun-colored and sooty. The critic seemed to shudder. We found our tickets, walked the runways, and we turned. There was the painted outfield and the diamond, Pee Wee Reese and Jackie Robinson and Gil Hodges wearing white and blue.

The Englishman stopped stock-still and fell speechless. Somebody bumped him. "Beautiful," the stately Englishman said. Although I had been journeying to Ebbets Field almost from the beginnings of memory, I would not have thought to call it so.

In time it became a divine prison. I had this job, covering the Dodgers for the *New York Herald Tribune,* and Ebbets Field was where I worked. Most days, across the brightness of mild seasons, I drove a honeydew Chevrolet convertible — honeydew, the salesman said, is the color of the Chevy *Dinah* drives — to an alley where a man called Frank barked, "Move it. Move it closer. Hell, you reporters can't drive worth a damn." Park the car and once a month slip Frank two dollars. That made sure no one, certainly not Frank himself, slashed the car's black canvas top. (Honeydew and black, the salesman said, is a *terrific* combination.)

Climb out onto McKeever Place and pass the rotunda, where tiles were worked into designs of ball and bat. Walk toward the creaking sign marked PRESS GATE. You could not help but swagger. If you covered the Dodgers regularly, you didn't have to show a press card. "Hiya," the gatekeeper said, and you answered with a magisterial nod. Press through the groin-high turnstile. Behind, laity milled and swarmed for tickets.

Once inside you had to go to work. Check the pitchers. "Yeah, my arm hurts," Billy Loes said. "It always hurts. A pitcher's arm hurts all the time. Write that." Read the team. How was it with the

Duke of Snider? "Damn you guys. I'm hitting .280 and you keep writing I should hit .320. What the hell's wrong with .280? And why are you always comparing me with Mantle and Mays? We're different guys." Snider and Mantle and Mays. What a beneficence of center fielders. Sure, Duke. Easy, Duke. Hit two tonight and you'll be up at six to buy the morning papers.

Try the other clubhouse. Warren Spahn skipping a turn? "Yep. Spahnie's having some trouble with his back." Actually, Spahnie had been having ten years of trouble with right-handed power hitters in Ebbets Field. His back would heal on the plane back to Milwaukee.

Ride the press elevator, small as a coffin, and ask the operator if the general had come. Douglas MacArthur was an Ebbets Field addict. Climb to the press box, hanging from the roof. Reach for the yellow Western Union paper and begin.

> Carl Erskine was on the mound seeking his 14th victory last night as the Dodgers faced the Milwaukee Braves before an estimated 28,000 at Ebbets Field. The Braves, nine games behind the Dodgers, countered with Gene Conley, a righthander, who is very tall for a pitcher.

Editions closed till midnight, and keeping up with them you typed constantly, trying to remember (or forget) that someone defined journalism as literature under pressure. After the game Dick Young of the *Daily News* would say, "I got a lead for you."

"What's that?"

"Under leaden skies."

"Good, Young, but I won't plagiarize your stuff. Now hold it. I have to write."

"Under cloudless skies?" Young said, smiling an evil smile.

I have been trying to find a single memory so vivid and so real that one can understand, with the shock of recognition, what the place called Ebbets Field once meant. It was my ball park, and before that it was my father's ball park. It served for ghastly Brooklyn teams and for the Jackie Robinson Dodgers. It was the

Elysium of boyhood, the one place above others where one was safe from algebra and other casual woes. It was secure. Then, so quickly there was not time to sort this change of circumstance, it became the building where I went to earn a living.

Furillo and the wall. Were ever man and magic better fused? A line drive crashed into that wall, the screen rising above, the scoreboard jutting onto the field. Carl Furillo calculated the carom. He gloved the ball and exploded a throw. How had he figured that carom? How could anyone throw a ball that hard? "This man," said the ancient reporter from the *New York Times,* "is armed."

Robinson in a run-down. One black man, dodging among whites, in those embattled times when baseball people said you couldn't hire a Negro. Robinson, the focus of an era, sprinted and stopped, feinted and skidded, sprinted and broke free. Above all ball players, Jackie Robinson would not be penned.

Alan Paton of South Africa arriving in the press box. I like to pretend that I met Paton, shook his hand, and thanked him quietly for *Cry, the Beloved Country* and *Too Late the Phalarope.* But that night I was off. "Mr. Paton," said Dick Young in the strident accent of New York, "what's a phalarope?" Paton answered solemnly, "It's a boid."

The wrecker's ball, crashing against Furillo's wall, destroying mortar, laying waste a monument. Steam shovels assaulting soil that had felt the spikes of Reese and Robinson. We thought, we had always thought, that Ebbets Field would stand for centuries. Isn't the oldest building in Rome the Colosseum?

The borough of Brooklyn, extending eight miles from the East River to the Atlantic Ocean, was once a vital collection of communities, with names like Greenpoint, Bay Ridge, Sheepshead Bay. Brooklyn was rich in middle-class high schools, thick with churches and populated by about three million souls. In one neighborhood called Brownsville, Jewish children who would grow up to teach philosophy lived beside incipient terrorists who became loan sharks, basketball fixers, even killers. Park Slope was heavily

Italian, mixing longshoremen, musicians, and goons. On Sundays the Irish of St. Theresa's parish worshiped a gentle Christ. Other days some of them distributed the fascist newspaper *Social Justice,* which warned of a revolution being organized by Jews. In bleak pockets near Atlantic Avenue a small, profoundly depressed black seedbed endured.

Brooklyn was troubled — it is a dangerous fiction that urban troubles are new — and contentious and disparate and joined. What joined all Brooklyn was a sense, when we were young, that everyone outside was laughing at us. If you listened to a radio quiz program and a contestant said he came from Brooklyn, you heard a clamor of laughter from the studio audience. If you went to a set-piece war movie there was one soldier out of Brooklyn. He might be heroic, but Gary Cooper never played him. The best we got was William Bendix throwing grenades and bawling, "Dis is for da folks on Flatbush Avenyuh." Sometimes the Nazis cut him down, but Brooklyn Bill Bendix never died like Hamlet. Nobility was reserved for taller figures from the prairie.

One's father's memories seem grander than one's own, which may be how gods were first invented. My father, a courtly, private, thick-wristed man, lighted my childhood with stories of ball players I had never seen. He had been rooting for the Dodgers since the first decade of the century. "They weren't called the Dodgers then. They were the Superbas, and there wasn't any Ebbets Field. The Superbas played in Washington Park."

"What was it like?"

"There was a hill behind the outfield. More people sat on the hill than bought tickets. That's why we had to build Ebbets Field."

He had admired a first baseman named Jake Daubert, who batted .350 in 1913, and a splendid outfielder, Zack Wheat, and he recalled, as an old general recalls his soldiers' victories, how Brooklyn had won pennants in 1916 and 1920. "We had a spitball pitcher named Clarence Mitchell, who was also a pretty fair hitter. But in the 1920 Series, Mitchell hit into a double play and a triple play in consecutive turns at bat. Two swings. Five outs. Efficiency."

By this time, the 1930s, my father had developed protective, defensive techniques of rooting. The Dodgers were a dreary club with no visible tomorrows, and a grown man learns to hide disappointments.

We first voyaged to Ebbets Field in 1935, traveling by trolley and on foot. We were to see Babe Ruth, who was drinking through a drab finale with the Boston Braves. Ruth didn't play that day. We went next to see an exhibition between the Dodgers and the Yankees. Lou Gehrig, the Iron Horse, passed up the game. A thumb was aching. Afterward we went four times a year, enough so that memories developed and not so often that the trip became routine.

Because the park was compact, you caught interplays between the players and the fans. "Hey, Schnozz," someone shouted at Ernie Lombardi of the Cincinnati Reds, "pick up your cap so we can see your big nose." Lombardi grinned and raised the bill of the cap. That nose could well have startled Cyrano.

"Hey, genius," someone bellowed at Dodger shortstop Lonny Frey, who made fifty-one errors in 1936. "What ya got the glove for? A decoration?" From the dollar-ten seats you could see Frey redden.

Bright moments came seldom to the Dodgers of the mid-1930s, and people said they ought to hire Alf Landon to manage. "I mean you need a man who's had experience getting beat." But once an old pitcher named Freddie Frankhouse held off the Cardinals with breaking stuff. "A roundhouse curve," my father said with great authority. "Very few can get away with that in the major leagues." A brilliant center fielder, Johnny Cooney, dived and somersaulted and stole a double from the grass. Van Lingle Mungo, fierce and black-haired, fired fastballs behind a mighty kick. "Whatever you hear about this team," my father said, "remember this. They're major leaguers. Nobody playing in Ebbets Field is a bum."

When you reached ten, you began to explore the ball park by yourself. It was curiously shaped, as most old ball parks were, lending variety to the play of baseball. It had been built of brick and mortar with repeating arches framing little windows, the kind that are always broken in old factories. Two tiers of pillared grandstand ran from the right-field corner toward home plate, then out toward left and behind the center fielder. There the stands ended.

The right-field wall sloped upward for perhaps eight feet and rose straight for another seven. Above the wall a stiff mesh screen extended forty feet into the air. A black scoreboard jutted out in right center, describing angles that Furillo would master. The playing field was a narrow cockpit: 297 to right, 348 to left, and 393 to straightaway center. Batting left-handed, Mickey Mantle hit a screwball into the upper left-field stands during the 1953 World Series. A good power hitter could drive a ball out of Ebbets Field at any point.

But long ago it seemed a fortress, and like all fortresses it had to be attacked. A seat in the bleachers, actually the covered upper deck in center, cost fifty-five cents. If you lacked that, there were other means to violate the place. Across Bedford Avenue, which ran behind right field, lived a popular boy named Herbie Friedman. Herbie was popular because his bedroom overlooked the screen. Standing at his window, you could see the infield, some of center, none of right. Every weekend Herbie, who did not like baseball, had to suffer sunshine friends.

In right center, where stands and wall met, two heavy iron doors formed the exit gate. The doors did not quite reach the pavement, and by lying on the ground you could peer through a crack twice as wide as an eyeball and see a game. Or part of a game. Eventually a policeman tapped a billy on the soles of your shoes and said, "Get going, buster."

"What's the matter?" you said to the policeman. "Weren't you ever a kid yourself, sir?"

It was a community ball park, set among apartment houses, frame buildings, and garages. The same cops worked there every day, and the same children loitered around the green in the middle of a city that was not a city but a borough. Early I rooted for journeymen Jersey Joe Stripp and Pete Coscarart, watching the way Stripp backhanded a shot toward third and how Coscarart sped behind second and set his foot and threw to first. Through the eyes of youth, a bad team in a tiny ball park looked glorious.

When boredom might have entered, a winning club was born. Larry MacPhail, trumpeted into town by Brooklyn bankers, assumed the leadership of the Dodgers in 1938. He set lights on the roof, and in the first night game — the first game *under arcs* the papers said — Johnny VanderMeer pitched a no-hitter. We were still losing, but now with style.

MacPhail bought the team satin uniforms that shone under the lights, and in a way no longer possible, with current baseball talent stretched to transparency, he began dealing and spending for strength. Babe Ruth came out of retirement to coach first base. According to Leo Durocher, Ruth never learned the Dodgers signs. Still, we went to see the big man clap hands and shout, "C'mon. Get holda one, kid." Durocher arrived from St. Louis, intense and loud and damned if he would lose. MacPhail rescued Whitlow Wyatt from the minors and snookered Kirby Higbe from the Phillies. He dealt for Dixie Walker, purchased Pee Wee Reese, and signed a young free agent named Pete Reiser. Dolf Camilli came to play first base — almost as gracefully as Jake Daubert, my father conceded — and Billy Herman, master of the hit to right, took over second.

Suddenly — the year was 1941 — the Dodgers were no longer funny. In a magnificent race with the St. Louis Cardinals, they won a pennant. Although the Yankees outmatched them in the Series, that pennant reinforced our sense of who we were, or would like to be. "So Brooklyn's a joke? Well, try a Wyatt fastball at your chin and see who laughs." The place where we climbed out of clown suits was dun-colored Ebbets Field, the ball park. That made the autumn of 1941 glorious in Brooklyn, although Hitler raged and Japanese admirals were preparing the devastation of Pearl Harbor.

Red Barber, the Dodger broadcaster, made splendid phrases. Durocher, ranting at an umpire, was "tearin' up the ol' pea patch." Fred Fitzsimmons ahead, 7–0, was "sittin' in the catbird seat." The public address announcer, gravel-voiced, porky Tex

Rickard, had his own encounters with the mother tongue. Once he announced, "Attention, please, a child has been found lost." One Sunday he offered, "Will the fans with their coats on the outfield railing please remove their clothes."

MacPhail himself had spirited moments. "What's the score?" he asked Bill Boylan, who tended bar in the cramped press room.

"We're losing, six to two," Boylan said.

"You're fired," MacPhail said.

Everything happened in Ebbets Field, Red Barber announced day after day. And then war came. MacPhail enlisted. Branch Rickey succeeded him, but the Dodgers, ravaged by the draft, fell to seventh place. "Lose 'em all," sang Roscoe McGowen of the *New York Times*. "The long and the short and the tall . . ."

There was one moment, and one only, when baseball truly led the country. That was in 1947, when Rickey brought Jackie Robinson to Ebbets Field. It is difficult these days to imagine the climate of a quarter-century ago, how the right of one lone black to play infield rent America. But after Robinson was signed, the man who ran the minor leagues declared, with leaden sarcasm, that a temple to Rickey would soon be built in Harlem. Major league owners sought a way to drum Rickey from the game. The Cardinals tried to organize a players' strike.

At the ball park in Brooklyn, people cracked small, uncertain jokes. "You can tell which one is Robinson. He's wearing number forty-two." You recognized Robinson by his color: imperial ebony. Watching the big, pigeon-toed, solitary man, you had to face what you had long repressed. Baseball everywhere, even in Brooklyn, had been racist.

In that small park the electricity that was Robinson, the bar of music that was the man, leaped from field to grandstand. In the boxes close to first, and just as surely in the poorer seats, you felt his vibrance. The crowds were bigger now, bigger than we had known them. In that bandbox the Dodgers drew 1.8 million, a record for the National League.

You couldn't hear the chatter anymore. Too many people. Too

much noise. But you could see a struggle waged in pantomime. The infield went: Spider Jorgensen, Pee Wee Reese, Eddie Stanky, with Robinson at first, a new position for him. They all wore white, the home team, with DODGERS written in blue script on their jerseys.

Some Dodgers were themselves racist. Later Robinson said that whenever he was on base and Dixie Walker hit a home run, he ran straight to the dugout, forgoing the handshake at home plate. "I didn't think he'd take my hand if I offered it," Robinson said, "and I didn't want an incident." But most of the Dodgers, including Reese and Ralph Branca, stood with Robinson. Waves of hate came from the other side.

Ben Chapman led the Phillies in cacophony. "Alligator bait" was his preamble. One or two players, running out a ground ball, tried to plant spikes in Robinson's Achilles tendon. And many pitchers sought to drive fastballs into Robinson's skull. The assault was ceaseless.

Here was a borough that had been torn by gibes. Hadn't Brooklyn always been something to laugh at? Here was a ball park where you sat so tightly that the field embraced you. The fans — Irish, Jewish, and Italian — pulled for Robinson, self-consciously, to be sure, but not for long. In the 1930s we had developed a simple New Deal view of life: pull for the underdogs. In 1947 the team looked really good. Now if this colored guy on first can make it big, we've got a chance.

After that came my newspaper job, and the magic fled. I came to know the Dodgers and to relish their company, as I still do, but Ebbets Field was at length a place of work. Watch a ball game every day and sensibilities dull. You could analyze the way the Dodger pitchers contended with Stan Musial. (Nervously and not well; part of Furillo's wall belonged to Stash.) You could find nuance and glory in watching Billy Cox play third. But as a professional, you came to recognize a formula of baseball. In an average week, two games will be good and two will be fair. Three will be exercises in tedium.

Nor did everything happen in Ebbets Field. When finally, un-believably, the Brooklyn Dodgers won a World Series from the Yankees, the seventh game was played at Yankee Stadium. Ebbets Field lay empty on that October day, and later I remember drinking with Pee Wee Reese and wishing that my father were alive.

When the wreckers came in 1957, I felt no pangs. Walter O'Malley was a money man. The place was too damn small. Let it go, let it go, like the past.

Now through the years it haunts me, like the fresh-faced, ardent girl you never married, maybe never even took to bed. I can see again a child's forgotten afternoon, when he walked with his father through arcs of sunlight and saw the bright flags, blue and green and white and red, the flapping flags that meant Ball Game Today. I wonder if a child can feel such stirrings walking toward the modular stadiums of the present. I wonder if children lack for having no neighborhood ball park, no preposterous right-field wall, no Carl Furillo; no sense that this park represents their town, which is itself unique, as cities were before the planners came with steel and glass skyscrapers.

One scene endures. Jackie Robinson is leading off third. The pitcher fidgets. Robinson glares at him, saying nothing. The pitcher winds up. Robinson breaks. "He's going," cry 30,000 voices. The big man slides, hurling his body at the catcher, intimidating him. Then, at the last instant, Robinson hooks his frame toward first and sweeps the plate with the tip of one spiked shoe.

Safe.

Jackie Robinson arises, smiling that inward smile. Everyone stands and cheers, and some men's eyes glisten. In Ebbets Field they have rooted for a ball player, some ignoring another person's color for the first time.

Well, Ebbets Field is gone, but perhaps we can preserve the bunting and the crystal of that memory.

1974

Rhapsody in Black

This is Don King's story. Having heard it, I don't think comments on his "electric hair" are funny.

From Don King's penthouse suite above the Rainbow Grill in Rockefeller Center, you look from horizon to horizon and see low hills sprawling in Westchester County and fat tankers nosing through the Narrows into New York Harbor and all the troubled city in between. But from sixty-seven stories, the city does not look troubled. No rat's alley, no ruin of highway shows. You see masonry, steel, glass, towers fixed in the neighboring sky, and beset Manhattan seems secure.

"My man, my man," says Don King, smiling. "How does all this strike you?" A portrait of Muhammad Ali hangs behind King's desk. The painter is LeRoy Neiman, a coloratura artist, more tone than substance usually, but this time Neiman has caught something distinct. Ali's arms are raised in victory. He has won his fight. Somehow Neiman makes the victory posture suggest crucifixion.

The penthouse ceilings are fifteen feet high. The rent is $85,000 a year. The elegance is anachronistic; I expect Ginger Rogers to come dancing in from a terrace and someone to offer me a sloe-gin fizz. "It's high living," Don King says, "and I don't know how long I'll stay on top, but at least I've gotten here. If a time comes when I have to leave, I'm taking the elevator down. I'm not stepping off the terrace." A second smile — a serious smile — and King follows with a rush of words, from Voltaire, Shakespeare, Machiavelli, Frantz Fanon, and the Cleveland ghetto.

Don King is the most successful fight promoter now practicing. That is, he has beaten a clutch of driving lawyers, a gaggle of Hollywood hustlers, and all by himself has promoted thirty million dollars' worth of boxing during the last two years. Before that he booked numbers in the Cleveland slums, and from 1967 to 1971 Don King was inmate no. 125734 at the Marion Correctional Institution in Ohio. The charge was manslaughter, and King concedes that he is guilty of a killing, without endorsing the severity of his punishment. "I had him down," he says, "and then I kicked him in the head.

"In there," he says of prison, "you find Barbaria. The jailers are like the white straw bosses on the plantations. The straw boss rode the horse, but he resented how the big boss lived in the big white plantation manor. He took his resentment out on the slaves. Your prison guard's education is nil, but his resentment runs high. Your hard-core prisoners want to penetrate young men. A young man resists; you get a murder. Your prison officials worry about boards of inquiry. Here comes a board. Boom. The menu switches. No more hot dog soup. A rib eye steak instead. But these murders keep happening, and you get no conjugal visits, and do we want to turn our men prisoners into women? It's all worse than the horrors of Dickens, man. In a prison we can recycle people, or we can burn them up. Our prisons are just crime factories. I worked days hauling hog manure. Nights I read."

King, who is forty-four, stands six feet two inches, with a chest as stout as a youthful oak and an Afro that springs from his brow to stiff attention. His vocabulary has grown so rapidly that it has outrun his pronouncing skills. King calls the German philosophers "Hee-gel" and "Neetsh," but he has also *read* Hegel and Nietzsche.

In the penthouse suite he races across literature and philosophy nonstop, offering a breathless, booming lecture on the humanities.

"I got no real degree," King says. "I'm a Ph.D. from the ghetto. I read everything in the prison library. I took extension courses. Still lots of people figure I'm just a nigger.

"But now I'm setting up the Ali-Frazier fight, and President Marcos of the Philippines is very proud of his wife's looks. And I say, 'Mrs. Marcos, age cannot wither you, nor custom stale your infinite variety.' The president blinks. That's from *Antony and Cleopatra.* They didn't expect to hear a Cleveland nigger spouting lines like that.

"I read in prison every night. I took every extension course I could take. Oh, the sweetness of adversity. I took the jewel out of the brow of adversity. Shakespeare. I read Voltaire. How to vilify but be accepted. Machiavelli. The strength of the lion and the cunning of the fox. It is better to be feared than to be loved. Frantz Fanon. You are either the victim or the victimizer. Demosthenes. He described a bribe as a promoter of friendship, but he also said a statesman was one who sees and foresees. The black condition. They promised us forty acres and a mule. They gave us neither." King blew air through his cheeks and studied a telex from the Shah of Iran.

"When I got out of that fucking prison in 1971, I was a dangerous character. I was armed with knowledge."

The ghetto is frightening, most of all to the people who live there and who die there, but it is vital and throbbing and heterogeneous and dynamic. Each ghetto is a graveyard of stunted lives, but now comes King.

The movies fooled us. They told us the ghetto people were Irving Berlin and George Gershwin and that a ghetto crisis was finding money to pay the music teacher. The movies left out tuberculosis, bookmaking, pimps, Murder Inc., Meyer Lansky.

Don King, whom *Time* describes as "one of the most successful black businessmen in America," lived among pimps and racketeers before he killed the man he now refers to only as Sam. King was famous in the ghetto and wealthy in the ghetto long before he crashed the boundary into the white world.

"We weren't poor," he said in the penthouse. Facing Neiman's Ali a print showed Aristotle contemplating the bust of Homer. "For black people, we were middle class. My father worked as a laborer at Jones and Laughlin, pulling the plug from a steel smelter. One day, easy to remember, December 7, 1941, the plug stuck. The smelter blew and killed my father. There was a settlement. In the ghetto we call that 'tragedy money.' My mother took the money she got for the flesh of my father, Clarence King, and there were seven kids and she went and bought a house. I was ten years old."

King liked boxing, dabbled at high school, drank the life around him in leviathan gulps. He considered ghetto religions. "They program black people for death. You get a band in spats for the funeral. Pie in the sky when you die. But when you're around, there's nothing sound on the ground." He learned street lore, the look of whores, the flash of pimps, as suburban children learn the rooflines of a Mercedes.

Contemplating careers, King thought of law, but that was remote, a world away, white man's stuff. Then he decided to work the numbers. "Doesn't hurt anybody much," King says. "Gets some people nigger rich. You know, like bingo in the white community."

To play numbers you buy a slip for a dollar or two or five, and you pick three numbers, say 6-8-5. If you hit, you are paid off at about 600 to 1. The actual odds are almost 900 to 1. Each day's winning combination — this varies with the ghetto — may be the last three digits of the U.S. Treasury statement. A well-run numbers game is probably as fair as a state lottery but, being illegal and black, it is more exotic.

Dream books flourish in the ghettos. They explain what a specific dream foretells in numbers. Did you dream of death? One book says play 9-6-2. Did you dream of sex? Try for 3-4-7. Keep buying. Keep trying. Keep dreaming. You'll hit, my man. Someday you'll hit.

In each community, numbers operators work in loose federation. If one man comes up with more action on a certain number than he feels he can handle, he makes a layoff. He replays some of his action with a bigger operator. "The numbers people have to work with each other to stay alive," King says. "You need a rhapsody in black."

King ran his own numbers games flamboyantly and soon bankrolled other operators. He says he always paid off in public and in full. "There's a psychology to paying off. I'd have the winners meet me in a bar. I'd be a few minutes late. Let the tension grow. Then I'd park my Caddy and come in and pay them off with small bills, looked like a fortune, and there'd be lots of people around. I'd say, when you win with Don King, you're guaranteed to get paid. I'd say, Don King is sound as the Federal Reserve."

Sam, the man Don King would kill, was an ex-convict whom King had set up in the numbers business. King himself placed a bet with Sam on 3-4-7, the sex number, and 3-4-7 hit. Sam never paid. "You've got to take care of this," King told Sam in a bar. "We've got to keep our reputations."

"I will take care of it," Sam said. "It's an overlook."

"You better take care of it," King said, "if you ever want to work with me again."

Voices rose. King walked out into the street. Sam followed him, shouting. The men began to fight. King knocked Sam down and kicked him. Sam's head hit a concrete curb. Seven days later he died.

According to King, the first charge against him was aggravated assault. "What the hell was it to white cops," he says, "two blacks fighting and one dies?" But King was famous in certain quarters of the Cleveland Police Department. "Numbers Overlord was my title of damnation, and when they found out I was *that* Don King, the charge escalated to murder two, second-degree homicide. I felt despair. How can you beat a charge like that? The judge reduced it to manslaughter, but at the trial I had no chance of getting another reduction or going free. I might have if ghetto people judged me, but I didn't have a jury of my peers. I was tried before a jury of middle-class whites shortly after the riots of the 1960s. When I was arrested, I was driving a new Caddy and I was carrying eighteen hundred dollars cash. That jury seethed when they looked at me. They thought, 'Jail him and we jail our own miseries.' They heard what happened, but they weren't listening. I got one to twenty years."

While King writhed and read in prison, his wife, Henrietta, maintained the rolling suburban farm he had bought, and the family remained solvent. Six months after his release, stirred by guilt and a new sense of mission, King organized a promotion for Forest City Hospital in Cleveland. Wilson Pickett sang. Lou Rawls told jokes. Muhammad Ali fought four different men in ten rounds of sparring. The promotion was a smash. King lifted his eyes from numbers to boxing.

"It's the damnedest thing about fight promoters," says Harold Conrad, who has worked for many. "The straightest guys get a license to promote, and they read it as a license to steal." Conrad mentioned some names. "Of course, we don't always get the straightest guys. Something King has going for him so far is that he delivers what he promises, and on time."

Something else is his ability to see and foresee. Booking a fight now, with Ali et al. demanding $10 million in guarantees, exceeds the resources of any arena and indeed most cities. King does not look for cities; he looks for countries. Through heads of state he has booked Ali into Zaire, Malaysia, and the Philippines, and while we talked, that wire from the Shah sat on his desk. "Saudi Arabia," I said. "You ought to book a fight there and bring home petrodollars."

"As a matter of fact, I have to meet an Arabian representative at the UN next week. I can talk to them at the UN, but I can still talk to young fighters, give them that jive talk, too."

Horatio Alger, rewoven into black on black. If you want to argue the morality of numbers, you'll have to do that with an honest ghetto cop, if you can find one. Not here. "Hell," Don King says, selling his former business, "for years numbers was the only insurance a black person could buy. Not guaranteed, but the best around. That's why they call the numbers 'policy.'

"I want to serve," King thunders above the Rainbow Grill, selling his new business. "What Muhammad and I and the rest of us make every fight, half of that goes to the government. We help the balance of trade. We show them a rugged image of America. I'm making money, two hundred thousand dollars some days, but I'm serving, too. I've made it because I'm straight. Being black helps me with Ali, but so does the fact that I work eighteen hours a day. I'm straight and I don't hesitate."

He smiled and asked if I'd like to visit his farm near Cleveland and meet his wife and his children and his pet elephant. "I told you straight about the numbers, about the killing," he said. "I hope you write it straight."

I said I'd try, but I was thinking about the pet elephant.

1975

The Fifth Ward
in Houston

George Foreman never got the chance he wanted to win back the heavyweight championship. A few years later he found work preaching from his friends Matthew and Isaiah. At forty, old age for a fighter, Foreman returned to the ring and found he had not lost a former habit. He continued to knock people out.

In a rambling suite at the Beverly Wilshire Hotel so ornate that I imagined Thalberg engaging it for visiting bankers circa 1933, George Foreman, a huge, sensitive, complex fighter, sat restlessly taking his ease. He had been heavyweight champion, and he had put a million dollars in the bank, and he had driven back to the wretched Fifth Ward in Houston at the wheel of a $56,000 Rolls-Royce; now he was preparing to act with Redd Foxx in a sequence of the television series "Sanford and Son." He had been reading poetry, a volume by Nikki Giovanni, learning and growing and traveling, but something had gone wrong. He was not the heavyweight champion anymore.

Foreman won the championship in 1973, when he was twenty-four, by devastating Joe Frazier within two rounds at Kingston, Jamaica. Nobody had devastated Frazier before. Foreman destroyed this splendid heavyweight, then went on and knocked out

José Roman of Puerto Rico in one round and Ken Norton, the man who broke Muhammad Ali's jaw, in two.

Through the mythology that springs up about strong heavyweights, George Foreman came to be perceived as both an immovable object and an irresistible force. Before fighting Muhammad Ali in Zaire in the autumn of 1974, he had won all forty of his professional fights, thirty-seven by knockouts. Just before the African encounter, certain people close to Ali feared that Foreman might kill him in the ring. Just before the bout Ali himself fell to his knees and prayed. At length rising, he said, "It's in the hands of Allah."

God, Napoleon reminds sophomore history students, is on the side of the army with the most cannon. Ali slipped, moved, covered up against the ropes until finally George Foreman, the indestructible, had punched himself weary. Foreman's artillery was silenced, and Ali knocked him out in round eight.

To this day Foreman believes that Ali did not defeat him. "I beat myself," he said. "I believed in my own indestructibility. Same thing happened to Sonny Liston."

Foreman's Zaire purse was $5,500,000, but with bountiful proceeds came hard times. In a single encounter his proud and hard-bought sense of what he was had been ripped from him, along with the heavyweight championship. Richer than he had known how to dream of riches, Foreman felt lost.

He consented to a boxing burlesque, for the glory of the American Broadcasting Company, and took on five mediocrities in a single afternoon at Toronto. He outmuscled everyone, but as Joe Louis remarked after one of his own poorer efforts, "Nobody got hurt but the customers."

Finally, after a fifteen-month layoff from serious boxing, Foreman knocked out Ron Lyle in Las Vegas last January. Lyle hurt Foreman in the first round and knocked him down twice before Foreman clubbed Lyle senseless in the fifth.

Now, as we sat in a suite beyond an endless foyer tiled in black and white, Foreman tried to explain where he was going. The problem was he couldn't be sure.

"After Zaire," he said, "Ali looked me in the eye and said, 'I'll give you a chance to get the championship back. You come ahead of Frazier and Norton.'"

"And?"

"He hasn't fought me." Foreman wore Levi's and a tan shirt. He stands six feet three, and his arms are so long that his reach measures seventy-nine inches. He smiled, mostly to himself. "I guess he was lying."

"Do you feel bitter?"

"I don't get bitter. I hate not being heavyweight champion, but I got other important things, too. My reading. I can't maybe explain all of Nikki Giovanni's poetry, but I look at her face and I associate that face with the poetry and I understand. My religion. I believe in God. I love to read Matthew and Isaiah. My daughter." Through French doors you could see the Hollywood Hills. "I'm not bitter, but I want that championship back."

George Foreman grew up in a slum so deprived that as late as 1959, only two families in the ward owned television sets. He was one of seven children, and he recalls that his great early delight was standing on a porch looking through a window at a Western movie on one of the sets. Westerns were his favorite. The cavalry charges thrilled him, the movie soldiers riding bravely, firing blanks, and waving flags furnished by the prop department of Republic Studios.

The one dream he remembers was wanting to be a defensive tackle. His school years at E. O. Smith Junior High were disastrous. "You hear about them integrated and partially integrated," he says. "E. O. Smith was unintegrated. All black. The way I was, to learn, I had to get the attention of the teacher, and there were other kids who were always better at that, so I didn't get the attention of the teacher, and I didn't learn. That took care of football. I dropped out in the ninth grade."

His diet was shocking. In such relatively affluent ghettos as Harlem and Watts, families serve dinners of chicken necks and chicken backs. Foreman remembers dinners of chicken feet. "I ate the toes," he says. There was no money, no food, no hope. He took to the streets.

He learned to rob, and when he had stolen money, he learned to spend it on cheap wine. He didn't like what he was doing. Wine drunks beat off reality. Then, sober, he would have to rob again. By sixteen, George had become a chronic offender, and his future seemed reduced to a single word: prison.

Suddenly and quite magically, George Foreman, the delinquent alcoholic of sixteen, decided to leave his ghetto and join the Job Corps, one of the social welfare programs born of the Kennedy-Johnson years. He worked as a lumber jack in the Pacific Northwest. There he met whites for the first time. "I had a mythology about whites," he said, "and the whites had a mythology about us. And we found out, whites and blacks, not all of us, but some, we weren't so damn different. And I learned to work, clear land, and make a living, and I flew in an airplane, and they were always kidding me. 'Big George. Big George. You're so strong you ought to be a fighter.'"

He began boxing and within three years won the Olympic heavyweight championship at Mexico City. That summer other black medalists raised clenched fists as a symbol of black power. George Foreman, the heavyweight champion, proclaimed his victory by waving a tiny American flag in the ring.

"The Job Corps made me a patriot," he said, "but people don't understand everything about that flag. I was holding it up because of what the Job Corps did for me, but I was also holding it up because I was crazy about flags. Remember, that's what I saw the cavalry wave in those old movies on television in the Fifth Ward."

George was restless on Stage Three at NBC. The actors worked for a few minutes, broke, and played the same scene again. They broke once more. Redd Foxx held a hideously misshapen walking stick. He put it between his legs. "I wonder what she gave me," Redd Foxx said.

Foreman played himself in a role that would not have challenged

Paul Robeson. He knew his lines. Redd Foxx, reading from cue cards, said he had been a fighter once himself. "Kid Death." More breaks. More retakes. Lunch time.

"This," George Foreman said as actors fled for the commissary, "motivates me to go back to training. All these breaks. This is not a challenge. Fighting is. I work out in Livermore, near San Francisco. I was going to go back to working on the thirteenth, but why mess with luck? I'm starting on the fourteenth."

He grew pensive. "I haven't always been like this, you know. I got to be champion and I bought three homes and a batch of cars and I took the $56,000 Rolls back to the Fifth Ward and somebody came up and said, 'Champ, now that you've made it, why don't you dump this thing and get a classy car, a Caddy.' I kind of laughed at him and thought it would take three days to explain to this guy what a Rolls-Royce is.

"All right. After I lose, I'm up in Vegas and a couple of guys see me. They're driving a pimp's car. A 'sixty-one Chevy with pink velvet interior. They wave, and I wave back, feeling like a big man. Then one of them says, 'I hope Ali whips your ass again.'

"I was a difficult guy when I was champion. Arrogant. I can beat Ali; I mean next time he's going to beat himself. When I get to be champion again, I'm not going to be difficult. I'm going to remember all these months. Next time I'm champion, I'll treat everyone as though I were just a contender, say number five."

Technically, Foreman is attempting to alter his style. For all his slugging power, he has tended to punch somewhat wide. A straight line and a tight hook are the shortest distance between points, and Dempsey is said to have possessed knockout power with a six-inch punch. Toward tightening his blows, Foreman has engaged Gil Clancy, a boxing scholar, as his new trainer.

Foreman's graceless performance against Ron Lyle could have been a symptom of rust or an uncertain moment in transition or the simple result of getting slugged hard as hell in the first round. But also it might mean, as in the case of Sonny Liston, that one whipping by Ali forever snapped something in the psyche.

With this in mind and Joe Louis in mind, I asked Foreman how he stood with that partner of every champion, the Internal Revenue Service.

"I'm not going to tell you where I keep my money," Foreman said.

"But you're OK?"

A small, warm smile. "IRS is the real undefeated heavyweight champ. They show you the left. You never see the right. They'll take everything, even your tears."

He grew serious. "Yes. I'm all right, and I can't complain about taxes. The Job Corps made me human, and income taxes supported that."

"My income taxes," I said.

"Thank you very much," George Foreman said.

1976

George Foreman never did get his rematch with Ali, but his comeback in the late 1980s made him a great national favorite. He talked about boxing until he was past fifty, or was it past sixty?

Ali in Whispers

Writing a column for Time *magazine didn't work out. An editor said, "We'd like you to cover Wimbledon, explain Chris Evert, and consider the women's movement in tennis."*

"I can't fit that into seven hundred and fifty words."

"Try," said the editor, a decent sort. "It means you get to London for free."

"I can afford to go to London on my own," I said.

We parted amicably, thanks to Ray Cave. This Time *column probably was the best.*

The fighter sat in semidarkness, talking in an urgent whisper. When you sit with Muhammad Ali, he talks in whispers. He knows that when the heavyweight champion speaks softly, you strain to hear.

"Why are you fighting this fight?" I asked. "Why are you going on?"

Rays of late afternoon sunlight angled against an off-white wall. Ali, who wore black, had positioned himself in darkness.

"To do good works," he said. "I helped a Jewish nursing home. You know I go in the ghettos. Two, three days after this fight, I may be on the South Side of Chicago talking with people. What heavyweight champion before ever done that?" Ali stroked his brows, which are unmarked for all the punches crashed against them. "I gives a lot away. I got a mission. God, if there is a God, he's gonna judge me. That's when I die. And I'm gonna die. Sonny Liston. He died."

I nodded.

"And you," Ali said. "You gonna die. Jimmy Cannon, he was once sitting right where you are, and he died. You ever think about that?"

I had driven cheerfully into the Catskill Mountains to observe two black men readying themselves for a fight at Yankee Stadium. The Ali I remembered was brave, young, and handsome, and as remote from death as spring. But now this man had turned contemplative and grave. He was telling me something with great sublety. Muhammad Ali was dying as a fighter.

Ken Norton, thirty-one, the opponent, is a child of the black middle class, a star in two dreadful movies, and the possessor of a body that Irving Rudd, a boxing publicist, called "mythologically hewn."

No rancor separated the fighters. Ali had been guaranteed $6 million. Norton would earn $1 million. September 28 was payday, but as they worked toward summits of conditioning, the world yawned. Ali is proud of his ability to sell tickets, and at the public prefight physical, he staged a vulgar, raucous demonstration.

"You a nigger," he screamed at Norton in a meeting room at Grossinger's Hotel. "You a yellow nigger. And your movies are bad." Ali lifted a poster displaying a photo of Norton that had appeared in the *Village Voice*. Posed next to a sink, Norton wore only a jock strap.

"You are a disgrace to athletics," Ali shouted. "You are a disgrace to your race. You are a disgrace to your country, posing for a picture with your balls hanging out."

Norton ignored the champion, and a doctor in a yellow and black sports jacket took pulses and blood pressures, complaining that he could not do his work unless Ali quieted down. Ali signaled to his retinue, and presently his seconds and Norton's seconds were calling each other flunkies.

"Both men are in superb condition," announced Harry Kleiman, the doctor.

"When Ali gets beat, you go on welfare," cried one of Norton's people.

"You're just a nigger," said Ali's man, Drew Brown.

The champion's eyes showed merriment. Privately he had given Joe Louis $10,000 to spend two weeks with him at the Concord Hotel. Publicly he refused to notice Louis wince whenever the word "nigger" rang out.

Such alternations tax credulity, except for this: Ali is the champion and he is locked into a style. He turned professional during the last days of Dwight Eisenhower's administration, and he has fought well, sometimes brilliantly, through five presidencies. Young, he was Cassius Clay, the "Louisville Lip," establishing himself with his fists, his doggerel, and his outrageous predictions. Now, four months away from his thirty-fifth birthday, he is Muhammad, the Muslim minister, pledged to peace and God. But he is also a ticket salesman. If vulgarity sells tickets, let it be.

Fight night broke chilly, and for all of Ali's noise, only 30,000 people appeared in the cavernous stadium. There was more violence outside the ring than in. Ali still moves with a lithe beauty, but he no longer punches in flurries. He had predicted, "Norton must fall in five." After five rounds Norton stood strong. Across the whole fight, neither staggered the other. Ali reddened Norton's face. Norton bloodied Ali's nose. Eight-year-olds would do more.

Norton appeared to win narrowly, but a law of boxing holds that no heavyweight champion can lose by a narrow decision. Dutifully the referee and two judges gave the fight to Ali. Dutifully Norton's manager protested. Norton wept in frustration. Ali stole off into the night, frightened by hoodlums clawing at the windows of his car.

"Not exactly your classic fight," I said to Harold Conrad, a boxing scholar engaged by Ali as a personal aide.

"Dorian Gray," Conrad said. "The face is still beautiful, but what's gone on inside the body? The kidney punches. Shots to the liver. That stuff and time have taken a toll. It just doesn't show on the champion's face."

"This isn't the fighter who took on Joe Frazier in 1971."

Conrad puffed a cigarette. "Nobody," he said, "makes love as well as he did five years ago."

Ali sees his future in evangelism. He would become a cross between Billy Graham and William Jennings Bryan. To do that, to take care of his children and his divorces, to work his private charities, he has calculated that he needs $83,000 a month. That is why he has gone on boxing with eroded skills. That is why, his mind heavy with death, he shouted "nigger" into the face of a decent man like Kenny Norton.

But three days after the fight, Ali was not on the South Side of Chicago. He was in Istanbul. The dullness of his performance had sunk in. "As of now," he announced, "I am quitting boxing and will devote all my energy to the propagation of the Muslim faith."

He meant it. He means a lot of what he says. But six months from now, when he is hoarse from preaching and someone offers him $10 million to fight George Foreman, we will behold a mighty crisis of faith.

1976

No one made such an offer.

The Sunshine Boy

Although he had the Tammany man's concern for what the New York Times *might publish, Walter O'Malley played a puckish game when we finished luncheon. He ignored the check. O'Malley was worth $100 million. He ignored the check.*

When I took it, he said, "All the years I've known you, since you were in the fifth grade at Froebel Academy, that's the first time you bought me lunch."

"Get the restaurant photographer," I said. "Then we can send the picture to Cooperstown."

"You'll have to settle for an affidavit," O'Malley said.

I filed an expense account. Arthur Ochs Sulzberger paid for the lunch.

Winter has laid an icy hand on McKeever Place, back of the old left-field stands, and there is nothing much for city kids to do but watch the new snow blacken under soot. In colder winters long ago, a magic sounded. You threw a rubber ball against a dun brick wall and calculated how many months and weeks and days would have to pass before Jackie and Duke, Furillo and Preacher, Campy and Pee Wee marched home again to Ebbets Field like heroes.

Already the red brick houses called Ebbets Field Apartments

show dirt, disorder, and other symptoms of incipient slum. Where generations of baseball crowds sorrowed and exulted lies only another corner of the urban wasteland. It is almost eerie in the whistling cold. The soul of Brooklyn shriveled and was lost when a baseball franchise moved and the wrecker's ball ravaged Ebbets Field.

"If we hadn't moved," Walter O'Malley mused over a Lucullan luncheon at Perino's Restaurant on Wilshire Boulevard. "If we hadn't moved . . ." Maestro O'Malley played a thoughtful look at a crystal chandelier.

"Sir," said a captain. "We have fresh raspberries today, flown in from New Zealand."

O'Malley's round face assumed a more practical expression. "Say," he said, "are you getting the tab for this lunch or am I?"

Walter Francis O'Malley is a feisty, visionary, manipulative adventurer of seventy-four winters who feels that politicians and circumstances booted him and the Dodgers out of the borough of Brooklyn. In what remains of Brooklyn, feeling runs the other way. *Benedict O'Malley deserted us.* The issue — who rejected whom — is native more to divorce than to the sports page.

Some remember the Dodgers of the 1930s with affectionate giggles. Frenchy Bordagaray, a Brooklyn outfielder, once tried to score standing up and was tagged out.

"Why the hell didn't you slide?" asked Casey Stengel, the manager.

"I was gonna, Case," Bordagaray said, "but I was afraid I'd crush my cigars."

One thousand on the laugh meter. Zero at the box office. The Dodgers spent the Great Depression shuttling between fifth and seventh place, playing before crowds of 1,208.

"Larry MacPhail brought in some decent ball players at the end of the 1930s," O'Malley said, considering with peculiar warmth a platter of calves' liver, blue. "Won a pennant, but then he went off to war. Now the Brooklyn Trust Company, a client of mine when

I was practicing law, had a note outstanding that the Dodgers would not repay. They asked me to look into it, and I smoked things out at once. The club would not repay because it couldn't. There was no capital. Dodger stock hadn't paid a dividend in a generation. Litigation persisted with the estate of a former owner. Even Ebbets Field was in hock to a life insurance company. Things were so bad, a twenty-five percent share of the team was practically begging. I obliged and bought in for $250,000."

Branch Rickey replaced MacPhail and passed a variety of miracles. He found Duke Snider, traded for Preacher Roe and Billy Cox, and integrated baseball with Jackie Robinson.

"A great baseball man," O'Malley pronounced at Perino's. "The greatest. But Rickey didn't have much organizational business sense. The contract he wrote for himself was unfair to every other stockholder. Why, the contract he wrote himself . . ." Looking up from the blue liver, O'Malley's eyes turned gelid. "We had to get him out of there if the club was ever going to make money, and we got him out of there in 1950."

As Dodger president and at length controlling stockholder, O'Malley played a multilevel game. To the press and public he portrayed himself as a fan, and it is true that he likes to watch baseball games. But the man within, the interior O'Malley, so to speak, burned with dispassionate brilliance.

Bad weather hurt attendance. Twenty-five years ago O'Malley ordered plans and a working model for a ball park with a retractable dome. No one took a domed stadium seriously in 1955.

Television was growing beyond the nine-inch screen. O'Malley charted receipts and concluded that "radio whets the appetite of the fan; television satisfies it." He tried to talk pay television with David Sarnoff but was dismissed.

He saw blocks of brownstone houses boarded up in Bedford-Stuyvesant. Customers, Dodger customers, were moving away.

The team was winning. Everyone knew that. But a winning team was not enough for O'Malley. He wanted victories plus profits plus opportunities for future growth. He saw himself wedged into an old ball park in a declining neighborhood, and it had taken him so long to get to where he was, he'd be damned if he'd stay wedged.

The New Zealand raspberries arrived, outrageously pink for January.

"I believed in mass transit," O'Malley said, "so I wanted a new park over the Long Island Rail Road Station at the intersection of Flatbush and Atlantic avenues. I envisioned a ball park, which we would build, which would not have cost the taxpayers a dime, right in the railroad station to deal with the suburban thing, and with a break on pay television, I could have given Brooklyn fans a dome. But Mr. Moses, Robert Moses, insisted that we move to Gravesend, at a site he was peddling, that lay between a cemetery and the sea." Los Angeles turned out to be more convenient.

If Robert Moses had been less rigid twenty years ago . . . if the mayor, Robert Wagner, had been stronger . . . imagine the continuity of things. The Koufax-Drysdale years. Maury Wills stealing bases. That string of great Septembers. And now Steve Garvey, who wears Carl Furillo's old number. The Dodgers in Brooklyn to this day.

The fancy deepens. Time suspends. Old Brooklyn, borough of steeples and stickball, could be old Brooklyn yet. But if you think that, then fancy has turned your mind to butter. Ball clubs don't save cities, or even neighborhoods. The Indians remain in downtown Cleveland. Around their park Cleveland wastes away. The Tigers linger in Detroit, which someone called "no longer a city but a rim around a bomb crater." In its new veneer Yankee Stadium is particularly irrelevant to the horrors of the South Bronx.

Had the Dodgers stayed in Brooklyn, justice would have been served, because the Mets [then in last place] and Los Angeles deserve each other. But Brooklyn today would still be a borough of decay. Buildings would rot. Rats would prowl within sight of Walter O'Malley's pleasure dome.

May the souls of Jack Robinson and Gil Hodges shine on in their glory; may the urban planners go to work.

1978

Walter O'Malley died at the age of seventy-five in the summer of 1979. He left the family business, the Dodgers, to his son and daughter.

No Moaning
at This Bar

Attempting naturalism in the New York Times, *I indicated, with the sixth letter of the alphabet and a dash, the word Joe Namath used in his sulk. Arthur Gelb, the managing editor, replaced that with the term "vile obscenity." Knowing few obscenities that are not vile, I have deleted Arthur's adjective.*

According to a newsmagazine I read in other days, "sportswriters are a notoriously sentimental lot." That is how they put it. Notorious. Sentimental. And lot. The same issue reported that if we were to stand any chance against godless, atheistic communism, we would all have to vote for Thomas E. Dewey. Although young, I let my subscription expire.

Recently Joe Namath, promoter, hedonist, and unemployed quarterback, said that he was retiring from the National Football League. He was not giving up much, since it was uncertain if he could find football work for 1978. But since then sportswriters have been behaving like a notoriously sentimental lot. They talk about Joe's private grace. They compose rhapsodies to his style. They report breathlessly that he is not broke.

It's enough to make a man rethink his position on Tom Dewey.

*   *   *

Joe Willie Namath was an entertainer; he was no hero. He threw a football well, with incredibly quick release; he liked to swagger. If he stood for anything at all, it was for the right of a quarterback to drink whiskey, cohabit with stewardesses, and speak with a southern drawl, even though he came from Pennsylvania. I respect these rights, but heroism demands more lofty themes.

He lent his name to employment agencies, restaurants, underwear, every fast-buck scheme that came along, and the one time true emotion surfaced, he embarrassed everyone.

Namath owned part of a lively restaurant called Bachelors III, and he enjoyed the pace of New York East Side life. People courted him. Scotch flowed. Girls flashed about in hot pants. The drawback, NFL security people claimed, was that Bachelors III became a place where some drug pushers gathered. At length Pete Rozelle heard that "a Treasury Department raid is imminent."

Rozelle reacted with healthy terror. He ordered Namath to sell his interest in Bachelors III or quit playing football. Namath called a press conference and said that he wouldn't sell out; he'd give up football. Then he began to cry.

Presently Joe dried his eyes and peddled the joint.

By any title, Sonny Werblin is an agent, with a glorious eye for publicity and talent. Last week he was trying to buy the best hockey players out of the Soviet Union and Sweden because the Rangers can't win with North Americans. Last decade he was recruiting quarterbacks and buying credulity. That is, he announced contract figures to make sure we understood that the New York Jets at last were big time.

John Huarte, a $100,000 beauty from Notre Dame, threw sidearm. Nice motion for baseball. Huarte failed. Namath, the Alabama bomber, had a superb arm, questionable knees, and a $400,000 contract. Werblin knows how to create news. The contract made Namath famous.

Joe had one ultimate week in Florida sunshine. He guaranteed that the Jets would defeat the Baltimore Colts in Super Bowl III and proved as good as his boast. That was on a Sunday in 1969.

The victory reinforced his arrogance. A publicity man from *Sport* magazine invited Namath to a luncheon at which he would get the keys to a car as most valuable player in the game.

"How much cash?" said one of Namath's advisers.

"There isn't any fee, but all the media are there, and he gets a car worth $6,000."

Namath felt that he was going to lunch too cheaply. He scowled from the dais at Leone's except when nibbling a model's ear, which he had confused with the tortoni. His demeanor put off sportswriters until one grabbed a child and said, "Sign for this youngster, Joe, and how's your arm?"

Namath signed and growled.

Twenty minutes later another reporter was smitten with the same idea. He approached the guest of honor with the boy.

"Get him away from me; I've signed for this kid already!" Namath shouted. He interpolated an obscenity before the word "kid."

I believe I'd object as strongly to that behavior even if the child had not been my older son, who was eleven.

Sport gives us emperors, clowns, heroes. Roberto Clemente played in a passion to prove that "Latins are not hot dogs." He risked his life and lost it out of what Milton calls "considerate pride." Casey Stengel was portable Americana. The old man knew who he was better than anyone else, and he laughed with the rest of us at the pap issued as his autobiography. Then he'd tell good stories, not for print. Muhammad Ali, that mixture of con man and idealist, follows his concepts of integrity. Three disparate sport figures. Three heroes.

Namath is only a performer, invented by Werblin and to an extent by himself. As he swaggers into the sunset, my eyes remain notoriously dry.

Other Super Bowls will come, along with other super arms. They may even be attached to more gracious men.

1978

Walter Wellesley Smith

In the late 1950s, the editor of Newsweek *magazine asked me to write a cover story on Red Smith. He said he had a wonderful cover line: "Shakespeare of the Press Box." That was hardly politic. John Lardner wrote a weekly sports column for* Newsweek, *and the two, Smith and Lardner, were competitive. Besides, Shakespeare wrote better than either. Killing the cover line consumed energies properly put into a story, but I couldn't kill another editor's description of prominent sportswriters as "titans." That is in the nature of what Luce called "group journalism." You debate things that should not have been brought up in the first place.*

Before The Boys of Summer *was published, Smith accepted an assignment to write a cover story about me for the* Book-of-the-Month Club News. *The interviewer was sharper than his subject. Smith asked what date I had begun at the* Herald Tribune. *I didn't remember.*

Smith loved his alma mater, Notre Dame, and when the university magazine asked if I could write a piece for them, Smith joked about our interviewing one another for fun and profit. The one "titan" here was an inside joke.

Tomorrow Red Smith would reach the age of seventy-four. He would be springy of step, ebullient with youth, and well tuned to a world newly born each day. Still, he would be seventy-four years old.

"When is your deadline?" Smith asked.

The day had broken cool autumn blue. I mentioned a target date.

"Maybe you'd better hurry," Smith said. "My contract at the *Times* expires in five weeks, and I haven't heard a word about renewal."

Paranoia is a classic affliction of writers. Somehow you will not be allowed to finish a work in progress. If you do finish, a dozen critics will hurl typewriters at your head. Should the critics be kind, the public will ignore what you have written. "Hell," says one durable writer of my acquaintance, "I admit I'm paranoid, but what else can you be when they're persecuting you?"

One of Red Smith's charms, across the thirty years I've known him, has been an abiding, diffidently expressed confidence. Pressed once by an admirer who hailed him as a titan of the press box, Smith winced but then conceded, "I know I'm a pretty good speller." He has not seemed to perceive the world as freighted with enemies. Rather, his views of sport, prose, and himself suggest that he is working for an audience of friends. The people he writes for are literate. They know which base is second. They delight in his stories, jests, insightful reporting.

"You aren't serious," I said. "Your column is the best thing in the *Times* sports section."

"You aren't the editor of the *Times*," Smith said.

The next day, as Smith entered his seventy-fifth year, I telephoned A. M. Rosenthal, a complex, gifted, unsentimental journalist who runs the *New York Times*.

"Not renew Red Smith's contract?" Rosenthal said softly, as though in shock. "His contract will never be over. Do you know what Red means to me? Personally? I get depressed sometimes editing this paper. But whenever I get down I say to myself, 'Wait a minute. I hired Red Smith.'"

*　　　*　　　*

The full name is Walter Wellesley Smith. The late Stanley Woodward, a sports editor of irresistible ferocity, found a women's school named Walter somewhere and thus could claim that Red was the only man in history "named after three girls' colleges." The claim goes undenied. Smith's style in writing and life is graceful and measured, sensible and joyous: culture without pomposity. He lost his first wife, Catherine, to cancer, and he himself underwent surgery two years ago for a dangerous growth deep in the gut. But he does not dwell on pain. I assume he can write a tortured sentence. I cannot remember reading one.

At work Smith avoids the terrible triad of sports journalism: shrillness (as in televised pro football), overstatement (as in Olympian battles under purple sunsets), and mindless emotionalism (as in the beatification of Thurman Munson). His eyes may mist for vanished friends, but he spares us shrieks, polemics, and grunting sobs.

A specially choice sample of Smith's style described the balance of power between the czar of all the Dodgers and Bowie Kuhn, a pleasant, somewhat stiff attorney who found gainful employment as commissioner of baseball. "When O'Malley sends out for coffee," Smith wrote, "Bowie Kuhn asks, 'One lump or two?'" Writers fifty years Smith's junior had spent a thousand words making that point less well.

It is an error to perceive Smith's civilized approach as mild. We were discussing one sportswriter who is gifted but so painfully self-important that he recently remarked, "I have perfected the magazine sports profile."

"Did you read his latest piece?" I asked.

"No," Smith said. "I didn't have the energy."

Once, when editors at *Sports Illustrated* were altering his stuff, Smith commented, "They put words into my copy that I've spent my life not using."

"Such as?" I asked.

"Such as 'moreover.'"

Boredom is the leopard that stalks the stag. Sports patterns repeat. Athletes say similar things from one decade to the next. Today's champion may not glitter like yesterday's hero, whom we remember in the soft focus of our own youth. Not long ago someone asked Smith if, after a lifetime in press boxes, he was beginning to find baseball dull.

"Baseball," Smith said, "is dull only to dull minds."

By its terse eloquence, the comment leads one away from the core of Smith's indomitable enthusiasm. The source is not baseball, his favorite sport. We are considering a professional, not a fan. The source is the newspaper business. "I love the newspaper business," Smith says, "whether I'm writing sports or anything else."

It's a brief journey from the urgent rattle of Manhattan to the quiet that presides on Martha's Vineyard. A shuttle jets you to Boston, and then a small, high-winged plane bounces through turbulence — pilots insist on calling such shuddering "light chop" — above southeastern Massachusetts, over Buzzard's Bay and an island called Cuttyhunk, until the final welcome bounce onto a runway.

Red and Phyllis Smith own a colonial home in New Canaan, Connecticut, but they take special pleasure in the cedar house they have had built near a Vineyard crossroads known as Chilmark. The house is airy and modern without being extreme. It is secluded, but in minutes the Smiths can drive to fishing boats that ride out through Menemsha Bite or to a sandy spit that commands head-clearing views or walk to a promontory 142 steps above a sandy beach backed by changing cliffs of clay.

This windy day Smith looked ruddy rather than red. He describes himself as ill-coordinated and four-eyed. He also says that he is prolix and maundering. Actually, he is only one of the above (he does wear eyeglasses). He wore a blue sweater and gray slacks as he approached the arrival gate, and his walk was quick. Though the red hair has gone white, his face retains a young expression and a look that suggests he is about to smile.

At the cedar house he set a fire within a white brick hearth. He has been trying not to smoke for several years, but my pack weakened his resolve. His hands shook slightly as he lit up. "I attributed this to alcohol once," Smith said, "but there was a time when I couldn't drink a drop and the shaking persisted. Turns out it isn't whiskey but senility."

He does not like to play the dean, much less the critic, but eventually he agreed to compare sports sections past and present. "There is truly a generally higher level of competence," he said, "than there was, say, thirty years ago. We had illiterates then who grew up from copy boy, if you'll pardon me."

I pardoned him. Thirty years ago at the *New York Herald Tribune*, I drew $26.50 a week putting away Red Smith's mail.

"Actually, there aren't as many big papers," Smith said, "so there aren't as many jobs for bums. On the other hand, there's a spreading tendency on newspapers to use a magazine approach. Newspaper editors are developing a notion that everybody has watched every event. I appreciate depth in coverage, but newspapers shouldn't abdicate who won and by what score.

"Then, even though the general level of competence is higher, I don't see anywhere a developing [Joe] Palmer, [John] Lardner, [Westbrook] Pegler, [W. O.] McGeehan, or [Frank] Graham."

It is hard to say exactly why. Television salaries attract some journalists before they really learn how to write. Education standards have sagged, and it is possible to win a journalism degree at certain universities without studying the American and English stylists who developed the written language. (Let alone Virgil or Aeschylus.) More people attend more schools. Each may learn less.

When Smith graduated from Notre Dame as a journalism major in 1927, he was equipped with both a sure sense of sports and a classical background. "The only team I tried out for was track," he said, "and that mostly as a way of avoiding gym. I couldn't run fast enough for the half mile, so I thought perhaps I could run long enough for the mile, and I competed in a freshman–varsity handicap. Soon I was last, about ten laps behind. Rockne coached track, and he said, 'All right. You can drop out now.' So I not only finished last, I didn't finish."

We began to play a game of capsule columns. I'd mention a name, and Smith would comment.

Sugar Ray Robinson: "At the St. Louis zoo in Forest Park, a black jaguar was the most beautiful thing I ever saw. I'd get in front of the cage some days and say, 'Good morning, Ray.' Robinson said I made him conceited when I wrote about him."

Frank Leahy: "I suppose he laid it on too thick. He made one of the seconding speeches for Eisenhower in 1956, and you thought he might really say, 'We've got to win this for the Gipper.' I took pleasure in needling him, but at the bottom Leahy was sincere. I believe Frank always stood up when his mother entered a room."

Muhammad Ali: "In nineteen years the act has never really changed. We've had telephone conversations where he's said, 'Do you have enough?' Whatever his positions, how can a guy in my business hate a subject that cooperative?"

George Steinbrenner: "When I was sick, I got a note from George saying we'd had differences, but he respected me. It was a lovely note, but George has gotten to be pretty impossible."

Eddie Arcaro: "He was the best at what he did, and he was always approachable, always candid. Most of the time that's true with the great champions."

Ernest Hemingway: "I didn't know him well, but I remember meeting him at Shor's, and I said, 'Thank you for putting me in the book.' [Smith draws praise in *Across the River and Into the Trees*.] Later in Cuba Frank Graham and I were watching an auto race on the Malacon, and afterward he invited us to his house. In the *New Yorker* profile, he seems to be a drunken braggart, but I found him diffident, a little shy. He was a big gentle guy with what seemed a very sweet disposition. After he won the Nobel Prize, he was quoted as saying that he used the first $25,000 to get even. I had the bad taste to ask him why he was broke. 'What bothers me,' I said, 'is that with the exception of Edgar Guest, you are the best-selling author in America, and the top guy should be able to afford anything.'

"He said that with his first successful book [*The Sun Also Rises*], he gave the royalties to the mother of his son. With the next [*A Farewell to Arms*], he gave the royalties to his own mother.

"Then he said, 'Red, a fellow's only got so many books like that in him.'"

No less a weight than Gertrude Stein postulated that being an artist begins with recognizing one's limits. She said that when Picasso showed her his poetry. Smith does not compose sagas or novels, and his style shimmers, like a bark at sea, rather than shattering waters, like a Leviathan. Certain dogged plodders, confusing easy reading with easy writing, see Smith as an airy sort, more concerned with lightness of line than with depth of thought. I know no one, Nobel laureates or Pulitzer poets, more serious about the craft of writing.

Smith came out of Green Bay, where his father ran a grocery, with ample native talent. His triumph is the way he developed the talent across five decades. He applied at the *Times* in 1927 but was turned down. He then worked at newspapers in Green Bay, St. Louis, and Philadelphia, hoping somehow to make New York. When Stanley Woodward finally brought him to the *Herald Tribune*, it was 1945, twenty-eight years after Smith's first newspaper job. His stuff had gotten better and better, but Woodward had to lie to the *Tribune* brass about the new man's age. He shaved the honest total by five years.

The *Tribune* was getting what Casey Stengel so admired, "one of them men with experience." Smith could and did and does write the hell out of a sport column. He also knew how to cover a warehouse fire. No one was better prepared or more anxious to play the Palace. His *Tribune* columns attracted a syndicate of ninety newspapers. Then, after the *Tribune* died, the *Times* hired Smith in 1971.

"The one trouble with him now," insists a younger writer, who might be radical if he had the patience to read Karl Marx, "is that he doesn't challenge sport's fascistic values."

Ah, but Smith challenges sham, pomposity, grandiloquence, self-righteousness, and the self-anointed priesthood of the arrogant. I believe those qualities sum up Mussolini.

Growing with each decade, Smith has lately become the most distinguished champion of the baseball players' union. That issue, the players' right to share the giant jackpot, is as political as sport has been getting. "Slot 44" is neither fascist nor communist; it is a way of making several yards. Sparky Anderson, who barred facial hair in Cincinnati, was not attacking the New Left. He wanted Bench and Rose and Morgan to look well groomed. Smith does not confuse the demands of a head counselor with the fiats of a dictator. He is alert to real issues, such as players' rights, without finding sociology in a line drive.

He describes Chris Evert Lloyd and Jimmy Connors as they are (self-occupied is what they are, before anything else). He does not constantly try, as Hemingway said of Jimmy Cannon, to write columns that "leave the English language for dead." His only demand is that the reader be able to think, which is probably the first demand he found at Notre Dame when he arrived there fifty-five years ago.

Newspaper libraries show no specific predecessor. Oh, Heywood Broun was literate and Pegler was irreverent, but both went global. Current sports pages are blank of an inheritor. Once I asked Smith if he had any superstitions, and he said immediately, "Only the Holy Roman Church." Seeking the source of such a response is as fruitless as analyzing laughter. You had better simply rejoice that the phrase is there.

One does not say that directly to Mr. Smith. He has lived a long time — he is twice a great-grandfather — but outbursts of praise make him uncomfortable.

Crisp Vineyard night was lowering on the cedar house. It was time, we all agreed, to open a bottle of wine.

1979

Red Smith died at the age of seventy-six in 1982, five days after publication of a particularly graceful column.

Past Their Prime

This won me my fifth Dutton Award as best sports magazine story of the year. Playboy's article department, in my experience, is distinct from the photo people. You can use rough sporting language as it is spoken, and the editing is of a high level. It has long since become tedious to hear someone, usually holding a drink, say: "Hey, did a bunny edit your story?"

The pitcher telephoned me, which should inform you that he was a veteran athlete. Young baseball players do not waste change telephoning writers who are male.

He was coming to town, the pitcher said, and he was going to start a baseball game in Yankee Stadium. There weren't many games left in his arm, and I knew he had become afraid of the rest of his life. But mostly his fear was stoic, wreathed in resignation, like the fear of certain brave, old, dying men. Anyway, after the game, he wanted a woman.

The pitcher felt a fulminating lust for a particular tennis star, and when I called her, she agreed to meet him with one proviso. I would have to date someone she called her "new best friend." That was the woman superintendent of the brownstone house where the tennis player cohabited with cats and fantasies.

The building super, I thought. A woman who spends days stacking garbage bags and reaming toilet drains. Dating her would be some enchanted evening. We would all turn into frogs, I thought. But I owed the pitcher certain favors.

"What should I know about the tennis player?" he asked me on the morning of the game. He didn't have to ask about opposing hitters anymore. He knew all their rhythms and their weaknesses. "I mean, gimme a little scouting report on the lady, so I can plan my moves."

"Miss Center Court," I said, "loves to talk dirty, and if you don't press hard, she gets wild and delicious. But she has one peculiarity. She has to be the one to talk dirty first. If the man comes on raunchy, Miss Center Court turns off."

"Got ya," the pitcher said, with a confident nod. He then lost to the Yankees, 3–1, in punishing sunlight.

When the ball player marched into an East Side bar at seven-thirty that night, he was swaggering bravado. Actually, of course, he was covering up. He had always despised losing, and he hated losses even more now that so few afternoons of stadium sunlight were left.

Technically, he suffered from an irreversible chronic tendinitis in one shoulder. The condition would be annoying, but not much more than that, for an accountant. But this man was a major league pitcher, and chronic tendinitis meant something more extreme. His major league arm was all but dead.

He looked at the tennis player and blinked and smiled. She was attractive, not merely for a lady jock. She was large-eyed and lissome, and she wet her lips before she spoke. Abruptly the ball player became desperately cheerful.

"Say," he said, dropping into a captain's chair, "you all know about the city boy and the country girl and the martinis? This here country girl had never heard of martinis, and the city boy got her to drink a batch." The pitcher's tongue was brisker than his slider. "Finally, the country girl says, 'Them cherries in them maranas gimme heartburn.'"

"The city boy, he says, 'You're wrong on all three counts. They're not cherries, they're olives. They're not maranas, they're martinis. And you don't have heartburn, your left tit is in the ashtray.'"

The pretty tennis player made a face like a dried apricot. Then she and my date, the woman superintendent, went to the washroom.

"Dead," I told the pitcher. "The German word is *tot*. I believe the French say *mort*. The Yankees knocked you out this afternoon, and you just knocked yourself out now."

"It's a good joke," the pitcher said. "I used it at a supermarket opening in Largo, Florida, and they loved it, even the mothers with kids."

"We're north of Largo. Didn't you listen to me? Miss Center Court has to set the tone herself. If she lets guys start the rough talk, it might seem as though she's an easy lay."

"Isn't she?"

"That isn't the question. The question is style."

The women dismissed us civilly after dinner, and the pitcher said the hell with them. He knew a Pan Am stewardess who could do unusual things with a shower nozzle. He called, and an answering machine reported that its mistress was in Rome.

"Forget it," I told the big pitcher. "Everybody has nights like this. John Kennedy had nights like this. The dice are cold. Let's go to sleep."

"Stay with me," the pitcher said. We rode down to a Greenwich Village club that was cavernous and loud with bad disco and empty of talent except for a dark-haired teenaged girl from Albany. The pitcher was quite drunk by now. He scribbled love notes and sexual suggestions on cocktail napkins, which a small Spanish waiter delivered. The girl from Albany paid her check and fled in fright.

A serious thought suddenly made the pitcher sober. "I can't pitch big-league ball no more," he said.

"You knew this was going to happen," I said.

His voice was naked. "But now it's happening."

One tear, and only one, rolled down the man's right cheek. "Shee-yit," he said, embarrassed. "Shee-yit."

"Like hell, shee-yit," I said. "You've got something to cry about."

He was thirty-nine, hardly old. He was well conditioned and black-haired, and every movement he made suggested physical strength. Most would have called him a young man. But because he was an athlete, his time was closing down. He had won premature fame at twenty-two, and now he was paying with a kind of senility at thirty-nine.

The adulatory press conferences were ending. He would not again travel as grandly as he had; he would never again earn as much money as he had been making. Already his manner with attractive women had regressed. He was finished, or he *thought* he was finished. The two often are the same. I remembered Caitlin Thomas's wrenching phrase, created after Dylan's final drink: *leftover life to kill.*

Santayana wrote:

> Old Age, on tiptoe, lays her
> jeweled hand
> Lightly in mine. —
> Come, tread a stately measure.

This may have been true for a philosopher who sought out the stony tranquility of cloisters, but time rings for athletes with a coarser cadence.

> Old age, in nailed boots,
> wrenches at my limbs,
> And stomps my groin.

In the usual curve of ascendancy, the American male completes so-called formal education in his twenties and spends the next fifteen years mounting a corporate trapeze. If he is good and fortunate and very agile, he will be soaring by forty.

Athletes follow wholly different patterns. They soar almost with puberty. Life for a great young athlete is different from other children's lives, even as he turns fourteen. Already he is the best ball player of his age for blocks or miles around. He is the young emperor of the sandlot.

With enough toughness, size, nutrition, and motivation, the athlete will feel his life expanding into a diadem of delights. He does not have to ask universities to consider his merits and tolerate his college board scores. A brawl of jock recruiters solicits him. If necessary, they offer him a free year at a prep school, finally to master multiplication tables.

Assuming certain basic norms, the athlete has a glorious pick of women. Pretty wives are not an exception around ball clubs; they are characteristic.

It is all a kind of knightly beginning to life, isn't it? Doing high deeds, attended by squires, moving from stately courts to demimondes? But most knightly tales conclude with the hero full of youth.

I remember a marvelous quarterback named Ben Larsen, who dominated high school football in Brooklyn. His passing was splendid, and he ran with a deceptive gliding style. Perhaps thirty colleges offered him scholarships. He chose one in the Big Ten, where the wisdom of football scouts proved finite. Ben was suddenly pressed harder than he had ever been, by athletes of comparable skills. He wilted quickly and never finished college. He was the first of my acquaintances to become an alcoholic.

Ben Larsen's life reached its peak while he was a schoolboy. For many the climax comes in college or as a young professional. Others (Carl Yastrzemski and Fran Tarkenton) can play well and enthusiastically as they approach forty. Once an eon a Satchel Paige or a Gordie Howe makes it to fifty. Technical literature doesn't yet tell us much. Studying human behavior is still a science of inexactitude. But broadly, and obviously, we're dealing with two elements.

The first is physical. An athlete must be granted a good body, a durable body, and — I hate to be the one to make this point —

he'd better take care of it. I don't know whether or not all those careless nights cut short Mickey Mantle's career, but unwillingness to do proper pregame calisthenics and to perform therapeutic drills on all those hung-over mornings sure as hell cut off his legs.

Then there is emotion, world without end. How long can an athlete hold all his passion to be an athlete? How long can he retain all his enthusiasm for repetitive experiences?

One hot afternoon last spring, Johnny Bench, Tom Seaver, and I were riding together to make an appearance at a book fair in Atlanta. Bench at twenty-six was the best catcher baseball has known. Not perhaps, not one of, just *the best*. Last spring, at thirty, he was in decline.

Bench's batting average lounged below his old standard. He was getting hurt frequently. His matchless play, his Johnny Bench–style play, seemed limited to spurts. "You get bored, John?" I asked in the car.

"With what?"

"Catching a baseball game every day."

"Do I?" Bench has a broad, expressive face, and he lifted his eyebrows for emphasis. "You know why I envy him?" he said, elbowing Seaver.

"For my intellect," Seaver said. "My grooming and my skills at doing the *New York Times* crossword puzzle."

"Because he's a fucking pitcher," Bench said. "He doesn't have to work a ball game but one day in four. All that time off from playing ball games. That's why I envy Tommy."

Seaver grew serious and nodded. Both men are intelligent, curious, restless. As they grow older and recognize that the universe is larger than a diamond, it becomes increasingly difficult to shut out everything else and play a game. It also hurts more. The human body was not designed to play catcher from April to October.

It was not designed to fight for the heavyweight championship at the age of thirty-six either.

Last September I flew to New Orleans to watch Muhammad Ali make a fight he really did not want to fight. He won easily over

Leon Spinks, but a new sourness invaded Ali's style. "It's murder, how hard he's got to work," said Angelo Dundee, the sagest of Ali's seconds.

The motivated athlete responds to the physical effects of age by conditioning himself more intensively. "That Spinks, he looks like Dracula, but he's only twenty-five," Ali said, in a house he had rented near Lake Pontchartrain. "So I have to make myself twenty-five. I been up every morning, running real long, real early for five months. Five months. I've done the mostest exercises ever, maybe three hundred and fifty different kinds, so's I could become the first man ever, in all history, to win back the heavyweight championship twice."

For the first two rounds in the New Orleans Superdome, Ali toyed with a dream of knocking out Spinks. But all the roadwork and the sparring could not bring back the snake-tongue quickness of the hands. Ali missed badly with two hard rights. Then, yielding to reality, he made a perfect analysis of Spinks's style and how to overcome it.

Spinks had *no* style, really. Move in standing up, move in, move in, punch, lunge. Devoid of style, he still is strong and dangerous. From the third round Ali simply moved around and about Spinks, flicking punches, holding, sliding, holding, always staying three moves ahead. It was a boring and decisive victory and it must've hurt like hell.

Afterward, at a press conference in the Superdome, Ali spoke in the crabbed tones of age. First of all, this huge crowd — 70,000, give or take a few thousand — had come to a black promotion. "Wasn't no blond hair or blue eyes doing no promoting," the champion said. That is accurate, but only in a lawyerly way. The man who put together Ali-Spinks II (and the marvelous undercard) is Robert Arum, whose hair is black and whose eyes are brown. He is, however, white. Under the Arum umbrella, so to speak, two blacks and two whites, all from Louisiana, were subsidiary promoters. They are now suing each other.

Having stretched truth until it snapped, Ali offered a brief return to his old form. "Was that a thirty-six-year-old man out there, fighting tonight? And not only fighting but dancing? Was that dancing man out there thirty-six?"

"Thassright," chirped a parliament of votaries.

"That *Time* magazine," Ali said, "that great *Time* magazine, goes all over the world, they wrote Ali was through. Could *Time* magazine be wrong . . . ?"

Crabby again, he was settling an account he had already closed in the ring, treating a buried story as though it were alive. It was a graceless effort from a man Dundee says now has to work too hard.

Why, then, does Ali drive on past his prime?

Supporting himself and his children and his wife and former wives and his retinue and properties, Ali said not long ago, costs about $60,000 a month after taxes. His investment income is short of that. He fights on because he believes he needs the money.

Over three recent months I explored cash and credit, concentration and distraction, professional life and professional death — in short, how the jock grows older — with thirty-one remarkable athletes. They have worked their trades — baseball, boxing, basketball, football, hockey — from San Diego to New England. One (Fran Tarkenton) was sufficiently sophisticated to evoke Thomas Jefferson. "Doing a variety of things, like Jefferson did, keeps you fresh." Others (Lou Brock, Merlin Olsen, Brooks Robinson) showed positively Viennese instincts for self-analysis.

"Did anyone say that money had nothing to do with why he kept on playing?" asked Fred Biletnikoff. He's been a wide receiver at Oakland for fourteen seasons.

"Some said the money wasn't primary."

Biletnikoff drew a breath to prepare his own comment. "You know," he said, "they're full of shit."

Generally the athletes were honest and direct. Away from cameras, one on one, athletes speak more honestly than entertainers or politicians.

Most shared annoyance at America's blinding obsession with

youth. They found subtle prejudice against age in certain executive suites. "In the front office I have to put up with," one veteran baseball player said, "they're always looking for a reason to replace me. Maybe it's because a young guy would cost less, but I think it's not just that. They got a mindset on the axiom that baseball is a young man's game."

Willie McCovey, the mighty first baseman who reached forty-one in January, is discomfited by a particular fan in Chicago. "There's this dude who sits behind the on-deck circle in Wrigley Field," McCovey reported, "and when I get a hit, he doesn't make a sound. But every time I swing and miss, I hear the joker holler, 'You're getting old, McCovey. You're washed up.'"

McCovey shook his head in annoyance. ''That's shit," he said. "Doesn't the guy know I missed pitches years ago? Does he think I never made an out until I was thirty-five?"

"He's just needling," I said.

"Well, I say needle with a little intelligence. Judge me by my performance. Forget my age. I try to forget my age myself. Too much thinking about your age can psych you. It can make you press and panic and retire before your time." McCovey believes that is what happened to his friend Willie Mays.

Every geriatric athlete that I talked to maintained an unabated passion for the game. It was a passion to win, to prove certain points, to keep on making money. To those men, sport was no small sliver of the consciousness; it dominated them.

Brooks Robinson, the fine third baseman who played until he was forty, said, "My whole life had been baseball. Passion? It sure was for me. In the eighth grade back in Arkansas, I wrote a whole booklet about how I wanted to be a ball player. That never changed. I kept on wanting to be a ball player until my reflexes told me it was time to stop. By then I'd played almost as many big-league games as Ty Cobb."

"Didn't age hit you like a rabbit punch?" I asked.

"The first time something was written about my age, I was thirty. 'The aging Brooks Robinson,' the story said. I thought, What do they mean by aging? I'm a young man. And I went out to play harder. When they called me aging at thirty-five, it didn't hit me either way. I knew they were accurate in sports terms. But then, when I was called aging at thirty-nine, the thing became a challenge all over again. It stayed a challenge until I accepted what time can do and got out."

A few old athletes remain absolutely juvenile in their enthusiasms. George Blanda, the quarterback and place kicker, was forty-eight when he played his last game in the National Football League. "Hell, I didn't retire even then," Blanda said. "*They* retired *me*. I enjoyed it. I always enjoyed it. Proving myself week after week. Ego-building week after week. Who wouldn't enjoy all that?

"If you have the right conditioning and you keep the right attitude, the air smells cleaner, the food tastes better, and your wife looks like Elke Sommer."

Across the past decade big-time sport has become an explosive growth industry. That's fine for many investors and some of the athletes, but "growth industry" is no buzz phrase for fun. It suggests hard-knuckled grabs for every dollar anywhere in the country.

Newspaper reporters have concentrated on the new high salaries paid to athletes. That doesn't mean simply, as some journalists suggest, that the rich athletes all become complacent. It does mean that many work longer and harder and so may wear out sooner.

A generation ago, major league baseball extended only from St. Louis to Boston. The professional hockey season was half the present schedule. Pro football was a secondary sport. The sporting life, the sporting pace was leisurely and more conducive to longevity than today's Sunday afternoon and Monday night fever.

I was fortunate enough to begin covering sports before the disappearance of the American train. Going from New York to St. Louis was a twenty-four-hour hegira. You traveled in a private car and you ate in a private diner, and a drink was never farther away than a porter's call button. Moving at double-digit speeds, trains gave your body a chance to adjust as you crossed time zones.

"But jet travel now is part of the package," said Lou Brock, a major league outfielder since 1961 and the man who broke Ty Cobb's record for stolen bases. "Mentally it doesn't make sense to eliminate or separate different aspects of a ball player's life. If you want the cheers and the fame and the money and the victories, you've got to accept the two A.M. jet rides. They go together."

I first traveled a sports circuit in high excitement. I had never seen the Golden Triangle in Pittsburgh or the lake shore north of Milwaukee or the drained malarial swamps around Houston, for that matter. Like the young men in the old stories, I ached for travel. Then, very quickly, sports travel — as distinct from a plea-sure trip to Cozumel — became a minihell.

You had to be in St. Louis on four simmering July days because the team you covered was playing four games there. Often that was the week when a Chicago blonde called and said, "Please visit." You had to be in Philadelphia when the team was there, or Boston or Cincinnati. Human nature being what it is, sports travel came down to a matter of always going to the wrong place at the wrong time with the wrong companions.

"I don't look at travel like that," said Brock. "Not like that at all. To me, travel is still exciting. When I think of travel, I ask myself, How else can I get to my opponent? Get to where he is and whip him?"

Various athletes play tactical games with time. Phil Esposito, the hockey forward, keeps his weight twelve pounds lower than it was a decade ago. Tony Perez, the first baseman, says that at thirty-six he is far better at anticipating pitches than he was when younger. If you guess low slider and the pitcher throws a low slider, you stay in business. "You can sometimes beat the younger guys with your head," said Dave Bing, the basketball player, who decided to retire last August when he was thirty-five. "You figure their weak-nesses and you play into them. But in the end . . ."

Merlin Olsen, the Mighty Mormon who played on the line for the Los Angeles Rams across fifteen seasons, believes that athletes who endure are able to anticipate danger. "It's a kind of sense you have," Olsen said. "Don't push yourself harder this time. Don't extend with everything you've got just now. There's danger out there."

I remembered the kindly horses in all those terrible Western movies. The animals always knew that a bridge was out or that a landslide would be gathering its roaring strength or that twenty-nine feet to the left, under a clump of gray-green sage, a sidewinder coiled.

"Good movie stuff, Merlin," I said. "Friends of mine have paid rent bills writing sixth-sense themes. But practically . . ."

"Practically," Olsen said, "I played in the pits on a pro football line for a long time; consider all that tonnage and the carnage. But I was never seriously hurt."

I have before me twenty-seven pages of single-spaced comments from professional athletes, but curiously, or not so curiously, I keep turning back to Lou Brock. "When I think of travel, I ask myself, How else can I get to my opponent? Get to where he is and whip him?"

Major sport is American trauma. Crumpled knees drive halfbacks into early retirement; pitchers' arms go dead; hockey players slammed to the ice twist in convulsion. Before this onslaught both the body and the psyche tremble.

The complete athlete measures pain against glory, risk against profit. He considers what is left of his body and then, I believe, he subconsciously decides whether or not he wants to go on. In the end, the difference between Carl Yastrzemski, a star at thirty-nine, and Mickey Mantle, an assistant batting coach at that age, is that Yaz wanted it more.

It is tempting to conclude with too much certitude on so-called qualitative distinctions among the experiences of various athletes aging into other men's prime time. Is Tony Perez, who grew up in the balmy poverty of Cuba, markedly afraid hard times will come now in the North? He says not. Is Gordie Howe, who still works hockey at the age of fifty, clutching the withered stump of his boyhood? Hell, no, Howe says. His wrists hurt and his legs are gone, but he loves playing pro hockey on the same team as his sons.

This temptation to conclude too much persists. To me, the core here is rather like what the saucy, lissome tennis player was to the veteran pitcher. The object looks so damned attainable: then, in a blink of too-bright eyes, it is gone.

My journalistic interviews are not excursions into therapy. You ask. The athlete answers. You press a little. He tries to be honest. You press harder. He thinks of his image. He also tries to be macho. He tries to keep his dignity. You ask some more. You think. And you move on.

So I fight temptations to write glibly about predictable crises, self-flagellation, or variable testosterone levels. If I can hear and share a little of the heartbeat of another man, I have my accomplishment.

The bravest and most competitive athlete I knew was Jackie Robinson. Breaking the major league color line in 1947, he played with teammates who called him nigger. Rivals from at least four teams tried to spike him. The best I can say for the press is that it was belligerently neutral.

What Jack did — his genius and his glory — was to make obstacles work for him. Call him nigger and he'd get mad. Mad, he'd crush you. Misquote him out of laziness or malice and he'd take his disgust out on rival pitchers, as though they were the boozy press. Barred from the dining room of your hotel in Cincinnati at lunch, he'd dominate your ball park in Cincinnati after dinner.

It was a cruel, demanding way to have to live. His career burned out in a decade, and his life ended when he was fifty-three. "This man," the Reverend Jesse Jackson intoned from the funeral pulpit, "turned a stumbling block into a steppingstone."

Only a few extraordinary athletes — Stan Musial and Joe DiMaggio — are able to prevail in retirement. Their glory intact, they move from the ball park to other arenas, still special heroes. Some, like Jack Dempsey and Casey Stengel, even achieve Olympian old age. All these men learned how to transform obstacles into stepping-stones.

"Did Robinson know he was dying?" my friend Carl Erskine, once a Dodger pitching star, asked after the funeral.

"I think maybe he did."

"How did he bear up?"

"It was amazing. He was getting blinder and lamer every day and working harder and harder for decent housing for blacks."

"He was a hero," Erskine said.

"Apart from baseball," I said.

"But don't you think," Erskine said, "that disciplining himself the way he had to and mastering self-control and commanding a sense of purpose — don't you think the things he had to do to keep making it in baseball taught him how to behave in the last battle?"

Before that moment I had a distaste for people who saw sports as a metaphor for life. Where I grew up, life was less trivial than a ball game.

"I never thought of that till now," I said, still learning.

1979

Sinatra's Friend

He is a showman, a jokester, a type that used to be called a "Broadway Sam." Within, he is a gifted baseball man and a relentless competitor. When the Dodgers lose a game he thinks they should have won, genial Tommy Lasorda throws chairs.

Tom Lasorda wants to know if I'd like to join him on a rapid run to San Francisco. It is twilight time in Los Angeles, and he has already presided at a press conference for Fernando Valenzuela and opened a mobile-home show behind the center-field stands at Dodger Stadium.

"When?"

"Now."

"Sure."

We are standing in the Dodger Stadium parking lot, but at twilight time in Los Angeles, it does not look like a parking lot at all. Mobile homes are moored about us, and landscape people have covered the asphalt with sod and pine bark. They've rigged lemon trees and small palms so that the parking lot has become a pretend village. The mobile homes have imitation stucco exteriors and real shake roofs, and the street before us, which is not a street at all, is marked with a sign. Lasorda Lane.

"How do we get to San Francisco?"

"There's a Learjet waiting at Burbank Airport," Lasorda says.

"Then what?"

"Tomorrow I talk to Boy Scouts in Palm Springs. Then Chicago. Then the Air Force Academy in Colorado Springs." Lasorda's eyes are alive with merriment. "You like to travel?"

"A bit," I say, walking into a punch line.

"I buried four writers who tried to keep up with me," Lasorda says.

I knew Thomas Charles Lasorda in three or four incarnations before he emerged last October as the greatest baseball manager on earth, pro tem. You can argue for Billy Martin, Earl Weaver, or Whitey Herzog, but in October Lasorda guided a good though hardly overwhelming Dodger team through two play-offs and the World Series with that sure hand seldom seen since the creation of heaven and earth.

You cannot consider Tom Lasorda without considering at least a few of his intimates. Frank Sinatra, whose blue-eyed visage stares from a half-dozen pictures in Lasorda's office. Don Rickles, whose pictures cover another wall. Bob Hope, Andy Granatelli, Norm Crosby, and someone Lasorda calls The Big Dodger in the Sky.

It may be more practical to remain on the planet. The Lasorda I knew earlier was eager, uproarious, agitated, combative, and even somewhat somber, but always charged with extravagant vitality. He appeared first in the early fifties, a smallish, left-handed pitcher who wanted to make the Dodgers. There was no fake cool to Lasorda, no affected nonchalance. He loved to pitch, and damn it, he wanted to pitch in the majors. He had drive and intelligence, but he lacked what his forebears called *fortuna imperatrix mundi* — roughly, good luck — and an overpowering fastball. He vanished into the minors with precious little trace, only a footnote to the boys of summer.

But he materialized again early in the seventies, somewhat stouter, still boyish, as an ultimate third-base coach. He sparkled so at third that NBC once wired him into a nationally televised game.

Lasorda to Pete Rose: "Hey, Pete. Every year the Dodgers vote for the handsomest guy on the other clubs. We just voted on the Reds."

Rose: "How did I do?"

Lasorda: "You finished second handsomest."

Rose: "Thanks."

Lasorda: "The twenty-four other guys finished tied for first."

But Tommy wasn't in baseball for coaching or for laughs. He had been denied his dream of starring for the Brooklyn Dodgers. Now he wanted to manage the Dodgers in L.A.

It was late one July night in 1976, and Lasorda was sipping soda water in a press room. "How many more years do you think Alston will want it?" he said of then-manager Walter Alston, a strong man devoid of color.

"He doesn't tell me," I said. "But what else is he going to do with his summers? Shoot pool in Darrtown, Ohio?"

"Damn," Lasorda said. "He could keep the job forever. Even if he quits, I got no guarantee that I replace him."

"You can always manage some other team. Doesn't Seattle want you?"

"I'm not allowed to say. Anyway, I don't want to manage some other team."

"Why?" I said. "Why does it have to be the Dodgers?"

"Cut my veins," Lasorda said, "and I bleed Dodger blue."

I thought he was kidding. The hand holding the glass of soda shook with intensity.

In 1977, after twenty-nine years in the Dodger organization, he finally got what baseball people call the big club. That spring his joy made a raucous song.

"Hey, we got some team. Take Lee Lacy here. Lee's momma told him to make money, but Momma never told him to spend it. That's why Lee has the first dime he ever made. There's Steve Garvey. Mr. America. Mr. Clean. When Steve goes to an X-rated movie, he puts on sunglasses. I got a couple pinch hitters, Manny Mota and Vic Davalillo, they gotta be fifty years old each. Do you know why?"

"Why?"

"I collect antiques."

Unlike football, baseball allows for a certain humor. But there is a wavering line that a man crosses at some peril. If you are too funny — and on a good day, Lasorda can stand off Rickles — you pay a price.

Casey Stengel was so great a comic that almost until his sixtieth year, few took him seriously as a tactician. In Stengel's triumphant seasons with the Yankees, he retained his wit, but the old man raged when anyone suggested that he was then or ever had been a clown. "You're fulla shit," Stengel would cry, in a ranting fury, "and I'll tell ya why . . ."

Lasorda has suffered similarly, without souring. Listening to his routines — Steve Garvey says he has heard the old ones in three languages — you can forget the intelligence at Lasorda's core. His memory is eidetic, roughly phenomenal. He can recite the names of every Dodger's wife and children, and he can tell you how the weather was on August 8, 1966, when he was managing Ogden in the Pioneer League. He recalls games, individual performances, good pitches and bad with absolutely specific detail. This gives him a gray-celled memory bank that is the indispensable basis for decisions.

Although he cut short his education as a high school senior to pitch professionally, he is fluent in Spanish and Italian as well as English. He faults himself for not having acquired French while playing for Montreal. He has taken self-taught courses in baseball, the psychology of athletes, public speaking, media relations and, most recently, the craft of selling tickets. Wherever Lasorda speaks — and he is gaining on William Jennings Bryan as the most available orator in U.S. history — he plugs the Dodgers. Ask for an autograph and this is what you get:

YOU AND THE DODGERS ARE BOTH GREAT!!!
                                        TOM LASORDA

Funny? Not really; nor is it supposed to be. The four highest attendance figures in the annals of baseball have been posted by the Los Angeles Dodgers. These cover Lasorda's first four years of managing. The record, slightly more than 3,300,000, is about 600,000 more admissions than any team but the Dodgers has ever drawn.

The name of one of our national games is plug. Write a book in the woods, and a year later you find yourself smiling at a TV hostess in Omaha, plugging. ("No, Lucinda. The sexual aspects of the novel are not autobiographical.") Want to run for alderman, sell unisex underwear, market a straight-line-tracking turntable? Plug, brother. Plug, sister. Plug.

Lasorda, the Ph.D. in self-education, has grasped this so clearly that he has redefined the baseball manager's job. Now, as always, you have to win or come close. A dreary team loses games and money. But you also want to sell tickets.

Before Lasorda, basic and even advanced managers worked hard from March to October, then took the winter off, like water-skiers in Maine. Not Tom. Allowing for Thanksgiving and Christmas with his wife and two children, he manages the Dodgers and makes speeches about the Dodgers 363 days a year. His line about bleeding Dodger blue is so well known in the Los Angeles basin that the official ball-club bumper sticker no longer mentions the team by name. Instead it reads simply: THINK BLUE.

The components of victory, that prerequisite to baseball salesmanship, are reasonably complex. A manager runs a game. He picks the starting pitcher and replaces him with a reliever. He mixes steals and bunts and pick-offs into each night's order of battle, and he had better ignore the risk of being booed. ("A manager who worries about boos from the stands ends up sitting there himself," Lasorda says.)

All right. You know your percentages and your people, and you're keeping your boss happy by selling tickets from a soapbox at Hollywood and Vine. Now you have to create a clubhouse environment. With their private jet, a magnificent training base at Vero Beach, Florida, and large, supportive home crowds, the Dodgers offer the best of major league worlds. Lasorda, who doesn't believe in understatement, constantly reminds the players of their advantages and demands that they in turn LOVE THE DODGERS even as he does. Behind closed doors he practices mass hypnosis, and with a single exception, it has worked. The exception, right-hander Don Sutton, says, "I didn't love the Dodgers. I just worked for them." Sutton is now pitching for Houston.

"I'm not bragging," Lasorda says, "when I tell you I'm a helluva motivator of ball players. I found out one day when I was managing Spokane and we were playing in Tucson with a left-hander, Bobby O'Brien, pitching for us. Bases loaded. Two out in the ninth. Three and two. I went to the mound.

"'Bobby, imagine that after you throw this pitch, the heavens open and The Big Dodger in the Sky grabs you up. I want you to throw this pitch as though it's the last pitch you'll ever throw on earth.'"

As Lasorda returned to the dugout, a line drive rocketed between his outfielders. Spokane was beaten. "Bobby, Bobby," he said. "What happened?"

"Skipper," O'Brien said, "you got me so scared of dying, I couldn't concentrate on the pitch."

A pause for emphasis. "Right then," Lasorda says, "I knew I could motivate."

Our ride from the pretend mobile home park to Burbank Airport is quintessential California. The car I've rented comes with a tachometer and an automatic transmission. The tachometer gives you rpm's, so you can shift or double-clutch smoothly, and the automatic transmission means you can't shift at all.

"We gotta make time," Lasorda says. "Budweiser distributors are meeting at the Fairmont Hotel. Ed McMahon is flying up with us. Bob Hope's in San Francisco already. For this talk I get a fee."

He sets off in his Plymouth Reliant, driving hard, and I push the rented turkey to keep up. My tachometer works fine, but the engine begins to whine as though in labor.

Burbank Airport. Lasorda tries the main entrance. No Learjet.

Another entrance. There is nothing like a Lear. Frustrated, he drives faster and faster in a wild, aimless rectangle, circumnavigating Burbank Airport three times. The rented car stops whining and begins to scream. Even the tachometer shudders.

At length a local Spanish-speaking grocer helps us out. McMahon and a gray-haired pilot are waiting, and they lead us to the airplane, which looks about the size of an economy tube of toothpaste. (But at least the pilot has gray hair.)

The seats are deep, plush leather, and the Learjet comes equipped with a small saloon and a refrigerator. Our takeoff defines the word *accelerate*. Soon digital readouts say we are flying at 32,000 feet at 469 knots. In this toothpaste tube (but the pilot has gray hair).

I ask Lasorda when his dream to pitch for the Brooklyn Dodgers was finally killed.

"You may remember the game. Walter Alston suspends Don Newcombe for refusing to throw batting practice. Who gets Newcombe's start?"

"Not Ed McMahon."

"Right. It's me. I go against the Cardinals. I walk a guy. A pitch gets away from Campanella. I walk another guy. Want the name? Bill Virdon. Another pitch gets away. I'm working on a hitter. This name is Musial. A third pitch gets away. The man on third comes roaring home. No way he's gonna score without cutting me in half. He hits me like a truck. Pretty rugged country ball player named Wally Moon.

"I strike out Musial. I strike out Rip Repulski. I get outa the inning and they notice in the dugout my uniform is getting red around one knee. I gotta make this club. Getting hurt is a mark against you as bad as losing. They got a doctor near the dugout. Name? Herbert Fette. He looks at the knee and says, 'Son, if you try to pitch on that you may never pitch again. You've been spiked so badly, every tendon and ligament is exposed.'

"The hell with that. I gotta pitch. I gotta make the club. Next inning I start toward the mound, but two other ball players who heard the doctor grab me by the throat and hold me back. By the throat! That's how I get taken out. Want the date? May 5, 1955.

"Then the front office sends me back to the minors. Before I leave, I go in to appeal to Buzzy Bavasi, the general manager, and he says, 'Put yourself in my chair; who would you send out?' I tell him there's another left-hander on this team and he can't throw a goddamn strike. Bavasi says, 'Maybe, but the other left-hander's been paid a bonus to sign, and the rule is that a bonus guy has to stick with the big club for two years or else you lose him.'

"Want the name of the bonus guy who couldn't throw a strike? Sandy Koufax.

"It hurt ten times worse than the spiking, being shipped out. But I say now that it took the greatest left-hander in history to get me off the Dodger squad." Lasorda smiles with neither mirth nor self-pity.

"Carson's a little upset at Howard Cosell," McMahon says.

"Why's that?" Lasorda says. Instant change of mood and tone.

"They showed a close-up of Carson at the Series," McMahon says, "and Cosell remarked that he was aging gracefully."

Hope does a full hour — songs, dances, even a Polish joke — for the beer distributors at the Fairmont Hotel. McMahon does a funny fifteen minutes. Lasorda talks motivation. "Everybody in the United States, including the president, has times when he needs to be motivated." Then he tells one of his special Dodger stories.

When his life ends, Lasorda has often said, he wants this inscription on his tombstone: DODGER STADIUM WAS HIS ADDRESS AND EVERY BALL PARK HIS HOME. After Walter O'Malley heard this, he arranged for a ceremonial press conference. He presented Lasorda with a replica of a tombstone complete with the inscription and a drop of imitation blood dyed — surprise! — Dodger blue.

"I'm honored, Mr. O'Malley, to have served the Dodgers, and I want to go on serving them after I die."

"Now, Tommy, how can you do that?"

"Hang a Dodger schedule on my stone. Then, when people visit their loved ones in the cemetery, they'll say, 'Let's go over to

Lasorda's grave and see if the Dodgers are playing at home today.'"

In Chicago he introduces me to Rickles.

"Kahn," Rickles says. "That was Cohen, wasn't it? Cohen and you changed it, right?"

"Far as I know, it's always been Kahn."

"Hey," Rickles says. "Don't be ashamed of what you are. Look at Lasorda here. He still misses Mussolini."

Lasorda works skillfully as master of ceremonies at the Conrad Hilton Hotel, where six athletes, including Mario Andretti, are being inducted into the Italian American Sports Hall of Fame. Rickles tells the dinner guests, in a Godfather voice, that it is too late to escape — federal marshals have the building surrounded. Norm Crosby says beauty is skin deep but ugliness runs clear to the bone. Andy Granatelli, introducing Andretti, speaks at length. When Lasorda recaptures the microphone, he says, "I'm glad Andy finished because I'm due at spring training in four months."

At a party later Granatelli seems ruffled, and it's not just his tuxedo. "Come on, Andy," Lasorda says. "Anyway, I got something to ask. How does it feel to have millions and millions of dollars?"

Granatelli sits up straight. "Seriously?"

"Very seriously."

"It feels very, very good."

Lasorda will gross perhaps $175,000 managing and speaking in 1982. He is curious about great wealth but does not lust for it. Fame is the spur . . .

"Look," he says as the party swirls around us, "when I was a scout making $5,500, I was happy. Managing in the minors, $6,000 up to maybe $9,000, I was happy. Now I make good money and I'm happy, but I was happy then. I've lived in the same house, a tract house in Fullerton, for twenty-one years. I've got a great wife, Jo, and she isn't any more materialistic than I am.

"Because we didn't need a fancy house, we could buy what we

wanted outright. When we were raising the kids — well, what's more important, money or love? Money wasn't the tough thing. The tough thing was having no guarantees that I'd ever move up in the Dodger organization. I once asked Pee Wee Reese where he'd have rated me, among the twenty-five Dodger ball players in 1955, as a prospect to manage the big club. Pee Wee said twenty-four, and that was only because one guy, Sandy Amoros, didn't speak English."

"Tommy," I say, "here we are at an Italian-American sports party, and guess where this delicious blonde was born."

"Where?"

"Israel."

Lasorda beams. "You found each other."

Five Lasorda brothers survived through the Depression to manhood in the blue-collar community of Norristown, Pennsylvania. Four — Eddie, Harry, Morris, and Joe — run a restaurant called Marchwood Tavern in Exton, some twenty minutes from their birthplace. Place mats at Marchwood Tavern show a left-handed pitcher throwing, under a logo that says EASTERN HOME OF THE L.A. DODGERS. At fifty-four, Tom is the second oldest.

All the brothers idolized their father. Sabattino Lasorda emigrated from Abruzzi, a hilly province eighty miles east of Rome, and married Carmella, fifteen years his junior, so that, he told the boys, "when I retire, she can go to work." Both Lasorda's parents are dead.

In the United States, Sabattino became Sam, and Sam Lasorda drove a truck out of a gravel pit six days a week. He played the concertina, sang, made up stories around a potbellied stove, preached education, and practiced discipline. Minor infractions were punished with a strap. Once, when Tom kept the family car out until two-thirty A.M., he was beaten with a wooden clothes hanger.

All the boys talk reverently about their merry, stern old man. "After I was pitching professional," Tom says, "whenever I saw

Dad, I gave him a kiss. I don't go for that stuff that it's weak for men to show affection. When cancer killed Dad, you know how glad I was for all the times I'd let him know I loved him? Maybe the greatest day in my life came when he was gone and I went back to his home town. Tollo, in Abruzzi. They had a big sign in Italian that said WELCOME TO THE SON OF SABATTINO LASORDA. I cried."

The other brothers remember Tommy as argumentative, funny, and a fighter. "He could fight good," says Harry Lasorda, who is fifty-two, "and he'd take on anyone who hassled him, no matter how big. And he had one helluva curve ball." Harry drives me to the old neighborhood, past Holy Saviour School, which Tommy abandoned for Norristown High because Holy Saviour didn't have a ball team. He shows me fields and streets where the La-sorda boys scrapped and played in front of stone buildings with brick fronts. He takes me to the Santa Secouri Maria Social Club, where Italian-Americans still gather and beer is thirty cents a glass. There is a boccie court outside, card tables within, and a sign above the bar that warns NO PROFANITY. It is a long way from Rickles and Hope.

We drive to 713 Walnut, in Norristown, where the Lasorda boys grew up. The brick-fronted house is gone because families who lived there later let the building go so badly that it was condemned. What was once 713 Walnut is an empty lot. All that remains to mark an extraordinary immigrant truck driver named Sabattino Lasorda is the sycamore he planted long ago. The tree looks ancient now and weathered and gnarled.

Out of Norristown, Tom pitched from 1945 through 1960. He had some fine minor league years but never won a game for the Brooklyn Dodgers. They sent him to Kansas City in 1956. He never won a game there, either. His lifetime major league record is 0 and 4.

He worked his way back into the Dodger organization and won eighteen games for their Montreal farm in 1958, a season when the L.A. Dodgers finished seventh. Two years later, when he was thirty-three, they told him to stop pitching. The era of career minor leaguers was winding down.

He moved to California and put in five years as a Dodger scout. He managed Ogden, Utah, to three straight pennants and was promoted to Spokane. He won the pennant there in 1970 by twenty-six games, moved up to Albuquerque, and won a pennant there as well. Then came four years as a third-base coach. The real job, managing the big club, didn't come until he was forty-nine, and it was a month after his fifty-fourth birthday before he won the Series. He sure as hell put in his time.

What makes Tommy run? Like so many other children of immigrants, he is foursquare in fundamental values. He says his wife, Jo, and the Dodgers are his two great, enduring loves. He drinks a little wine and not much more. No serious drinker could survive his schedule. He is no stranger to depression but has an enduring, ecumenical religious faith and an optimistic, cheerful view of humanity. He is your basic upwardly mobile second-generation American, who knew early and profoundly that he did not want to spend his life driving trucks out of Pennsylvania gravel pits.

"You know," Lasorda says on one of our plane rides, "when I took over from Alston, they asked if I was worried about filling the shoes of a guy who'd managed the Dodgers for twenty-three years. I told them no, but I was worried about the guy who someday was gonna have to fill mine. You like that?"

"Brash," I say, "and pure Lasorda."

"Now," Tom says, "I'm beginning to believe it."

We split in Chicago. He is going west to speak to air force generals and cadets, and I am heading east, toward Norristown. As we say good-bye, he thanks me for traveling with him and touches a few memories we share. I feel a surge of admiration: for his spirit, his poise, his lack of hubris, his baseball knowledge and, certainly not least of all, his salesmanship.

Hell, I think, my old friend Tom Lasorda could sell the Democratic platform to Ronald Reagan. Provided that it was printed in Dodger blue.

1982

Carl Anthony Furillo

Scores of people wrote that this piece moved them to tears. In a profound way that pleased me, as it might have pleased the strangely solitary subject who, like Stan Musial, wore number 6.

Gil Hodges was the first to go. Then Jackie Robinson. Next after a brief remission from death, Billy Cox. And suddenly there stood a journalist asking Pee Wee Reese, "How does it feel to be the last person alive from the great Brooklyn Dodger infield?"

I gasped. I was not the one who asked that wicked question. Reese stood his ground and said, in the full flower of his poise, "I don't think about things that way. If I did, I might go crazy."

Carl Furillo's death commands such memories to mind. Even as it does, I cannot believe Carl Furillo is dead. He was so skilled, so handsome, and so strong, I thought he'd be throwing out base runners, some smart, some dumb, until he passed his one hundredth birthday. Furillo was granted sixty-six birthdays. That was enough time to brighten life for everyone who took the time to know him.

Quite simply, he was a great player. Some write about his arm, the human cannon. He was not the man you'd ask to join you in a casual game of catch. Or how he played the right-field wall at Ebbets Field. That wall, a mystery of dead spots, bounces, angles, and planes, was a wonder of baseball before the dream destroyers wrecked it. Furillo never attended high school. Plane geometry remained a mystery to him. But he knew every angle, every carom. The way Furillo played the wall describes an art form.

Carl Erskine says he was a "Bible hitter." First pitch anywhere, in the dirt or at the eyes, Furillo took his mighty swing. Why, then, was he a Bible hitter? Erskine says, "Thou shalt not pass" (Numbers 20).

Furillo gathered 1,910 hits in fifteen major league years. He pulled the ball sometimes, or went to right. No one ever banged a baseball harder up the middle. If Furillo ever misjudged a fly I never saw it.

In the whispering rush of memory I hear my father saying: "We'll go out to the ball park early, son. They have a feller who can throw." And so the Dodgers did. A young center fielder. Others came out, thousands of others, long before formal competition started, to watch the warm-up throws. You could hear gasps at Ebbets Field and sometimes, an hour before game time, bursts of applause.

The Dodgers moved Furillo into right field, making him yield center to the exuberant grace of Duke Snider. Where a dandelion could not grow — right field in Brooklyn — Furillo flowered.

George (Shotgun) Shuba said that when Billy Herman hit fungoes in warm-up, he told Herman, "You better hit to left field first. *I'm not going to throw after that guy.*"

Doing a retrospective radio program with Roy Campanella I said, "Campy, how did you like that throw off wet grass?"

Campanella remembered certain moist nights. "You know," he said, "I had to go to Carl one time and tell him: 'Please bounce the ball closer to first base. No one in the world can handle that one-hopper the way you're giving it to me.'"

So there was, I suppose, an element of awe. Beyond that, there stood an extraordinary person. I knew Furillo for thirty-seven years. I do not believe he was capable of telling a lie.

Early on he had a hard time accepting the integration of base-ball. He grew up in all-white country and was never schooled beyond the eighth grade. But Furillo changed and grew, a quiet man learning from his times. In 1953 the Dodgers added Jim Gilliam to the roster, and a few players complained about another black in an ugly way. I wrote a story using no names, and Buzzy Bavasi, running the Brooklyn Dodgers, said, "Who talked to you?"

"We don't work that way, Buzzy."

"I'll find out," Bavasi said.

By this point Furillo was warming up each night by playing catch with Campanella. He had surpassed his boyhood and grown color-blind.

Into the clubhouse I went, and Furillo called me over. "That stuff was years ago," he said. "I was wrong. I got nothing against the colored playing ball."

"I didn't write that you had anything against the colored."

"Bavasi says you did."

"Carl, I swear I never wrote that. I'll show you the story."

"You don't have to swear and you don't have to show me the story, just giving me your word is good enough."

Such seems to be the stuff of friendship, even love. Long after-ward, a career later, he mentioned that he was afflicted by chronic leukemia. "Some of the tests are bad," he said, "but you know I never made real money playing ball. So what can I do? I always worked. I got to work."

When I last saw this elegant gentleman, he was putting in four nights a week as a night watchman, fighting off leukemia, and not complaining. Hell, Carl said, we all have to work, even writers.

In 1987 I lost a gifted son to heroin. Roger Laurence Kahn had just passed his twenty-second birthday. The telephone rang a few days later, and the caller said: "This is Pee Wee. You remember I was captain of the team."

I do remember.

"I just want to say," Reese said, "for all the fellers that we are very, very sorry."

Our turns come and go. I mean only to say, for all the fellers, Carl, may you walk in green pastures.

1989

Story Without a Hero

A healthy economy, we are told, while inner cities seethe with drug wars, and homeless humans rot on Manhattan sidewalks. Gorbachev appears, and for the first time nuclear missiles are dismantled. AIDS invades the vocabulary and the society, and two men running for president in 1988 bicker about who most loves the pledge of allegiance. We live in the time of the hustler.

There are bullies pushing about, bucks ogling the women, knaves picking pockets, policemen on the look-out, quacks bawling in front of their booths and yokels looking up at the tinselled dancers and poor old rouged tumblers, while the light-fingered folk are operating on their pockets behind. Yes, this is Vanity Fair; not a moral place certainly; nor a merry one, though very noisy.

— Thackeray

The man who led me onto the midway at Vanity Fair today — Vanity Fair Contempo some would call it — has not heard of William Makepeace Thackeray. That sort of irony amused the scholar-sportswriters of my youth, gentlemen too wise to look for wisdom in the infield. They looked for snap throws in the infield. Wisdom, if it existed at all, resided with philosophers.

walk away from a million dollars." (Eventually he would become my *former* agent.) A few days later, after half a dozen phone calls, the agent had an actual offer of the million, half to Rose and half to me, or not quite half. The agent would extract fifteen percent of my half million, a commission of $75,000 for six phone calls.

I said I wasn't sure about the project. It seemed synthetic, manufactured, bizarre. A book was something to be taken seriously. Who the hell was ungrammatical Pete Rose to write a book with me?

Couldn't I just agree to compose something entertaining? the agent said. That's all that was being asked for the million bucks. Later I'd have the money to retire and write poetry, if that's what I wanted to do. "Faulkner," said this agent, who claimed to know such things, "worked in Hollywood to finance serious writing. I'd say if Faulkner did that, you can do something similar."

My misstep, the first of several on the long walkabout through the Fair, was not to cut off the siren song forthwith. For a very long time I have financed my "serious" writing by selling my serious writing. I wrote each book as well as I could, and four (out of nine) appeared on best-seller lists.

"Ah," said the agent, a former high school pitcher. "But aren't you curious about what makes the great Pete Rose tick?" And, to be sure, I was. How could *anyone* get more major league hits than Cobb, Musial, DiMaggio, Ruth, Willie, Mickey, and the Duke? Besides, now that I thought about it, a million bucks for a book had an appeal. Among a roomful of agents, lawyers, and publishers I signed the contract numbly. Then I walked out to a press conference called to celebrate "America's first million-dollar sports book."

I said a few ordinary sentences about how I looked forward to studying what made the great Pete Rose tick, or anyway hit. Rose smiled warmly and said that he looked forward to working with me "on a book. That would be like working on a painting with Andy Warhol."

When the questioning began, a reporter shouted, "How are you guys splitting the advance?"

I was disappointed, which was naive. This was not a press conference called to celebrate baseball writing. Mostly it was about money.

Rose grew up in Anderson Ferry, on the west side of Cincinnati, among steep slopes rising from the Ohio River. His father, a bank clerk, was renowned as a Sunday semipro football player, still running with the ball on hardscrabble fields at the age of forty-four. Harry Rose lived long enough to see his firstborn son make the Cincinnati Reds, an accomplishment that caused him to cry with joy. But Harry barely survived the decade.

Pete was sitting in a barber's chair one day in December 1970 when a telephone rang. The barber answered it, turned solemn, and said, "Pete. Your father died."

"My father?" Rose said. "You must mean my mother."

This story, a dreamboat for the psychological folk looking in on Vanity Fair, came directly from Rose. Little else that revealing ever did. Rose had worked radio and television talk shows and press conferences for so long that he had developed patterned answers to questions and — worse than that for my needs and, ultimately, his — patterned thought processes as well. As I found him first, he was quick rather than deep, a swift-running brook, always ababble.

Tell me about your father, Pete.

"Greatest guy I ever knew."

Was he affectionate?

"He wasn't a hugger, if that's what you mean. But I knew he cared for me. Nobody never had a better father than me. Hey, Jewish people hug a lot. Why are Jewish people hugging all the time?"

"Hold it, Pete. Tom Lasorda, who hugs all the time, is no more Jewish than the Polish Pope."

Pete's answers were quick and diversionary. From what I hoped would be a discussion about the nature of affection in his family, I was sidetracked and in a fairly interesting way. Is hugging ethnic?

That set a pattern. I had no more luck on other occasions, and when I said to Rose that a book, a real book, the kind of book we wanted to do, didn't we, was going to have to reach for depths beyond television chatter, Rose said, "Yeah, I know. That's *your* job."

When first we met, he was resolutely set in his ways. And why should he not be? His career was like no other. Here is Rose on Rose before the fall.

"Look, I'm the guy with all the hits [4,256] and when I was chasing Ty Cobb [who totaled 4,191] I had to do a coupla press conferences every day, and every writer will tell you I handled them great. I give 'em jokes. I was available. I helped 'em all. So what am I gonna tell you sitting here. That I got a little lucky and that's how come I hit in forty-four straight games [during the season of 1978] and went five for five ten times, that's the National League record. I played in more games than any major league player, more *winning* games, that ever lived, and I made the All-Star team sixteen times and at five different positions. It ain't luck."

Rose ran out bases on balls, and a couple of laid-back Yankee professionals came up with the famous nickname Charlie Hustle. It was a wonder of a quarter-century to watch hustlin' Pete Rose leap into his head-first slide. To me a greater wonder, and a more subtle one, was how well he knew how to play ball.

He said over and over that baseball was a simple game and that all he did in the major leagues was live by rules his semipro father preached in the big green house on Braddock Avenue long ago. "I mean, on defense you're always moving toward the ball. And on offense, after you swing, you're moving away from the ball. That's not complicated, am I right?"

But, of course, baseball is a complicated game, as an example of Rose's gamesmanship reminds me. One night in Cincinnati, Barry Larkin led off against the Giants with a twisting grounder along the foul line. Hurrying, first baseman Joel Youngblood misplayed the ball. Buddy Bell lifted a high pop fly that Youngblood lost in the lights. Men on first and second.

Suddenly Larkin faked a steal of third. That is, he ran off second base as the pitcher threw, and then ducked back. It was a stratagem of more exuberance than good sense. Buddy Bell, fooled by the fake, broke for second just before Larkin retreated. Bell had to stop far off first. Second base was occupied. Bell stood still, shriveling in embarrassment as the Giant catcher ran from behind home plate all the way to the base path and tagged him out.

"If it was me," pronounced Rose, the great gamesman, "I wouldn't have stood still, like Buddy did. I woulda run back to first, and the catcher would have had to throw to Youngblood. Joel messed up two plays. Now I want to make him handle the ball again.

"My Dad woulda known that. You can bet me."

I'm not so sure.

The ball field, before those madding thousands, was a place of escape, eventually the only place of escape for Rose from Vanity Fair. Working between the lines, performing the exquisitely difficult tasks of major league baseball, came to be relatively easy for Rose, and clear and pure. What can be purer than a line-drive single? We even call that kind of base hit "clean." It was the rest of things, *living*, that Rose found so difficult.

He was not happy at schoolwork and he resisted serious education. His father wanted him to be a ball player and he wanted to be a ball player, and he completed only the schoolwork necessary to maintain eligibility. Although the father made a reasonable living at the Fifth Third Bank, Rose cast himself as a poor, rough kid. He talked tough, he *was* tough, and he picked up the harsh vocabulary of the ball field. Needling presides in professional baseball, some racial, some sexual. Rose developed a bristling exterior, a studied inelegance.

When he played with Art Shamsky at Macon, Georgia, the two became fast friends. Still, Rose's nickname for Shamsky was Jewman. "Hey, Jewman. You wanna go to a movie?"

This is offensive, of course, but is it indicative of bigotry or the mores of pro ball? One of Joe DiMaggio's few close friends on the

Yankees, Joe Page, sometimes greeted the star: "Hiya, Dago."

When Rose was promoted to the Reds in 1963, the older players found him grating. He was replacing a well-liked veteran, and according to Rose, the only established Cincinnati players who would associate with him were Frank Robinson and Vada Pinson. Indeed, Pinson let the rookie share his hotel room one night when Rose's roommate bolted and chained the door. He was embarked on a sexual adventure; the cocky rookie could damn well sleep in the hall.

Bleating, Rose knocked on Pinson's door. The veteran took him in, and in the morning suggested a room-service breakfast. Rose, twenty-two, had not heard of room service. "It was somethin', that first time, havin' a great breakfast in the room. Vada taught me how to do it. I still remember my tab. Twelve ninety-five."

Both Robinson and Pinson were black. Rose says that someone in the Reds' "front office" soon told him to "stop hanging out with those colored guys. It's bad for your image." Commenting, Rose said, in a nice moment, "There's so much hate in the world as it is. How can anyone be so stupid as to hate a man because of the color of his skin?" That was Baseball Rose, the indefatigable, clear-eyed professional, beyond reproach.

But often, in the manner of other superstars, Rose's focus was wholly on himself, on doing what he wanted. Away from the field discipline, limits, even good sense, vanished. He failed to pay tickets for speeding. He smuggled money into the country. He ran about with underworld characters. He was a neglectful father. Probably he suffered from satyriasis.

George "Sparky" Anderson, who managed Rose at Cincinnati, said once that he never had to wonder where Rose was late at night. "Our Peter always finds a nice warm place to put his peter."

The private lives of heroes and heroines fuel an industry of gossip that ranges from supermarket tabloids to pretentious full-length books. Elvis. Sinatra. Marilyn. JFK. Lennon. Olivier. Jackie. The best of gossip stuff is naked in its prurience. The worst is moralistic.

If Jacqueline Onassis's gynecologist's nurse reports that the lady is somewhat sloppy, what can we say about the reporter who bears this tale to a book-buying public? One does not need a master's degree in journalism to respond. Nor does one need a doctorate in psychology to recognize that many high-achieving people are prone to willfulness, thoughtlessness, sloppiness, and excess. I suppose in those ways Pete Rose is every bit as bad as Elvis, Jackie, Sinatra, Marilyn, JFK, and the rest.

A clubhouse attendant told Rose in 1978 that the hostess at a downtown disco called Sleep-out Louie's has "the best ass in Cincinnati." On April 11, 1984, the hostess, Carol Woliung, became the second Mrs. Rose.

But before Rose's second marriage, a quiet ceremony at the home of his principal attorney, Reuven J. Katz, the first Mrs. Rose, Karolyn, hired a divorce lawyer who tried to put the ball player into bankruptcy. She asked for half of Rose's total worth — $3 million at the time. She and her lawyer included Rose's pension rights in their calculations. That pension was still twenty years away. Thus Karolyn Rose was asking for $1.5 million in cash when Rose actually possessed no more than a third of that. She knew that. Her lawyer knew that. Rough stuff is the nature of contested divorce.

Close to his fiftieth birthday, Rose was reconsidering priorities. A well-written magazine article charged that he was distant from his daughter, Fawn, and that Pete Rose, Jr., the reluctantly hugging son, had to go through lawyer Katz for the father's home number. ("Yeah," Rose said. "I'm unlisted and I gotta keep changing it.")

Rose told the press that he had given Fawn a Mercedes to celebrate her graduation from college in Kentucky, and how was that for distant? He had done more than that. He had chartered a plane and flown into Kentucky from St. Louis so that he could attend the graduation. He didn't tell this to the press because "they don't care about that kind of stuff." Softness, signs of caring, embarrassed him. (And maybe, too, the press really doesn't care.)

He spent February 1989 living with young Pete in Florida, helping the boy with batting and perhaps with life. "This is the best our relationship has been," Petey said.

A suggestion arose screamingly loud, and ignored by sports reporters, that at long last Pete Rose was growing up.

Then, before Rose could begin to savor maturity, his world caught fire.

Marketing taints professional baseball. Give nothing away except (up to now) drinking water at the ball park. Sell everything for what the traffic tolerates. Load the soda cups with ice, boys; ice is cheaper than Coke. The most popular whipping boy is the ball player who sells autographs at a baseball card show. But jumping card shows (and ball players) is cheap. A genuine imitation Brooklyn Dodger baseball cap — a Replicap, really — sells for fifteen dollars, complete with a label from Major League Baseball, Inc., certifying that the cap is "Authentic." A genuine *authentic* imitation.

Pete Rose seems always to have wanted to make the most money possible. But he was no Marner caring to add more gold to the cottage in Raveloe. Rose liked to make money, but he *loved* to spend it. While still a minor league player in Macon, Georgia, Rose put his life savings into a racy mint-green Corvette. (This left barely enough to pay his first speeding ticket.)

Rose was alien to contemplation. Living on the surface of things, he was drawn to glitter and vulgarity. Ted Williams said, "I want to be the best hitter in the world." Pete Rose said, "I wanna be the world's first $100,000 singles hitter." One came across as an *artiste*. The other, though clearly a champion, smelled faintly of Gruyère.

Even before the debacle, before the baseball investigation and the grand jury indictment, two expensive lawyers "handled" Rose. They pushed his baseball salary ever higher. Three people from a marketing company helped Rose become a spokesman for candy bars, hair tonic, chili, baseball bats, a bank. Slowly Pete Rose, not a bad feller, melded into Peter Edward Rose Enterprises, Inc., a characteristically greedy small company. The blend produced a third entity: Pete the Peddler.

As the company sold endorsements, Pete the Peddler sold shirts and uniforms and bats and balls. On the night he broke Cobb's record, Rose changed his uniform shirt three times. That way he would have three shirts, each worn on the record-breaking night, to sell.

None of his advisers deplored such excess. Unlike Rose, they had read more books than they had written. They knew about the goose and the golden egg.

Katz dominated. He was a decent country-club athlete, a graduate of Harvard Law School and, he protested, a passionate Cincinnati ball fan. He and Rose played tennis, praised and ragged each other, and from time to time got on each other's nerves. Katz was senior partner at a law firm (Katz, Teller, Brant & Hild) prosperous enough to occupy three stories of an office building on Walnut Street in Cincinnati. When introduced as Rose's lawyer, Katz often added, "And surrogate father."

As I came to know both Rose and the lawyer, Katz cast himself as pepper pot, irritant, sage. "Should you be writing this book *now?*" he said. "Or in five years? Who knows where Pete will be."

"Oh?"

"But when this book is done, I want you to be famous as the author of the greatest baseball biography that ever was."

"Oh?"

Rose resisted my efforts to make him think or feel in ways he had not felt before. Whenever I probed, he cringed. He didn't know why I wasn't happy with the stuff he was "feedin' newspaper fellers." I was supposed to be a good writer, wasn't that right? Wasn't that why we got Big Bucks? Well, if I really was a good writer, why couldn't I take the same stuff and write it better than them newspaper guys. "That's your job."

Would Rose introduce me to his mother?

"Introduce yourself. She knows about you."

How about touring the old neighborhood together?

"You know where it is. You find it."

I insisted on a talk, out of his presence, with Carol Woliung, once "the greatest ass in Cincinnati," now the second Mrs. Rose. We met of an afternoon, and soon Carol was speaking of loneliness with a desperate intensity. Not knowing what to say, I had enough sense to say nothing, merely sigh.

After a while Carol began to cry and hugged her baby son. "Tyler, Tyler. I don't know what I'd do without you."

I had to leave, I said, and Carol lent me the family's number-five car, a red Chevrolet Blazer. I drove to Riverfront Stadium, playing with the radar detector and hoping that I had not made a difficult marriage worse.

"What Carol tell ya?" Pete said, in the most challenging tone he ever threw into my face.

"We had a talk."

"What she tell ya?"

"Good talk. Then she lent me your Blazer. I gave the keys to the clubhouse boy."

Rose dialed his home. Glaring at me, he said to Carol: "Why the fuck did you lend *him* the car?"

Rose was hardly secretive. He went to lengths in 1987 to introduce me to a dark-haired Cuban refugee, a tall, attractive woman, successful in advertising, whom Pete dated when he could get away. He spoke also of how he enjoyed gambling. That same spring he sent someone from his clubhouse office in Tampa to place bets on a college basketball tournament. He explained what he was doing and why he liked the particular teams he did. Maybe I'd like to bet along with him.

Control, not secrecy, was at issue. Rose wanted to control my access, control what I knew about his life. That way, he felt, he could control the contents of the book without subjecting himself to reading all those pages. (To this day I don't know if Rose suffers from a clinical reading disorder or is merely handicapped by his short attention span.)

But I intended to control the book myself. To me this wasn't Pete Rose's fifth or fifteenth book. It was my tenth.

Reuven Katz wanted so ardently to control my book that he slipped in a clause, somewhere in the sheafs of contracts, providing himself with the right to review the manuscript. Rose wouldn't read it, Katz claimed, and it was his duty as attorney to protect his client.

Only after a counterproductive war of attrition did Katz let control revert to where it belonged in the first place: to the writer who was doing the work and to the publisher who, however flawed, was paying the freight.

My question was voice. Whose voice should tell the story? That becomes a literary issue, and Vanity Fair is not a literary place.

The first publisher said that the Rose book was so important he would edit it himself. The man had a business degree. He had not edited a book before. But now he would. That was how important my Rose book was to him and his company.

When I suggested I was having a problem with voice, the publisher looked uncomfortable. "You see," I said, "Pete is intelligent, but in a gamesman's way. Pete is gin-rummy intelligent. His vocabulary is limited and his grammar is shaky and I'm trying to resolve . . ." The publisher left me for a convention of book sellers, where he posed beaming in front of a large mock-up of the jacket for the book I had barely begun.

I continued to agonize about voice, until the publisher wearied of nuance and fired me with a fusillade of lawsuits.

The next publisher, William Rosen at Macmillan, asked if I thought Rose's memory in baseball was comparable to Nabokov's memory in literature. I felt more relieved than I had a right to feel.

The voice, the dominant voice, would be mine. Rose could appear talking, a recollection here, a vignette there, an insight into a ball game or a ball player somewhere else. But with no more literacy than he truly possessed. I was casting the book as dialogue, and

I was happy about that. Rose and I were producing an honest collaboration. I was three chapters shy of the finale when Major League Baseball, Inc., hired a gumshoe to investigate my partner.

Angelo Bartlett Giamatti, the late commissioner of baseball who presided over the Rose gambling investigation, is remembered for eloquence and romantic passion. In 1977 in the *Yale Alumni Review*, Giamatti wrote of baseball:

> It breaks your heart. It is designed to break your heart. The game begins in spring, when everything else begins again, and it blossoms in the summer, filling the afternoons and evenings, and then as soon as the chill rains come, it stops and leaves you to face the fall alone. You count on it, rely on it to buffer the passage of time, and keep the memory of sunshine and high skies alive, and then just when the days are all twilight, when you need it most, it stops.

He was fascinated not only by baseball but by power. "The notion that absolute power corrupts absolutely is a sentimental axiom of a time grown blurred," Giamatti wrote in 1984 while employed as president of Yale. "Power can no more corrupt than light or wind can corrupt. Power itself can never spoil or be spoiled." That essay is less renowned than the earlier one, but it is just as relevant to Rose. There is a ring of absolutism in these Giamatti sentences. The thoughts might please a czar.

Giamatti moved from Yale with dreams of leading professional baseball into a golden age. What Giamatti admired, he adored. Elizabeth I, that queen of power, was a special favorite. Giamatti wrote of Elizabeth's "gorgeous, glittering self." He seemed to see baseball as a gorgeous, glittering panoply, the best and brightest, purest, truest institution in all America. "With some of these guys," says wise old Dave Anderson, the Pulitzer Prize sports columnist at the *New York Times*, "I want to remind them. Hey. It's a business, not a religion."

Giamatti focused on the spiritual and hired business helpers, including his successor, the lawyer and present commissioner Fay

Vincent, for bookkeeping and other earthly chores. "Above all," Giamatti wrote of his adored Elizabeth, "she learned that power lies in seeming."

What then would be the power of A. Bartlett Giamatti, essayist, polymath, Commissioner of Baseball. It would be Absolute. As Absolute as Giamatti could make his power seem to be.

The Rose mess leaked into the commissioner's office under a side door, sewage from a ruptured pipe. The Rose mess smelled to heaven and threatened Giamatti's golden age. Suddenly two extraordinary formidables were arrayed against each other. Neither can be said to have survived.

As Rose became the most durable major league batter of all time, he moved away from normal social patterns. Driven by the hawkers around him and by needs rooted somewhere in a battering childhood, he pressed his income higher, ever higher. Indeed, he earned enough to please a banker.

His success on the playing fields matched the grandest dreams of boyhood, that boyhood with the bank-clerk father demanding, ever demanding. Run faster. Throw harder. Swing quicker. A father who drafted little Pete to be his water boy but never hugged him. Grown up, Pete Rose always had so much to prove to his father in the coffin.

Following the divorce in 1980, Rose moved away from old friends. The cut and thrust of challenging conversation came to annoy him.

"Whatever happened, Pete, between you and Karolyn?"

"Hunnert percent my fault."

"Are you friendly now?"

"I talk to her. She hassles me. I don't want to be hassled so I don't talk to her."

Nor did he like talking to *anyone* who hassled him. Soon his hours away from the ball field were peopled by characters like Katz — paid employees or advisers — and sycophants. An unappealing demimonde coalesced. A headwaiter from the dining room at a Florida dog track, a gambling man. A serious bettor who ran a pizza house where Rose memorabilia was for sale. A vacuous weight lifter who trafficked in steroids and later cocaine. It is easy to postulate, as one psychologist did in *Sporting News,* that Rose had a neurotic need to risk. Beyond that, he seemed to love flirtation with the edges of the underworld. (So did Bill Veeck and John F. Kennedy.)

In February 1989 Rose was called from the Reds' new training camp in Plant City, Florida, to meet with Peter Ueberroth, the outgoing commissioner, and Giamatti, already named as successor. This was an administrative hearing, not a trial, the sort that any boss might call to check out a questionable employee. Rose brought a lawyer, a decision not lost on Bart Giamatti.

Ueberroth ran the hearing. He asked questions about gambling, and Rose said finally, "I lost $2,000 on the last Superbowl. I figured it wrong."

Ueberroth said he didn't care about that. Had Rose bet on major league baseball?

"No, sir. I got too much respect for the game."

The hearing adjourned. Ueberroth told a reporter from the *New York Times,* "There's nothing ominous. There won't be any follow-through." A few weeks later *Gentleman's Quarterly* published the article in which Rose came through as a parent who completely neglected his children.

In this gamy climate, late in March, Bart Giamatti learned that *Sports Illustrated* was investigating serious charges. Ronald Peters, a bookmaker out of Franklin, Ohio, had offered to sell the magazine a story in which he would charge that Rose had bet on ball games and that he had booked the bets. The story was presented by Peters's lawyer. (Peters had just been convicted of dealing cocaine.)

The magazine declined to buy the felon's story, but its editors did not discount the information. Two young reporters, Craig Neff and Jill Lieber, were directed to investigate further. They spoke to people who they thought would help them: players Rose had traded, the former Mrs. Rose. Rose damned these "vultures" of the press. Word got around.

Ueberroth was history now. Giamatti had taken over. His office moved quickly, before *Sports Illustrated* could break its first damaging Rose story, to demonstrate that the new commissioner was in absolute control of his new-won empire.

He hired tall, beefy-faced John Dowd to run baseball's own sweeping examination of Rose. Dowd, a "power lawyer" out of Washington, D.C., had built a reputation in government service as a prosecutor of thugs and racketeers. This was no sweetheart session. This was nasty.

"The careful cultivator of power," Giamatti wrote, ostensibly about Elizabeth, "always stores more than enough, keeps much in reserve, never wastes, uses the power of others so as to conserve one's own." Giamatti used Dowd (and paid him lavishly: some say Dowd's final fee was $500,000).

Now all the forces rode toward combat. Rose and his votaries. Dowd and his investigators. Against Angelo Bartlett Giamatti, that first-class medieval mind, what chance did modern functionaries have?

Rose cooperated with Dowd. He turned over years of telephone and banking records. His lawyers argued that this cooperation demonstrated innocence, but that is not persuasive. Under the bylaws of Major League Baseball, Inc., a manager *must* cooperate with an investigation ordered by the commissioner or face expulsion.

Dowd brought in a dozen assistants and kept interrogating until he had filled seven large black-bound volumes. Although his assignment was gambling, he gathered crumbs about Rose's philandering as well. He worked in the style well practiced by federal prosecutors. Cajole. Threaten. Deal. He interrogated people without Rose's being present and without allowing Rose's attorneys to be present either. Obviously this denied Rose the right to confront his accusers and have his attorneys cross-examine them when they gave the testimony on which Dowd relied.

In Giamatti's view, it was not required that Rose have that opportunity. This was not per se a criminal proceeding. Dowd was just preparing an "administrative" report. It might mean the extinction of Rose's career, but that was not a good enough reason, apparently, to extend to Rose the kind of rights that a criminal judge would give to an accused jaywalker.

Dowd wheeled and dealed with felons, as criminal prosecutors say they have to do. Ronald Peters faced sentencing and prison. Talk to me, Dowd told Peters, and we'll talk to the judge. He'll make the sentence lighter. At Dowd's urging, Giamatti wrote to a judge in praise of Peters. (Elizabeth of England might have been less hasty.) Thus motivated by the commissioner of baseball, Peters warbled.

Yes, Rose bet baseball, Peters said. Proof? Well, he'd taped Rose making baseball bets. The, uh, tape, was in a shoe box that, uh, his ex-wife had. In an affidavit Mrs. Peters said no tape existed. "It's the product of my ex-husband's fantasy." Yet in his report Dowd said merely that the tape "cannot be located."

Dowd asked another felon, who had been Rose's intimate, to state his case while looped into a polygraph machine. Thus wired, Paul Janszen also said that Rose bet baseball. But the expert who analyzed the readings, one William Robertson, reported to Dowd: Janszen is lying.

Dowd did obtain "gambling slips," records supposedly kept by Rose. They indicated baseball betting. But the experts Dowd hired and those engaged by Rose disagree about the authenticity of these papers.

Finally, curious telephone logs exist, much telephoning from Rose's office or hotel suites — when the team traveled — just before ball games began. Calls to make bets, Dowd insisted. Not that the logs prove that Rose was calling bookies. According to Dowd, Rose used Janszen to cover his tracks, giving him bets to pass on to bookies. Maybe. Rose's lawyers postulate that the suspicious telephone activity powered a scheme by Janszen to blackmail a fortune from Rose. Maybe. And maybe both sides are wrong. Dowd's report claims that Janszen himself bet baseball, possibly on tips from Rose, and the logs show much the same kind of telephone activity on days when Janszen's records do not indicate betting by Rose as when they do. Maybe Janszen was betting baseball for his own account.

A quick professional reaction to Dowd's work was provided by Samuel Dash, formerly chief counsel to the congressional committee that investigated Watergate. "If John Dowd turned in a report like that to me," Dash said, "I'd fire him." Giamatti and his successor, Fay Vincent, elected not to hear Sam Dash.

Rather, Giamatti and Vincent hinted at mysterious evidence quite beyond the Dowd report and said in effect to journalists: "Boys, if you could only see what I've seen, you'd have no doubt. Pete Rose bet baseball. It's a tragedy." This shopworn, simplistic "trust me" strategy carried the day, or rather the press, for the accusers.

Certainly Pete Rose may have bet on baseball. His lawyers are slick and his denial skill is most ornate. It is impossible, of course, to prove the negative, that Rose did *not* bet baseball, but it seems important here for both sides to go beyond assurances and pleas of "trust me."

The Dowd report presents the hardest evidence that has come to light and probably will come to light that Rose bet baseball. That charge, not related accusations, *really* is what has been threatening him with exclusion from the Hall of Fame.

Persuasive in spots, the Dowd report overall is an unconvincing mix of allegation and distortion. As I say, I don't know if Rose bet baseball. I do know, however, that he was railroaded out of the game.

With the Dowd report in hand, Giamatti scheduled a hearing. Here Rose and his attorneys could at last present their defense.

Would Rose's accusers be present? Katz asked. He wanted to prepare cross-examination.

Giamatti said no. He lacked the power to subpoena them. However, Big John Dowd would be there. Dowd would answer relevant questions. Rose could call his own witnesses, of course, but if he wanted to examine his accusers he would have to persuade them to appear and take the stand. These people, of course, had given damaging testimony against Rose. They were hardly friendly. For his part, Dowd had no obligation to make them available for Rose's lawyers to examine.

Katz asked for a hearing with someone else, not Giamatti, presiding.

Giamatti said that would not be practicable. He had a responsibility to preserve and protect the authority of the commissioner of baseball.

Katz challenged Giamatti's authority and impartiality in an Ohio court and obtained a stay. Lawyers for Major League Baseball, Inc., argued that the matter belonged in federal court. Whenever the Cincinnati Reds played ball at home, they pleaded, Manager Rose in Ohio and Commissioner Giamatti in New York were transacting interstate business.

A federal judge in Dayton agreed to hear the case, and the battle was done. No federal judge has been willing to limit the power of a commissioner in the seventy years since organized baseball assumed the outline of its present structure. Giamatti had won.

In New York a few days later, he read an announcement for network television. Rose was banned for life. He could apply for reinstatement in one year. Giamatti looked wan. He had been smoking too much. A reporter asked if Giamatti personally thought Rose had bet on baseball games. Giamatti said yes, in his personal opinion, Rose had bet on ball games.

One of Rose's lawyers said Giamatti's statement violated the spirit of the agreement — which made no finding on baseball betting — and broke a tradition of the English common law. A king, a royal presence such as a baseball commissioner, may not have any personal opinions. A king may only reign.

A week later Giamatti died on the magic island of Martha's Vineyard and his innermost secrets were silenced.

The publisher insisted on a book in the stalls before Thanksgiving. But Katz and Rose appeared to have lost interest. The press pounded Rose and ridiculed his case, his case to stay in baseball.

Against this backdrop I argued that it was more important than it had ever been before for Rose to be forthright. A span of five months had passed from the onset of *Sports Illustrated*'s investigation (March) until Giamatti banished him. During that time Rose continued to manage the Reds, which left him exposed to daily scrutiny. Rose and his people held discussions on media strategy. They decided that Rose would be as available as he had been in his triumphant days. But he would answer only "baseball questions." Gambling, the furor that had attracted the reporters, was off limits. Talking gambling could only lead Rose toward the sewers, where he had already spent too much time.

The press flocked about him. Day after day reporters asked: Did he bet baseball? Again and again Rose's answer was the same. "No comment."

The effect was devastating. Had Pete Rose broken the primal ordinance of Major League Baseball, Inc.? Had Pete Rose bet on major league ball games?

"No comment."

Another client of the Katz law firm, Johnny Bench, spoke for millions when he burst out, "If Pete hasn't bet on baseball, why the hell doesn't he come right out and say it?"

William Rosen, the publisher of Macmillan books, asked if I thought Rose had bet on baseball. I wanted to believe Rose had not. Did I have enough to write a chapter toward that point? I did not. Rose was being evasive, I reported. Katz, once the soul of cooperation, clearly was ducking me.

William Rosen flared. Unless Rose and Katz made themselves available to me, as they had agreed to do before the trouble, Macmillan would cancel their contract and sue for a return of the money, plus damages. Millions. Bloody millions. It was only after I recounted Rosen's threat to Katz that the lawyer made available his defense team. Rose himself then held still for a three-hour session during which a young editor and I threw every question at him we could imagine.

Rose: "Let me give you more stuff that is just plain wrong.

"There are stories that I sold one of my World Series rings to pay off gambling debts.

"There is a story that I gave a World Series ring to a bookie to settle a gambling debt.

"There is a story that I had to get a second mortgage on my house here to pay gambling debts.

"Every one of those stories is simply wrong. I helped a guy who I liked, Joe Cambra, to have a *copy* made of one of my Series rings. Cambra is a gambler. I gave him permission to order a ring which he paid for himself: $3,150. Isn't that a little different than paying off a bookie with a ring?

"A writer in spring training said: 'We understand you've taken out a second mortgage on your house to pay gambling debts.'

"I called Reuven Katz and I said, 'Do I have a second mortgage on my house?' Reuven said I did. When I won't be seeing him for a long period of time Reuven has me sign a lot of stuff. Reuven said, 'Remember those papers you signed last time. I told you one of them was for a second mortgage.'

"I didn't remember. I said, 'Where's the money?'

"Reuven Katz said, 'The money is in escrow — it's $150,000, Pete. I wanted it there in case all of a sudden you wanted to pay cash for some fancy new car. Right now we're thinking about taking the money out and giving it back because you're not going to buy any car.'

"We explained this as clearly as we could. And what happens? There are more stories that I took out a second mortgage to pay a bookie.

"I've made my mistakes and I've accepted a pretty good hit for them. I've lost a half-a-million-dollar-a-year job.

"Ball players are all the time making mistakes and heavy ones with things like drugs.

"To be honest with you, I don't think all in all I've damaged baseball.

"That's my own personal opinion.

"What has damaged baseball I believe is the media's one-sided coverage."

"Dowd fed the media, Pete."

"The media says I should have been more careful. I say the media should be more careful."

Quite apart from baseball, a grand jury was looking into charges that Rose had evaded his federal income tax for several years. Rose said he was told by his team of attorneys not to discuss the grand jury and directed me toward the criminal lawyer, Roger Makley of Dayton, who seemed to be running this aspect of the defense.

"Nobody is ever absolutely certain of anything with IRS," Makley said in his office in Dayton. "They are trying to see if Pete concealed huge gambling winnings. The truth is, Pete lost his ass gambling. They are putting the screws to Pete. They are trying to get out of him anything he knows about gambling in Cincinnati. A fishing expedition with news leaks."

When Katz noticed this passage while reviewing the manuscript with William Rosen and myself, he begged me to excise it. Would I please not publish anything that might trigger a criminal indictment of Pete Rose?

I said that maybe we shouldn't be publishing the book right now, with the grand jury still out. William Rosen said that question had been settled. Macmillan *was* publishing the book right now. Katz said to me, very quietly, "You're worried about a book. I'm worried about somebody's survival."

Was this simply a lawyer writing melodrama? (Katz played in student Shakespeare years ago.) Or, if I followed him correctly, was Katz making a soft-voiced plea for the life of the man he called his surrogate son? I responded emotionally and directed that the passage on Internal Revenue be deleted.

Three months later Rose pleaded guilty to income tax evasion without my help.

I called the work *Head First*. That was how Rose slid into base and that was the way Rose lived. Macmillan changed the title. Instead of *Head First*, a book written by me with oral supplements from Rose, we now had something called *My Story,* by Pete Rose and Roger Kahn. That was not a representation of the book, nor was it grammatical. (How can two people write a singular tale?)

Someone, I never found out who, provided misleading jacket copy. "That day has finally come. To demolish the case against him." More poor grammar. Nor could the baseball case against Rose be demolished. It consisted of three charges: bad associations, incessant gambling, betting on baseball. Rose pleaded guilty to the first two counts.

I made no pretense of demolishing anything. I merely interposed reasonable doubt on charge number three.

I proposed a press conference to help the book and more or less reopen the case of Major League Baseball v. Pete Rose. Let one tough lawyer summarize the defense. Bring in Sam Dash to pick apart John Dowd. Present the expert witnesses who believed the betting sheets were forgeries. Let Rose deny, as he was finally denying, that he had bet on baseball. Let him express remorse for some heedless ways.

Rose's people ignored the suggestions. Instead, Katz, a newly hired publicity woman, and Rose submitted to Macmillan a list of sportswriters to whom Rose would speak. The man was banned from baseball, en route to jail, but he and his advisers still wanted to call the shots.

Rose quickly became a nationwide object of ridicule. A cartoon in *The Sporting News* depicted him trying to sell an autographed ball from a yard in federal prison. The ball was iron and fastened to his leg.

In another context the critic Richard Schickel wrote of a fictional character: "He finally recognized that awful congruity between what he has been and what the modern world has become." Without great effort you can list negative attributes Rose shared with the era of his glory: greed, acquisitiveness, superficiality, flippancy. Was ever a ball player more a man of his time?

The boiling Rose mess scalded everyone it touched. But there are no villains stirring the pot. Some charge the press protected Rose for years, then overreacted the other way. (Do we want a press that avidly snoops and tells, practicing rottweiler journalism, offering up pornography disguised as investigation with our morning coffee?) When the press turned on Rose, excess and distortion did carry many days. But that is the nature of the press, living with deadlines. It is history, not daily or weekly journalism, that gives us balance.

The editors of *Sports Illustrated,* who decided to investigate a felon's tip, really had no choice. With a story that Rose bet on baseball up for sale, *somebody* was going to do something with it. Although significant errors appeared in the magazine's coverage, in sum the people at *Sports Illustrated* acted responsibly.

Katz's role is more complicated. In the view of another attorney connected with the case, Katz let himself get too close to Rose. He overlooked some excesses and remained blind to certain others, like, perhaps, a loving parent. I don't subscribe to one reporter's view that Katz cynically put up with Rose because the publicity attracted business for the law firm. They genuinely cared for one another, Reuven and Pete.

The case — the two cases, really — turned out in combination to be beyond the depth of both lawyer and client. The two were, of course, Baseball v. Rose and Internal Revenue v. Rose. Rose and Katz lost both.

Was Katz protecting himself, his own role, in a lawyer-client situation as well as protecting Rose? Of course Katz was protecting himself. But that isn't villainy.

The publisher, William Rosen, wanted to sell books. He is a marketing man, in no way literary, although he has read Nabokov. He could as well work for Peter Edward Rose Enterprises as for Macmillan. He decided that a highly hyped presentation would work, poetry be damned. Had Rose promoted the book — had he not been cowed into hiding by the tax grand jury — Macmillan might have made $5 million on the project. Bill Rosen would have drawn a substantial raise.

As for myself, I felt drawn, if not quite quartered. Katz and Rose were ducking. The publisher demanded the book. Just as Giamatti stayed deaf to Samuel Dash, the publisher stayed deaf to my insistence that the time was wrong, the grand jury was still out. Vital sections were deleted without my consent. Inserts appeared, ill written and poorly punctuated.

As for Rose, as I knew him, he was hyperactive, self-absorbed, brilliantly disciplined on the field, wildly undisciplined beyond. During the last summer that we were close, 1989, his harsh edges were beginning to soften. He is not a violent man, in no way hateful, and I suppose he will spend the rest of his days wondering what went wrong. No more the dashing warrior, he has become the poor old rouged tumbler, sad, even pathetic, in Vanity Fair.

The damnedest thing. After all these pages, approaching half a century in sport, I conclude by setting down a story without a hero.

1990

Words of Thanks

The following helped ingather exile essays and have my appreciation:

Nicole Aron of the New York Public Library; Alfred Baman of *Sports Illustrated;* Jill Bower of *Esquire;* Ann Callahan of *Time* magazine; Jack Curry of the *New York Times;* Edward Falcone and Elena Falcone of the Field Library, Peekskill, New York; Stephen Gencarello of *Newsweek;* Phyllis Halliday of *Playboy;* Richard Hill of the New York Public Library; J. K. Hvistendahl of Iowa State University; Stefanie Krasnow of *Sport* magazine; Lawrie Mifflin of the *New York Times;* Peter Miller of *Sports Illustrated;* Lora Porter of the Putnam Valley Free Library, Putnam Valley, New York; Nina Postle of *Notre Dame Magazine;* Steve Saks of the New York Public Library; and Peter Wessley of the Field Library, Peekskill, New York.

Carol Sevelowitz punched the manuscript into a word processor. (The author himself uses a manual typewriter crafted during the late Jurassic age.)

Charles (Cy) Rembar, who appears in the first essay as a "creditable shortstop," is my attorney and literary agent. I am grateful to counsel for finding this book a happy home.

At that home, Ticknor & Fields, I was assisted mightily by the editing and by the kindness of John Herman, and the efforts of his accomplice, Celina Spiegel. They had strong hands in shaping

Games We Used to Play, and I am grateful. Peg Anderson did the copy editing with care and style. Susan Kilgour ran down some slippery facts.

Despite these co-conspirators, if I have split an infinitive or sinned in other ways, that responsibility is mine alone.

R.K.

ACKNOWLEDGMENTS

"Willie Who?" was first published in *The New York Herald Tribune*, Feb. 28 and Mar. 3, 1954; copyright ©1954, New York Herald Tribune, Inc. All rights reserved. Reprinted by permission.

"Intellectuals and Ball Players" was first published in *The American Scholar*. Copyright ©1957 by Roger Kahn.

"The Life and Death of Howie Morenz" was first published in *Sport*. Copyright ©1956 by Roger Kahn. "The Original Sugar Ray" was first published in *Sport*. Copyright ©1959 by Roger Kahn. "'Toonder' on the Right" was first published in *The Nation*. Copyright ©1959 by Roger Kahn. "The Last Summer of Number Six" was first published in *Sports Illustrated*. Copyright ©1960 by Roger Kahn.

"The Death of John Lardner" was first published with the title "Death of a Writer" in *The World of John Lardner*. Copyright ©1961 by Hazel Lardner. Reprinted by permission of Simon & Schuster.

"The Press and Roger Maris" was first published in *Sports Illustrated*. Copyright ©1961 by Roger Kahn.

"$C = \dfrac{(\text{Frank Ryan})}{2}$" was first published in *The Saturday Evening Post*. Copyright ©1967 by Roger Kahn.

"The Game Without the Ball" was first published in *The Saturday Evening Post*. Copyright ©1967 by Roger Kahn.

"An Hour or So of Hell" was first published in *The Saturday Evening Post*. Copyright ©1968 by Roger Kahn.

"Kareem Arrives" was first published in *Sport*. Copyright ©1970 by Roger Kahn.

"The Mick" was first published in *Esquire*. Copyright ©1971 by Roger Kahn.

"Jack Roosevelt Robinson" was first published in *Esquire*. Copyright ©1974 by Roger Kahn.

"Sportswriters" was first published in *Esquire*. Copyright ©1974 by Roger Kahn.

"Cheer, Cheer for Old Ezra Pound" was first published in *Esquire*. Copyright ©1974 by Roger Kahn.

"The Shrine" was first published in *Sports Illustrated*. Copyright ©1974 by Roger Kahn.

"Rhapsody in Black" was first published in *Esquire* with the title "Elephant Man." Copyright ©1975 by Roger Kahn.

"The Fifth Ward in Houston" was first published in *Esquire*. Copyright ©1976 by Roger Kahn.

"Ali in Whispers" was first published in *Time* with the title "Doing It Just One More Time." Copyright ©1976 Time Warner Inc. Reprinted by permission.

"The Sunshine Boy" was first published in *The New York Times* with the title "Walter O'Malley in the Sunshine." Copyright ©1978 by the New York Times Company. Reprinted by permission.

"No Moaning at This Bar" was first published in *The New York Times*. Copyright ©1978 by the New York Times Company. Reprinted by permission.

"Walter Wellesley Smith" was first published in *Notre Dame Magazine*. Copyright ©1979 by Roger Kahn.

"Past Their Prime" was first published in *Playboy*. Copyright ©1979 by Roger Kahn.

"Sinatra's Friend" was first published in *Playboy* with the title "Sunshine Boy." Copyright ©1982 by Roger Kahn.

"Carl Anthony Furillo" was first published in *The New York Times* with the title "Carl Furillo's View of Sports." Copyright ©1989 by the New York Times Company. Reprinted by permission.

The lines quoted on page 164 are from *The Cantos of Ezra Pound*. Copyright 1948 Ezra Pound. Reprinted by permission of New Directions Publishing Corp.

The quotation from "Into My Heart an Air That Kills" is from "A Shropshire Lad," Authorized Edition, from *The Collected Poems of A. E. Housman*, Copyright 1939, 1940, © 1965 by Holt, Rinehart and Winston. Copyright © 1967, 1968 by Robert E. Symons. Reprinted by permission of Henry Holt and Company, Inc.